THE INCORPOREAL GOD

An Insight Into The Higher Realms

Dr. Feridoun Shawn Shahmoradian

authorHOUSE®

AuthorHouse™
1663 Liberty Drive
Bloomington, IN 47403
www.authorhouse.com
Phone: 1 (800) 839-8640

Published by AuthorHouse 12/17/2018

ISBN: 978-1-5462-7041-6 (sc)
ISBN: 978-1-5462-7040-9 (e)

Print information available on the last page.

This book is printed on acid-free paper.

And Jesus said "Foxes have holes, and birds of the air have nests, but the Son of Man has nowhere to lay his head."
Mathew 8: 20

The Incorporeal God: An insight into the higher realms

In the name of the Omnipotent, omnipresent, Omni-temporal, omnibenevolent, and the Omniscient God. The most merciful, the most gracious, and the most compassionate. The proprietor of patience, time, space, and beyond. The Fiduciary, Custodian, the Adjudicator (Arbitrator, Judge) to all there is and the nonexistence. In the name of the almighty God.

Watch your thoughts; they become words.
Watch your words; they become actions.
Watch your actions; they become habits.
Watch your habits; they become character.
Watch your character; it become your destiny

Lao Tzu

"The only thing I know is that I know nothing" – Socrates

"That man is wisest who, like Socrates, realizes that his wisdom is worthless" – Plato

Why? Because as Anaxagoras puts it:

"In everything, there is a share of everything" – Anaxagoras

If so, it will be of no possibility to exponentially know the infinitely driven share of everything, in everything else.

Bar Elaha (oh God) I have a countenance (appearance, facial expression), a façade, bas- (enough) shoorideh (mentally dispersed, with anxiety, not intelligently gathered, nervous, and a bit frightened), an inside in deep sleep, an un-awakened spirit lost in dreams. Occasionally I burn in fire and often drown into my tears. Bar Elaha (oh God), when I know the almighty, my troubles narrow, and when I don't, I am lost with self into dark alleys and plunged into the abyss. Bar Elaha (oh God), when I look upon you, I am the crown holder, and then look upon the self, I am not but just a speck of dust with massive ego tied to insatiable greed. Conveying unfathomable potential to advance, infinitely honored, which, I am. And exhilarated (intoxicated, elated) to know you, but so deprived (needy) in demeanor that I desperately seek your mercy.

SCIENCE AND PHILOSOPHY

> A little philosophy inclineth man's mind to atheism; but depth in philosophy bringeth men's minds about to religion.
>
> – Sir Francis Bacon

It is of utmost important to analyze some of the preliminary subjects that most atheists cling to when discussing God and existence. For instance, non-believers mostly purvey arguments utilizing Newtonian science, quantum physics, how's of the visible world, Darwinian evolution, the big bang, existence, matter, nothingness, infinity, entropy, and so on. In contrast, the believers resort to the philosophy of existence, whys of the world, metaphysics, the unseen world, consciousness, the quantum realm, the Omnipotent Designer, God and creation, believing in a destiny with purpose, entropy, and so on. When philosophical subjects are done without being angered or frustrated, the mind can act resolutely in finding valuable outcomes. "Leisure is the mother of philosophy" – Thomas Hobbes

"Philosophy is a battle against the bewitchment of our intelligence by means of language" – Ludwig Wittgenstein

Both atheism, and theism views are typically based on their emotional approach of the world, neither one is nimrod (stupid, foolish). What we know and grasp is that: God is unknown, and cannot be seen, proven or unproven. What we are left with is making sense of an amazingly marvelous universe, in which is either the effect of an absolutely competent creator, creators or none. They all require some type of faith, correct, or not? Is to be left with one's own insight, and choosing to decide, where no coercions should ever make any one to believe in God, or not. I said emotional, because so many non-believers are sad and angry with an unjustified world that we live in, mistakenly holding God responsible for our pain and agony implemented by the mighty and the "pharaohs" of our time. And bear in mind that: the absence of belief is not atheism. Atheism is saying something on God. The absence of belief is agnosticism.

Obviously, enough subjects as such are byzantine (intricate), and culminating enough in which they must be coagulated with grave reasoning power. And unless they are answered correctly and insightfully, the repercussion for an undermining discussion can manifest abstruse (convoluted) outcomes.

This can leave dire socio-cultural and socioeconomic issues, with ill morals and a spiritual impact, where humanity can lose ground for hope and justice; where everyone's moral imperative can become questionable, since man's relativity in judgement cannot be taken as an absolute, since no man is free from making mistakes as we must take refuge to the all-knowing, infinitely resourceful, with infinite wisdom, and omnipotent God to render precise sagacity (judiciousness).

One should meditate on and examine one's own character conduct before delving into metaphysical realms in search of God. As Socrates said, "The unexamined life is not worth living."

We need to distinguish and understand the differences between the two concepts of science and philosophy, since both terms relate to whys and how's of the world, especially when dealing with metaphysical views, God, and existence.

It is important to clarify the differences between philosophical analogy and scientific undertakings, and to discern which is which. Philosophical inquiries need to be precise, not sporadic; they need to betoken (presage, denote) perspicacious (insightful, penetrating) answers for proving the existence of God. Philosophy and science are essential, as they are needed to be logic-oriented, where philosophy is also very decisive in metaphysical discussions beyond the physical domain.

Science can often help with comprehending natural phenomena. It conveys empirical data, meaningful information that can be investigated; it quantifies; it does examine and repeat if necessary. Science is what we know, it is the objective truth. It is normally in terms of mass, energy, velocity, and position. Science is based on perceptual realty.

Science is methodical (orderly) by nature; it follows scientific methods, which makes its founding based on the outcome of experiments and facts. It commonly starts with experimenting with a certain hypothesis (educated guess) in which it can be corroborated (verified) as truth, or it can prove maquillage (artificial, not genuine), and even wrong.

"Science is what you know. Philosophy is what you don't know" – Bertrand Russell

For philosophy, measurements and observations, statistics and numbers, are not as crucial, since not even a laboratory is required to dissect findings and examine results, as they are as crucial for scientific endeavors that demand empirical validity with an equipped laboratory for hands-on participation.

Science is good at answering the 'how' questions. 'How did the universe evolve to the form that we see?' But it is woefully inadequate in addressing the 'why' questions. 'Why is there a universe at all?' These are the meaning questions, which many people think religion is particularly good at dealing with. (Brian Greene)

Philosophy makes subjective and objective questions. It also generates answers, while science is involved in finding answers. Science also takes answers and proves them as objectively right or wrong. Philosophy meditates on a variety of issues to produce knowledge through savvy thoughts, where science accomplishes the same thing often by observing. Science can be applicable to many areas of discipline.

Science investigates the physical world and learns to exhibit results in a correct way that shifts the responsibility to science in how things are actuated, since science delivers its findings due to probing into physical phenomena.

"An experiment is a question which science poses to Nature, and a measurement is the recording of Nature's answer" (Max Planck)

George Wilhelm Friedrich Hegel said, "Philosophy must indeed recognize the possibility that the people rise to it, but must not lower itself to people." Many philosophers believe the issue of existence is the origin of all philosophical principals; they believe the subject of existence is the core value in which all metaphysical teachings (i.e., information, knowledge, religions, and God) are centered.

Frank outlaw Referencing to the philosophy of God and the existence, validity embraces testing our reviews, where Conclusion should avoid challenging the infinite regression, and not to continually ask why?

One must warrant that reasoning and the power of inference can guarantee a rational and true conclusion.

Existence, or quiddity (nature, disposition, character), is the focal point and the essence of Existentialism. We often approach the concept of existence, since existence or existent is well-regarded as the subject of philosophy (i.e., the mind has to consider existent as belonging to all things and where the mind simultaneously does not behold it in the same way in two things). This is because man's mind cannot contrive (devise) even a single assertion (statement) unless it can narrate (relate) it to existence.

It seems that beautiful minds are influenced with premonition (foreboding, a sense of something happening in the future, anticipation of an event without conscious reason), as if they are mandated with a mission to perform gynecology into the womb of Mother Nature and give birth to yet another treasure, leaping into unveiling the mysteries of nature's obscurities to emancipate man from the clutches of ignorance.

For instance, it is heresy to believe the end justifies the mean; that you should make money every which way you can, which I am afraid a market exhausted from fair and just competition certainly ends up with a disparaging (demeaning, insulting, derogatory) outcome. Extreme income inequality materializes a huge gap between the haves and have nots, creating so much violence, crime, pain, and suffering beyond repair. Thousands and thousands of innocent lives are annually lost, solely because of financial depravity, as billons are globally being forced into poverty with no way out of their misery. One asks why that is the philosophy, and how to fix it; it takes scientific notion and expertise in economic and financial management to fix it—that is science.

Be aware of "predatory philosophy," where the culprits use psychology on masses of believers, prejudicially saying that if you are rich and influential, you are good and blessed, and if you are poor and disadvantaged, you are bad, and perhaps ungodly. But then again, Jesus was not rich.

Why a just and loving God should be so discriminatory in victimizing billions beyond repair; that is philosophy. How to fix it—in unleashing peaceful revolt without murdering innocent lives—is the science. When they use bogus anthropology and utilize false sociology to conceptualize sadistic (cruel) justification to keep different races, different nationalities apart, and crucify millions as misfits, implying they are of an inferior God, and you ask why; that is philosophy. Doing something about it—that is the science behind good socio-cultural conduct.

When neurologists tell us that billions of neurons and trillions of synapse at neurons' junctures spark in one's brain to produce thoughts; that is science. But why should they fire to create thoughts, insights, release hormones, create feelings, emotions, and thousands of other things? That is philosophy. (Which no one has been able to know why so far.)

The bottom line is, we must change the abusive narratives in which the consequences don't direct humanity into the cul-de-sac of socio-cultural and socio-economic impediments; where an intelligence-oriented society should question the root causes of our misfortunes manufactured by the few; where the epistemology (the theory of knowledge, especially with regard to its methods, validity, and scope) and the nature of every word and deed is questioned to avoid further exploitation of the children of God, as we all are, since humanity originated from the same undeniable source. And stop taking God hostage for our misdeeds and sins, as Fredrick Nietzsche said, "God is dead and we killed him."

THE MAGIC OF THE QUANTUM WORLD

The world of subatomic particles, the quantum world, has changed the physicist's mind and prominent scientists' thought process on subatomic particles and the quantum world, since the quantum realm is much different from the world we live in. What we should expect in Newtonian's laws of physics and the material world is quite different and ought not to be expected in the subatomic world.

What makes sense in our world, the world of Newton's laws of physics, does not make any sense in the realms of quantum mechanics because what is practical in our world cannot be experienced in a subatomic situation. Human beings are accustoming and in tune with the visible world. The human brain has gone through evolutional processes for millions of years, but it is solely practical in the world we live in, as we also are relatively the product of our environment. This makes the quantum world quite strange, and not so comprehendible. That is why scientists say that those who claim knowing the quantum world should realize, they know not much.

For instance, as defined, "The term classical vacuum is used in classical electromagnetism where it refers to as an ideal reference medium, devoid of all particles, with ideal properties." Electromagnetism is referred to by scientists as free space, or the vacuum of free space, and sometime as the ideal vacuum. Also as defined by the physicists and the scientists: "In a quantum field theory, the quantum vacuum state (also called quantum vacuum state) is the quantum state with the lowest possible energy generally" it contains no physical particle. Zero-point field is sometimes used as a synonym for the vacuum state of an individual quantized field.

Here is the catch, as "perfect vacuum" is defined and believed by physicists and scientists as the empty space with no atoms or any particles in it. But they also believe there is no such thing as a perfect vacuum, or better said, nothingness, because virtual particles are always popping in and out of existence. Even empty space is seething (come to a boil) with virtual particles. And weirdly enough, in a quantum vacuum, or supposedly in the nothingness state, there is no matter or space, but it's filled with the fundamental subatomic particles that are nowhere until they are observed, and when seen, they cannot be located. Their position is never identified; they can be in more than one place at the same time.

How odd! These particles are nowhere until they are observed, then, when they notice the observer's attention, they disappear, as if they know they are being spied on, therefore making the whole power of intention futile. Scientists believe the space within the world, like a balloon getting bigger and bigger, where there is space within the balloon, but there is no space, or any place outside of it, and without dimensions.

The strange thing is that there must exist some place, some sort of coordinates, for the balloon to have room as it expands, but to no avail; there is no place to accommodate the balloon as it grows bigger and enlarges, which is evidently beyond the human mind to grasp. To postulate (assume) having a place with no dimensions is significantly odd, or imagining things appear in and out of sight in a millisecond from nowhere, from nothingness, and disappear into nothingness, is extremely anomalous (unfamiliar, eccentric, unusual), as their whereabouts cannot be determined, and it only happens in the quantum world of subatomic particles.

The subatomic quantum particles have zero mass, which should mean not having any weight or heaviness. Fundamentally, quantum physics is based on subatomic particles that carry mass, but strangely enough, with zero mass. In other world they lack mass, as they have no heaviness, but they simultaneously carry mass. It would be wacky in our physical world for something to carry weight and not carry weight at the same time, and be in several places at the same time. It just would not make any sense. But they are normal occurrences in quantum realms. Quantum physics is today the strongest theory standing, and very reputable in the science of physics, which is based on uncertainty; there is no definite assessment in quantum physics, since it entirely depends on accidental events.

This is the reasoning behind most atheists' science, since they believe that the full-fledged, the integral nature of the worldly existence from infinitely minuscule (infinitesimal, diminutive, microscopic) to macro existence is based on quantum physics, in which quantum physics is comprised of, and related to, subatomic particles. And then they say, accidental events are the fundamental and the real nature of our material world. They further utter that, since quantum physics is the substratum, the ground for the physical world, and because quantum physics is based on accident, then we must conclude and be sensitized (aware) that the material world has also occurred accidently.

From what many scientists believe and say, we should interpret: the visible world, the tangible world, is created by the unseen realms, the immaterial world, from which it cannot be touched, experienced, cannot be seen, positioned, or even conceived. This should remind us of the meta-physical realms, in which holy sages, renowned philosophers, and many eminent and scholarly minded scientists, such as Ibn-Sinai, Galileo, Nicolaus Copernicus, Johannes Kepler, Francis Bacon, Sir Isaac Newton, Luis Pasteur, Blaise Pascal, Gottfried Leibniz, Werner Heisenberg, Marie Curie, and thousands of others, have explained the metaphysical realms, saying we are not as differentiated as we think. They have warned us of the world we do not see, the immaterial world, which apparently is the very exact reason we live, over and over through most of human history, and since what we do not see evidently controls and is affiliated with the world we see, the world we live in, and the entire universe. Why affiliated? Because if not, then the scientists, the physicists, and other inquisitive minds would not have been able to detect the world of subatomic particles, the quantum world, where utopias become real and further substantiated as we propel.

What they also are missing is interpreting the interactivities of the unseen world, the world of subatomic particles, as accident. Not giving it the probability of what we know as accidental, in which the meaning of an accident can often make sense in our world, might not mean accident in the imperceptible (undetectable, indiscernible) world, which should be better known as the "realms of magic." Where God can also laugh, when one thinks of manifesting a "theory of everything" that can perhaps be the answer to the mysteries of the universe.

The infinite power of God, which is beyond the human mind, is limitlessly diversified by nature, and is magnificent in creation, cannot be constrained in any one formula. We simply lack the ability to seek what is past our competency to delve into infinite a planetary system with trillions and trillions of galaxies, and trillions of universes, where we naturally are not able to dig into the boundless cosmos in trying to answer them with one formula known as the theory of everything.

Let's take a brief look at the Heisenberg uncertainty principle, which is a physical law that molds part of quantum mechanics. It basically says that the more accurate one measures the position of a particle, the less one learns about its exact motion (momentum of velocity and vice versa) in that instant. It is naturally difficult to comprehend the principle behind such an occurrence, but it apparently is harder to elucidate (explicate) it.

The Heisenberg uncertainty principle referencing quantum mechanics states that there is a fundamental limit to how well you can simultaneously know the position and momentum (where momentum is classical mass times velocity of a particle.)

The uncertainty principle, also known as the Heisenberg uncertainty principle or indeterminate principle, statement, articulated in 1972 by the German physicist Werner Heisenberg states that "the position and the velocity of an object cannot both be measured exactly, at the same time, even in theory." It also states that the exact position and momentum of an electron cannot be simultaneously determined. This is because electrons simply do not have a definite position and direction of motion at the same time.

Physicists often quote from T. H. White's epic novel *The Once and Future King*, where a society of ants declares, 'Everything not forbidden is compulsory.' In other words, if there isn't a basic principle of physics forbidding time travel, then time travel is necessarily a physical possibility. (The reason for this is the uncertainty principle. Unless something is forbidden, quantum effects and fluctuations will eventually make it possible if we wait long enough. Thus, unless there is a law forbidding it, it will eventually occur.) Michio Kaku, *Parallel Worlds: A Journey Through Creation, Higher Dimensions, and the Future of the Cosmos*

By now we should know that first there is no such thing as nothingness, or perfect vacuum, which should clearly question Professor Hawking saying in his 1988 book, entitled The History of Time, that the world was created from nothing. Also, in his book, he did not deny God. Then, in his 2010 book titled The Grand Design, he says that gravity is responsible for creation. Therefore, what he is saying is that because of gravity, the world was created from nothing.

The outstanding question that remains is: does gravity mean something, or does it mean nothing? If gravity means something, then the world is made of something, which clearly contradicts saying the world was made of nothing; and if gravity is not something, then gravity cannot be responsible for creating the world; unless perhaps the big bang created gravity. Or maybe gravity made the big bang possible? Which begs for asking the questions that if existence comes from nothing, is it matter that is the real reason for creation; is the big bang responsible for everything? Or is it gravity that made life possible? And on and on, in which such persistence for reaching nowhere land will hopelessly disappoint us all to the end of times.

The fact is that, unless we believe in an infinitely awakened consciousness and limitless cosmic force, which has eternally existed before the dawn of time and prior to any event, then humanity will never overcome being haunted by demonically spirited thoughts that eventually could drag us all into the cul-de-sac of callousness and irresponsibility. There, no just and constructive judgement can ever be mustered, for a convincing argument in imperative philosophical and scientific issues that could ill-effect mankind for the worse, because the repercussions of a godless society are as baffling and meaningless as believing in idolatrous icons.

Quantum physics thus reveals a basic oneness of the universe.

-Erwin Schrodinger

WHAT ARE WE?

Our daily engagement in having a financial life is as demanding as it is time-consuming; because of this, most people are numb toward exploring what we are, or perhaps do not even care to reference it as important at all. This is strikingly sad. Unless we can correctly assess the answer to what we are, the subtle captivity inherent in the lack of such knowledge will negatively affect our individual and social interactions and welfare, regardless of how advanced we seem to be in our modern lifestyle; the negative repercussions will eventually impact us all.

Historically, there are two major viewpoints on this rather intricate question. One is the materialistic view, which holds that humans are physical, behaviorist beings that act mechanically in response to external stimuli, experiencing a robotic-like reaction to environmental processes.

This view leaves no room for closeness to God, spiritual training, or any soul-searching activities. Science is materially based, and looks at the world objectively; it cannot explain it subjectively, and cannot understand the way innate forces operate. Materialists are trying to locate the center of the awareness, not realizing that cosmic awareness is predominant and is magically experienced through many forms and shapes; animals, plants, humans, planets, stars and galaxies, through the billions of universes, and so on.

What really matters is how we express it. Humans express consciousness dynamically, and are at the pinnacle of this awakened chain. The unexplained epiphany happens when the essence of the phenomenal world is not matter, but consciousness. When thoughts and the awakening mind elevate a few degrees. It is then what we knew as a miracle becomes reality. Cosmic energy makes our cognition and experiences possible.

On the other extreme, we have idealists who accept and proclaim the physical world does not exist, everything is just perception, and the material world is nothing more than our imagination.

Which answer we grasp over the other, either materialist or idealist, affects the way we think and how we respond to sometimes very delicate matters that we might face in our lives.

From a mechanical and reductionist perspective, man is perceived as a reduced entity; we are being lowered in status to resemble hardware and machinery, thus are better qualified in our robotic programming to deal with environmental changes. That, I say, is a rather senseless indoctrination, short-sighted in definition of man's attributes and a deadened evolution of a human being's characters.

Let's give the materialist view the benefit of the doubt. If so, should we remove the idea of having a programmer or not? If not, are we all programed the same and therefore must react uniformly to external stimuli? And if yes, what are the differences, if any, that distinguish us from lower species of animals that behave homogeneously by instinct? Which then means that any other human attributes and characteristics should not be immune to external changes or counted as intrinsically worthy, other than being solely behavioristic and instinctual. Either way, there must be an innately animated force that is conscious and sensitive to outside changes causing us to respond accordingly. There is also the need for some proprietor of awakening power in the animal kingdom to spur millions of them into survival of the fittest behaviorism, propelling beasts with brute strength to retaliate being haunted by humans who savagely kill their victims by overpowering them, assisted by camouflage and stealthy maneuverability. Which by the way, would become a recipe for disaster to follow if we were to become a disciple of atheistic views and hence regarded as "mechanically" oriented entities.

You might contest that the survival of the fittest mentality and belief is accepted as truth by many godly societies. To speak to that, I can reassure you we are dealing with hypocrisy in action by many, where self-centeredness and greed have taken over. The effects of this are worse than the work of any honest atheist or materialistic individual. The question that remains is: do human beings have intrinsic values? Do animals have intrinsic values and experience feelings and emotion deeply, as humans do?

When plants react to external stimuli like rain, sunshine, fertilizers, proper gardening; when they bear fruits with nutritional value and eventually dry out and die, are they also behaviorist, since beings react to outward catalysts, including humans? But it sure does not mean we are intrinsically barren, as we are far from it.

When you evaluate people from a mechanical point of view and deplete them of feelings and emotions, do they have the right, for example, to seek justice and react by taking revenge if one's innocent family is slaughtered by criminals? And if yes, then what exactly is it that pushes one to want revenge? Finally, do animals feel and react the same way towards such injustice when their kind is beheaded for dinner?

When one covers a ticking bomb and explodes to pieces, saving others from getting killed, is it the outside stimuli forcing one to sacrifice his or her life to such an extent, or is it because of intrinsic values?

If it is because of external stimuli, why would everyone present not be inclined to perform such extreme self-sacrifice? Or when one pulls his finger so fast from a burning-hot stove, reacting quickly to an outward incident so that one does not get burned, as compared to when someone jumps to his or her death trying to save a child's life, not to get killed by an oncoming bus? Should these two reactions to external stimuli be considered the same, and if not, what causes the extent of such sacrifice inherent to the latter one? Do all people react the same to fear of punishment, rewards, death, worries, justice, revenge, self-sacrifice, excitement, love, beauty, ambition, risk-taking, courage, hunger, wealth, poverty, loyalty, caring, kindness, compassion, philanthropy, benevolence, in giving and generosity, intuition, IQ and intelligence, insightfulness, wisdom, greed, uprising, or when they are discriminated against?

Are the reactions exclusive to each person and situation, or common to all of us? If not common, why not? I thought we as members of the human species should react the same to particular occurrences, since we are all mechanically labelled and descended to behave instinctually. How about when a soldier volunteers to be sent to the front line at a time of war—is it the same motivation as someone who spies for the enemy, no matter how many innocent lives are endangered or are wasted?

Do our emotions and feelings, our thoughts, imaginations, and dreams, our laughter and joy, pain and anguish, the language in which we communicate, and the sacrifices we make have weight, affect chemical composition, or occupy space? If yes, I thought only what carries weight, has chemical composition, and occupies space is manifested and bound to as materialistically real—as compared to agenda which are not manifested the same and are considered as superficially idealistic.

Look, there are intrinsic human values that are explored and put to work by heavenly characters every day and many times over that stem from human compassion and caring, from love and devotion, from loyalty and sacrifice, from dignity and honesty, from passion and longing for justice.

If some hard-headed ideologue behaviorist wants to turn a blind eye to blundering (error, lapse) and prove a miracle-like situation real, then well-known wisdom should apply; if it looks like a duck, swims like a duck, and quacks like a duck, then it is probably a duck. And if we are behaviorists who should mechanically react to environmental changes and automatically respond the same to circumstances facing us, why would anyone need to think or seek solutions to one's problems? We shouldn't have to, since we are supposedly programed to act by instinct, collectively interacting in a herd-like manner to address any auspicious or dire circumstances.

We ought to cling to the core of humanity, which contains the remnants of stardust as recently claimed by cosmic scholars, physicists, and space scientists. Since humanity should identify with people's pain and suffering, with their hunger and displacement from their abode and habitat, from natural tragedies that might have faced them, it should not let them die in vain. It takes time to discard "junk knowledge," ill-received information deliberately instilled in people's heads for the benefit of the few that sadly have become blinded with love of money, and numb to human compassion.

Their incriminating behavior forces the survival of the fittest mentality on desperate masses of people, making it a cutthroat society rather than creating a culture of cooperation. A true culture of compassion has proven to be immensely positive and very productive in bringing people closer together; this would certainly make a huge difference in improving people's lives, their prosperity, and in honoring God.

Let us capitalize on what in heaven's name we are all about. We are about light, we are about love, we are about healing. Stop brewing evil in the name of God, and in the name mankind, misleading them to believe they are cursed and perhaps do not deserve to live. Because you have appropriated and accumulated so much wealth, then you have been blessed and ought to have a clear conscience—this is far from the truth.

Your misconduct is exactly why atheists and behaviorists, agnostics and the like, are emboldening to doubt God. Because of the consequences of your misdeeds, mankind is ignorant enough to hold God responsible for human misery and their pain and suffering. The all-rounded patriarchal system compounded with irreparable ills should be stopped, which has yoked and damaged millions for the worse, if not billions of whom you find inferior, and not up to your discriminatory standard.

When Jesus was asked by his disciples, "Where do we come from?" he said, "We come from light." Contemporary scientists, with all of their might, scientific research, and magnificent telescopes, are now attesting to what Jesus said more than two thousand years ago.

The bottom line is that we are sacred beings, but unless we have the freedom to experience, to keep the good, repel bad and evil, we cannot progress as efficiently as possible. And without experimentation, no dynamic improvement should be expected.

"No man's knowledge here can go beyond his experience"

– John Locke

We should also know, where there is no democracy and human rights, people's happiness will be hampered.

What Immanuel Kant said becomes a reality, especially in dictatorial countries: "Happiness is not an ideal of reason but of imagination."

"God is not willing to do everything, and thus take away our free will and that share of glory which belongs to us"

– Niccole Machiavelli

"Liberty consists in doing what one desires"

– John Stuart Mill

WHY BELIEVE IN GOD?

Things alter for the worse spontaneously, if they be not altered for the better designedly.

– Sir Francis Bacon

The most imperative protectoral move you can ever take is to believe in and seek God. In a consumer-oriented society that is intensely materially based, profit is becoming the sole purpose and is replacing God. It is as if God exists today only as an empty shell with no kernel.

It is more urgent than ever to truly and sincerely call upon the omnipotent, omnipresent God and seek to know him with all your might. The conventional method of reaching God, as practiced by some charlatans, is nothing more than a joke; it is only about getting more dollars in their pockets. This form of practice uses scare tactics and sleazy maneuvers to fool and undermine people's normal rational thought.

This happens even though we live in the twenty-first century, and most people and civilized nations have become quite sophisticated, naturally questioning such phony religious practices. God does not deserve this kind of treatment, and neither do his true followers. Yet we see many instances of those who preach such a wrong message about God—and they should, in this writer's opinion, be dealt no mercy.

When you are spiritually broken and in need of spiritual shelter and help, and you seek refuge with those who claim to be men and women of God, and then receive nothing but trouble, it would take a strong, sane mind not to curse and deny God. We should discern that such false prophets are just more hypocrites that live among us. Their corrupt deeds spiritually kill and maim people's spirit, which has no remedy other than the true God. He is not the cause of human misery.

Rather, the causes are in large part from those who bludgeon others in the name of God. Never before has the existence of God been so well-substantiated, with so much hardcore support and proof that is heavily backed with reason and philosophical and scientific knowledge. Yet so many are becoming remote islands, getting further and further away from the vicinity of their Maker, no longer tethered to or encompassed within his territory. People of high moral fiber are asking why so many nations, peaked in education and immersed in civility of mind and manner, have such rampant and pandemic levels of crime and wrongdoing. Catastrophes are everywhere, as we are bombarded on all sides by disasters, wars, and hunger that are void of tranquility, serenity, and security of mind.

You need to question, why should a child die because of an untreated infected tooth, enduring it for so long, if his parents are unable to buy proper medical care? You should object when people are forced to sell their kidneys because they are financially pushed to the limit and exhausted from having the bare minimum to survive. You should object when so many commit suicide because they are fired and out of job, not being able to find proper vocation to sustain their family's livelihood.

And so many other tragic ordeals that happen because of extreme income disparity in which the real culprits extenuate (make a crime, or a mistake seem less serious or deserving of blame) misallocation of resources and ignore its devastating effects. In actuality, inordinate (exorbitant, extreme) income inequality is the real reason behind so much pain and agony.

You should ask why so many individuals insanely go on shooting sprees, often killing twenty, thirty, fifty, and more innocent bystanders in common places, even at places of worship, because of easy accessibility to guns and military-style machine guns, etc. These and hundreds of other justifying questions should be asked with honest intention, done in good faith, and through purity of heart to fix what is long overdue in many broken sociocultural, socioeconomic nations, to aim at preventing societal maladies (ailments) with lingering psychological effects and spiritual numbness hatching so much violence beyond repair. Caring to become part of the solution and collectively trying to remedy the problems facing mankind are the first steps toward believing in God.

Every day our livelihood is questioned and hanging by a thread. In such an environment, the lower self is praised so much that it cannot be changed without God's help.

The principle of causality states that if there is no intelligence in the design and the effect, there could not be intelligence in the cause. Therefore, if there is intelligence in man, there must be—not should be—must be intelligence in man's cause. It is of solidified reason that a being must exist as some form of mass in space and time. No creator can be part of what was created or within it. God, our Maker, does not visibly exist in created space, matter, or time as we know and perceive them.

Still, some theorists ignorantly inquire, "Where is God? Show him to me," or, "I went to space and did not see God anywhere."

We are not the products of chance; we are intelligently designed. A principle of modern science emerged in 1980 called the anthropic principle, the basic thrust of which is that human existence by accident or chance is not valid. Believing otherwise invalidates all laws of chemistry, all laws of conservation, angular momentum, and every other scientific law, such as physics, conservation of electric charges, and so on. To believe that matter is uncaused is to believe against and discard all the known laws and principles of science. Dealing with conservation of matter and energy would be nothing but an obtuse, insane approach to reason. Unless directed by some being endowed with knowledge and intelligence, whatever lacks intelligence cannot intentionally move towards an end. As the arrow that is shot to its mark by the archer, anything worth living has a purpose and is here to accomplish its goal and objective.

These facts can be seen throughout nature. The whole is made up of the parts, and if the parts have destiny and purpose, then logic dictates that the whole that comprises these parts also has a destiny and purpose.

To say we come from nowhere and we are going nowhere—that this is all just an accident—simply does not add up and is both wrong and contradictory.

Even the famous phrase "the survival of the fittest" presupposes the arrival of the fit. If Darwinists wish to maintain this purely biological theory, that the entire vast order around us is the result of random chance and random changes, then they are also saying that nothing of any empirical evidence can ever be confirmed, and no empirical science can be demonstrated.

Thomas Aquinas argued for God being the "Unmoved Mover." We know that there is motion in the world, and it follows that whatever is in motion has been moved by something else. This other thing, in turn, must have been moved by something, and so on. To avoid regression, we must posit a first and a prime mover that is beyond our space, matter, and time. That ultimate, prime, or unmoved Mover is our God. The late Steven Hawking, arguably today's most famous physicist, did not believe in a God at the end of his life, although he did earlier on.[1]

Yet he claimed, ironically, that the unseen force of gravity is what keeps life and the universe grounded and is also the root cause of existence. For those who do not have to see God to believe in him, gravity is merely an unseen force in the world that is subject to God's power, as are all the other unseen forces in the world, such as electromagnetic, atomic energy, and so on. One has to wonder why it is so difficult for Hawking to see the glory of the unseen God as the root cause of the infinite complexity of existence and the obviously intelligent design of the universe.

With all due respect to Professor Hawking, his is nothing but a vaingloriously (arrogance, vanity) prosaic (humdrum, ordinary) statement, uttered by a fallible man who was willfully blind to the obvious on all sides, as well as both macro- and micro-realities, both of which are beyond human perception. Only God provides the best explanation for DNA codes contained in and controlling the design and function of life on earth. Only God provides the best explanation for the absolute complexity inherent in every element of the universe, including cosmological, planetary, chemical, biological, physical, atomic, natural, electromagnetic, and gravity forces, all interconnected with utmost precision and balance to be optimal to support human life.

The impossible alternative is that every one of our highly complex inventions, such as binary code, sophisticated and powerful computers,

---

[1] Jamie Ducharme, "Stephen Hawking was an atheist. Here's what he said about God, Heaven and his own death." Time.com, March 14, 2018, accessed November 3, 2018, http://time.com/5199149/stephen-hawking-death-god-atheist/

and wireless and digital technology, occurred without any programming, testing, debugging, or planning. This impossible alternative, called the theory of random chance, holds that our modern engineering marvels are not the result of intelligent design but simply fell into place accidently, and it is all without purpose or meaning but simply exists infinitely as it always has, meandering aimlessly and vacuously (lack of intelligence, empty, void, no meaning.)

However illogical, improbable, and impossible, many have subscribed to this theory, despite the cognitive dissonance that inert, random matter is neither self-perpetuating (lengthening, prolonging), nor self-aware, nor capable of creating intelligence, purpose, or meaning. While it is true that all the phenomenological and biological systems could not and did not take a huge and unseen leap from simple, to complex, and to maturity, they are under the influence of and are being conducted with intentional, gradual effort and purpose.

Everything is part of a guided process and forward-looking instruction. One can only produce nature and invent science from an orderly cosmos and scientific blueprint; one can only create human complexity from a discipline-coded and superior source of life. Nothing orderly and disciplined, such as the theory of relativity or other imperative scientific laws and principles, could have come from a disorderly, chaotic, randomized, universe.

If physics is the heart and the soul of science, as physicists and scientists claim, then they are more aware than anyone that mathematics—the ultimate in logic and order—is the heart and soul of physics.

It is a vital principle that applied mathematics reasoning and logic produces harmony. It is a no-brainer that this could not and does not happen randomly but rather by intelligent design. It is only another baby step of inference that the universe, with such a conscious, infinite magnitude in intelligence, a disciplined Creator not only brought order, balance, beauty, harmony, logic, and endless complexity into being, but also has an eternal purpose and meaning for human existence. God's intelligent design is viable and enduring, which otherwise would have been extinguished in the very preliminary stages of its existence.

"It is undesirable to believe a proposition when there is no ground whatever for supposing it true"

– Bertrand Russell

"There is only one good, knowledge, and one evil, ignorance"

– Socrates

"If God did not exist, it would be necessary to invent Him"

– Voltaire

SOME METAPHYSICAL CONCERNS

When something changes or transforms, and after transformation takes place, is it necessarily the same thing, is its identity maintained?

Can consciousness (or ideas, or soul) exist without the body? Is there anything other than physical reality?

Does everything happen for a reason? Should we believe in being predetermined? Is there free will? Is there a cause behind everything that happens? And so on. It is not far from wisdom to believe that existence is causal, but then some believe existence has come about from nothing.

Philosophy begins with curiosity and wondering why things are the way they are, so the inquisitive mind has historically wondered what constitutes the basic stuff of the universe; why and how this basic resource progressed into the diverse forms we experience, and how it arrived to be. Those questions, and other related puzzling inquiries of existence on metaphysical dimensions, is the subject of our concern.

First, why is there anything at all, or something at all? This question becomes clearer when put in comparative form; why is there something rather than nothing? Some doubt whether we can ask this question because there being nothing is not an option. "What exactly is nothing at all? What would nothing be?" We analogize nothing with the idea of empty space, in which we can conceptualize nothing. Why do things exist now or at any given point?

This is the inquiry that Thomas Aquinas was interested in, not in a beginning cause but in a sustaining cause, for he believed that the universe could be eternal—although he accepted it on the basis of revelation that it was not eternal. He manifested his cosmological arguments around the question of what sustains things in the universe in their existence.

In the apparent world, cause and effect play a scientifically convincing and practical role, in which denial of causal relationship should mean futility in the assessment of any sensible technological endeavor. In the realms of cause and effect, Newton's laws of motion are still the proprietor and pioneer of so many reliable experimental accomplishments, but it seems they become irrelevant in the subatomic domain, the quantum world.

Quantum physics maneuvers in search of scientific breakthroughs to manifest rationale in the sphere of the unseen, as reasoning power changes course and spurs scientists to adjust to new laws that need to epitomize different criteria, motivating physicists and scholarly minded people in related fields to identify with revolutionary concepts in the invisible environment.

Even cutting-edge technology, such as the most advanced magnifiers and complex telescopes, have a difficult time making sense of intricacies of the imperceptible (hidden, inconspicuous) world where subatomic particles dance with much different rhythm. It seems that the laws of physics, mathematics, and applied mechanics are unable to substantiate reliable answers from the infinite dancing subatomic particles.

Scientists are rendered helpless to calculate homeostasis (equilibrium, balance) in particles smaller than the atom; it is the world of quantum physics, quarks, string theory, and beyond that has bewildered the magnificent minds of our time.

In particle physics, the notion of a particle is one of several ideas handed down from classical physics. But it also cerebrates (cogitates, meditates, reflects) the modern understanding that at the quantum level, matter and energy act very differently from what much of everyday experience would guide us to expect.

The new elementary particles, "quarks," have replaced protons, neutrons, and electrons as the fundamental particles of the universe.

"In quantum physics, the study of material at the subatomic level, you get down to the tiniest levels. When they take these subatomic particles, put them in particle accelerators and collide them, quantum physicists discover there's nothing there. There's no one home – no ghost in the machine" (Dr. Wayne Dyer)

The Greeks believed the atom was the smallest thing in the universe; they accepted that the atom was not divisible any more. Modern science has since smashed that assumption to pieces, as in the past century physicists have discovered hundreds of particles more diminutive (minuscule, tiny) than an atom. These subatomic, indivisible units are called fundamental, or primal, particles. For example, matter is composed of molecules that are made up of atoms that are made up of protons, neutrons, and electrons.

While protons and neutrons can be further split into fundamental particles known as quarks and gluons, electrons are themselves fundamental—at least for now. As physicists and astrophysicists further sharpen their knowledge of the universe and deploy more powerful technologies, they will probably discover how to deal with the unseen world reliably and to formulate transcendent concepts (ideas) that presently might seem utopian. They could then present revolutionary scales in our comprehension of how things actually work in the sub-realms of existence.

Fundamental particles of both matter and antimatter (in the form of antiparticles) exist.

Corresponding to most kinds of particles, there is an associated antimatter antiparticle with the same mass and opposite charge (including electric charge). For example, the antiparticle of the electron is the positively charged positron, which is produced naturally in certain types of radioactive decay. Likewise, photons mediate electromagnetic force, gluons mediate strong force.

"Scientists currently believe that the tiniest particles are in the form of vibrating strings associated with the world of the unseen that sustains us." String theory has the potential to show that all of the wondrous happenings in the universe – from the frantic dance of subatomic quarks to the stately waltz of orbiting binary stars; from the primordial fireball of the big bang to the majestic swirl of heavenly galaxies – are reflections of one, grand physical principle, one master equation. Brian Greene

"Just as our nervous system and senses are applicable to the visible world, then it is the infinite potentiality of our brain in which we should thrive for to one day have access to ultimate reasoning power that should clearly resonate with the intricacies of the unseen world."

"We need a theory that goes before the Big Bang, and that's String Theory. String Theory says that perhaps two universes collided to create our universe, or maybe our universe is butted from another universe leaving an umbilical cord. Well, that umbilical cord is called a wormhole." Michio Kaku

If we do get a quantum theory of space-time, it should answer some of the deepest philosophical questions that we have, like what happened before the big bang? Michio Kaku

Professor Michio Kaku, professor of theoretical physics and the co-founder of string field theory, states that the latest version of string theory is called "M theory" (M for membrane), so we now realize that strings can coexist with membranes. So the subatomic particles we see in nature, the quarks, the electrons, are nothing but musical notes on a tiny vibrating string. What is physics? Physics is nothing but the laws of harmony that you can write on vibrating strings. What is chemistry? Chemistry is nothing but the melodies that you can play on interacting vibrating strings.

What is the universe? The universe is a symphony of vibrating strings. And then what is the mind of God that Albert Einstein eloquently wrote about in the last thirty years of his life? We now for the first time in history have a candidate for the mind of God. It is cosmic music resonating in eleven-dimensional hyperspace.

So first of all, we are nothing but cosmic music played out on vibrating strings, a membrane obeying the laws of physics, which are nothing but the laws of harmony on vibrating strings. But why eleven dimensions? It turns out that if you write theory in fifteen, seventeen, or eighteen dimensions, the theory is not stable. It caves in and has anomalies; it has singularity.

It turns out that mathematics itself prefers the universe to be in eleven dimensions. Now some people have toyed with twelve-dimensional theory. A physicist at Harvard University has shown that twelve dimensions actually looks very similar to eleven dimensions, except it has two times, double times, rather than one singular time parameter.

What would it be like to live in a universe with double time? If you walked into a room you would see people frozen in a different time than yours, since you beat with a different clock, yet the clocks are running perpendicular to each other. That is called the F theory, "F" standing for the Father of all theories. It seems M theory in eleven dimension is the Mother of all string theories, since it works perfectly well in other dimensions.

Beyond eleven, we have problems with stability; the theories are not stable, and they have deviations from the norm. They have singularity that kills an ordinary theory, so the laws of mathematics themselves force you into an eleven-dimensional theory. Also, because this is the theory of everything, there is more room in higher dimensions to put all the forces of gravity, electromagnetics, and nuclear forces together, where the four-dimensional space is not big enough to accommodate them all. When you expand into eleven dimensions, bingo, everything works well.

Currently, cosmologists claim that the fabric of space and time based on Einstein's relativity theory has culminated in "gravitational wave theory," which might be the answer to how space and time originated. The collision of two black holes approximately 1.3 billion years ago—a colossally powerful incident detected the first time recently by scientists—resulted in gravitational waves that created a ripple across space and time. This was initially hypothesized by Albert Einstein a century ago when he plugged the idea of space and time curvature into curiously minded scientists in related fields. Hence, we should expect the impossible, since planet Earth is only a tiny cell in the body of the cosmos, leaving an infinite number of other planetary cells and universes still to be explored.

Despite scientists' grand attempt in related fields for answers in the unseen world, they only become more puzzling and elusive, making belief in the world of magic more credible. It is the world of the impalpable (undetected, intangible) that has actually made what is seen possible. A world that human senses cannot detect, and fooling some people to crudely say that the invisible world does not exist. It should remind us of the big bang theory, where many also unreasonably claim that it popped out of nowhere.

The big bang, "The role played by time at the beginning of the universe is, I believe, the final key to removing the need for a Grand Designer, and revealing how the universe created itself. … Time itself must come to a stop. You can't get to a time before the big bang, because there was no time before the big bang.

(We have finally found something that does not have a cause because there was no time for a cause to exist in. For me this means there is no possibility of a creator because there is no time for a creator to have existed. Since time itself began at the moment of the big bang, it was an event that could not have been caused or created by anyone or anything. ... So when people ask me if a god created the universe, I tell them the question itself makes no sense. Time didn't exist before the big bang, so there is no time for God to make the universe in.

It's like asking for directions to the edge of the Earth. The Earth is a sphere. It does not have an edge, so looking for it is a futile exercise." It seems "timeless" does not exist in Mr. Hawking's lexicon since he does not realize the "Grand designer" as he puts it is timeless.)

Stephen Hawking

Then Mr. Hawking carries on to say, "If the rate of expansion one second after the big bang had been smaller by even one part in a hundred thousand million-million, it would have re-collapsed before it reached its present size. On the other hand, if it had been greater by a part in a million, the universe would have expanded too rapidly for stars and planets to form."

Ironically, what Mr. Hawking says is a clear testimony to phenomenal intelligent design, mighty supervision, order, discipline, decisiveness, absolute precision, objectivity, management, and purpose, which it seems are not included in Professor Hawking's dictionary. He says if the rate of expansion one second after the big bang had been smaller by even one part in a hundred thousand million-million, it would have re-collapsed before it reached its present size. On the other hand, if it had been greater by a part in a million, the universe would have expanded too rapidly for stars and planets to form."

Mr. Hawking attributes the cause to nothingness, where no cause or time existed, and then abracadabra boom, suddenly primordial (time worn, primeval) existence appeared, which should remind anyone of magic, where miracles can happen, but then again, miracles are also God's attribute. Think about it: out of nowhere, with no cause, no space and no time, without a promulgator, and no creator, things can happen. This type of reasoning could send anyone for psychiatric evaluation, at least in our modern industrialized world. Alarmingly enough, unwarranted thoughts can become normality and eventually the law.

The big bang is now a dominant scientific fact where certain prominent scientists claim there were no activities before the big bang—meaning no matter, no motion, no time or space, just the void, and bear in mind that matter, motion, time, and space go hand in hand and operate in concert.

This should again affirm the view that life was produced from nothing. But then what we are incompetent to figure out is—what should be counted as magic or a miracle? This is obviously beyond our comprehension because as humans, our senses and nervous systems cannot comprehend miracles or deal with them in the name of science.

But reason still questions: did the big bang just present itself out of the blue, from nowhere? If yes, then that is magic, since no matter, no motion, no time, space, or energy could have ever existed before the big bang. To accept this is to believe that cause and effect as we know it in our physical world was not in existence then. Not accepting a prime mover in our regression analysis can go forever unless a prime mover for all moves is manifested indisputably.

If we do not accept an eternal God for the reason behind the sudden occurrence of the big bang, then we need to accept gradual movement and steady accumulation of energy and matter with an unsurpassed degree of lava and heat so focused that potentiated singularity and a very colossal explosion became a turning point in causing the big bang.

This, by the way, would have led to a chaotic and unorderly world. That is what any explosion must do, rather than implementing an utter miracle like a fabulously designed, majestically disciplined and displayed universe. I am not hesitant to say that the incremental build-up of matter and sharp concentration of molten (melted by heat) lava, explosive material, and gasses is more favorable and attuned with scientific communities than an enormous eruption taking place out of nowhere.

But if a gradual accumulation of matter was the case, matter is accompanied with motion, and motion is associated with time and space. They must have existed before the humongous explosion, and they must have been the preliminary requirements for what we know as the big bang because where there is matter exists motion, and where there is motion exists space and time.

We are often left with no idea but to believe nothingness should mean no activity of any sort. But we ought not to be remiss (thoughtless, heedless, lax) in saying that the so-called void should mean nothingness, which on the contrary, nothingness is the womb impregnated with all there is, and all there ever will be, patiently waiting to be sought for generating more miracles.

WHERE DO WE COME FROM?

> Everything that exists is born for no reason, carries on living through weakness, and dies by accident"
>
> – Jean-Paul Sartre

This saying above by Jean-Paul Sartre should leave mankind with no hope, and frankly, vulnerable to suicide, and host of other violent behaviors.

What is consciousness?
What is existence?
What is the universe made of?

Gospel of Thomas Saying 50
Previous -Gospel of Thomas Home -Next
This Gospel of Thomas Commentary is part of the Gospel of Thomas page at Early Christian Writings.

Nag Hammad Coptic Text

> 50. (1) ⲡⲉϫⲉ ⲓ̅ⲥ̅ ϫⲉ ⲉⲩϣⲁⲛϫⲟⲟⲥ ⲛⲏⲧⲛ̅ ϫⲉ ⲛ̅ⲧⲁⲧⲉⲧⲛ̅ϣⲱⲡⲉ ⲉⲃⲟⲗ ⲧⲱⲛ ϫⲟⲟⲥ ⲛⲁⲩ ϫⲉ ⲛ̅ⲧⲁⲛⲉⲓ ⲉⲃⲟⲗ ϩⲙ̅ ⲡⲟⲩⲟⲉⲓⲛ ⲡⲙⲁ ⲉⲛⲧⲁⲡⲟⲩⲟⲉⲓⲛ ϣⲱⲡⲉ ⲙ̅ⲙⲁⲩ ⲉⲃⲟⲗ ϩⲓⲧⲟⲟⲧϥ ⲟⲩⲁⲁⲧϥ ⲁϥⲱϩ(ⲉ ⲉⲣⲁⲧϥ) ⲁⲩⲱ ⲁϥⲟⲩⲱⲛϩ ⲉ(ⲃ)ⲟⲗ ϩⲛ̅ ⲧⲟⲩϩⲓⲕⲱⲛ (2) ⲉⲩϣⲁϫⲟⲟⲥ ⲛⲏⲧⲛ̅ ϫⲉ ⲛ̅ⲧⲱⲧⲛ̅ ⲡⲉ ϫⲟⲟⲥ ϫⲉ ⲁⲛⲟⲛ ⲛⲉϥϣⲏⲣⲉ ⲁⲩⲱ ⲁⲛⲟⲛ ⲛ̅ⲥⲱⲧⲡ ⲙ̅ⲡⲉⲓⲱⲧ ⲉⲧⲟⲛϩ (3) ⲉⲩϣⲁⲛϫⲛⲉ ⲧⲏⲩⲧⲛ̅ ϫⲉ ⲟⲩ ⲡⲉ ⲡⲙⲁⲉⲓⲛ ⲙ̅ⲡⲉⲧⲛ̅ⲉⲓⲱⲧ ⲉⲧϩⲛ̅ ⲧⲏⲩⲧⲛ̅ ϫⲟⲟⲥ ⲉⲣⲟⲟⲩ ϫⲉ ⲟⲩⲕⲓⲙ ⲡⲉ ⲙⲛ̅ ⲟⲩⲁⲛⲁⲡⲁⲩⲥⲓⲥ

BLATZ

(50) Jesus said: If they say to you: Whence have you come? say to them: We have come from the light, the place where the light came into being of itself. It [established itself], and it revealed itself in their image. If they say to you: Who are you? say: We are his sons, and we are the elect of the living Father. If they ask you: What is the sign of your Father in you? say to them: It is movement and rest.

LAYTON

(50) Jesus said, "If they say to you (plur.), 'Where are you from?' say to them, 'It is from light that we have come -from the place where light, of its own accord alone, came into existence and [stood at rest]. And it has been shown forth in their image.' If they say to you, 'Is it you?' say 'We are its offspring, and we are the chosen of the living father.' If they ask you, 'What is the sign of your father within you?' say to them, 'movement and repose." and

What we now hear from the most prominent scientists at the most advanced laboratories is that we are made of stardust.

For many years, advocators of science have believed that human-beings are made of stardust, and presently, a fresh

DORESSE

55 [50]. Jesus says: "If people ask you: 'Where have you come from?' tell them: 'We have come from the Light, from the place where the Light is produced [. . .] outside itself <or: of itself?>. It [. . .] until they show (?) [. . .] their image.' If someone says to you: 'What are you?' say: 'We are the sons and we are the elect of the living Father.' If <people> ask you: 'What sign of your Father is in you?' tell them: 'It is a movement and a "rest."'

survey of more than 170,000 stars exhibit how true the old platitude (cliché, buzzword) is: they have realized that: humans and their galaxy have approximately 97-98 percent of the same sort of atoms, and the elements of life seem to be more prevalent directed at the galaxy's center, the research found.

The imperative components for life on Earth, frequently known as the building blocks of life, can be abridged as CHNOPS: carbon, hydrogen, nitrogen, oxygen, phosphorus, and sulfur. For the first time, many astronomers have categorized plenty of these factors (elements) in a monumental embodiment of stars.

The astronomers
ranked each element's
abundance via a method
known as chromatic
(spectroscopy); each
feature (element) vents
multifarious (unequal,
unlike) wavelengths of
light from within a star,
and they size the depth
of the dark and bright
patches in each star's
light gamut (spectrum,
range) to decide what it
was made of.

Abstract questions of who are we? Where do we come from? Why are we here? What happens after we expire? What is existence? What is consciousness? and so on, historically have seen many views these questions, but the contemporary scientific approach by many scholarly minded scientists and prominent philosophers is that "our bodies are made of remnants of stars and massive explosions into galaxies," according to astrophysicist Karel Schrijver of the Lockheed Martin Solar and Astrophysics Laboratory and his wife, professor of pathology at Stanford University in their new book titled Living with Stars, how the human body is connected to the life cycles of the Earth, the planets, and the stars.

They believe that everything we are, and everything in the universe and Earth originated from stardust, and it continually floats through us even today. It directly connects us to the universe, rebuilds our bodies over and over again over our lifetimes.

The six most common elements of life on Earth (including more than 97 percent of the mass of a human body) are carbon, hydrogen, nitrogen, oxygen, Sulphur, and phosphorus. Those same elements are abundant at the center of our Milky Way galaxy.

Credit: Dana Berry/Skyworks Digital Inc.; SDSS collaboration.

The proportion of each element of life differed depending on the region of the galaxy in which it was found. For example, the sun resides on the outskirts of one of the Milky Way's spiral arms. Stars on the outskirts of the galaxy have fewer heavy elements required for life's building blocks, such as oxygen, than those in more central regions of the galaxy.

"It's a great human-interest story that we are now able to map the abundance of all of the major elements found in the human body across hundreds of thousands of stars in our Milky Way," Jennifer Johnson, the science team chair of the SDSS-III APOGEE survey and a professor at Ohio State University said in the statement. "This allows us to place constraints on when and where in our galaxy life had the required elements to evolve, a sort of 'temporal galactic habitable zone.'"

Consciousness is infinite energy, an awakened source, extremely resourceful, that is non-local, which means universal. Thoughts, ideas, insight, imaginations, dreams, creativity, ingenuity, feelings and emotions, mindfulness, space, time, qualia (the internal and subjective component of sense perceptions, arising from stimulation of the senses by phenomena), etc., are all interconnected within consciousness.

It is not tangible. All things maneuver within consciousness. It is the super glue holding what is animated, or not, what is instinctual or not, those with mind, or not. The entire existence is contained within consciousness. It is the very fundamental foundation to all there was, all there is, and what will ever be, as only the effects of consciousness are seen, as no experiment is ever possible without consciousness.

The power of semantics (related to the meaning of words and phrases) is connected to consciousness, since things do not exist if one is not aware of them.

It seems consciousness is the common denominator for the entire existence, and unless humanity comes into accord with this extremely potent force, no viable explanation by modern science can actually take place for explaining what is driving our universe.

For instance, the two major scientific revolutions of modern physics are first Albert Einstein's theory of relativity.

In the equation, the increased relativistic mass (m) of a body times the speed of light squared (c2) is equal to the kinetic energy (E) of that body.

$E = mc2$ Proof of Albert Einstein's special-relativity equation $E = mc2$, it means that mass and energy are relative, they are interchangeable, as they are not fixed.

The second theory says that space and time are relative; they are interchangeable and not fixed, they are equivalent. The formula is as follows: $s2= -t2-c2$ where space, time, matter, and energy are not absolute.

The actual physical reality of the world, and the experiences that we acquire from out there, what appears in our consciousness from maneuvering in the physical world are fundamentally different; they are not the same.

What we see, hear, taste, touch, and smell are just the illusion of the reality. the new paradigm is shifted in the assumption that CONSCIOUSNESS is the premier merit (capital) of reality.

Consciousness is prioritized for two reasons; first, it is potentiated for infinite experimentation, which is proffered (available) in all things. Secondly, because we do not directly experience the external world, what we grasp are the contents of consciousness, not to exclude our emotions, feelings, thoughts, and perceptions, and all the sensations that originate in our mind.

Immanuel Kant, the German philosopher, made a very clear distinction between the forms that appeared in the mind, known as "phenomenon," meaning that which appears to be, and the world that produced our perception of things and activities, known as "noumenon," meaning that which is grasped, apprehended, or detained. Kant emphasized, and insisted on phenomenon, where noumenon permanently stays beyond our knowing.

Many philosophers and prominent thinkers have insisted on the idealism theory saying that only the mind and mental contents exists.

A century ago, British philosopher John Locke argued that all knowledge is based on perceptions, caused by external objects acting on the senses. But Locke thought that perception was passive, the mind simply reflecting the images received by the senses.

Kant proposed that the mind is an active attendee in the process, constantly shaping our experience of the world. Reality, he thought, is something we each build for ourselves.

For Berkeley, the theologian bishop, he denied anything existing apart from our perception, that only mind and mental contents exist. His doctoring is generally associated and identified with "immaterialism," the doctrine that believes material things simply do not exist since they have no reality except as mental perceptions.

The difficult question for George Berkeley is that what happens to the world when no one is perceiving it. But Kant less radically believed there is a fundamental reality, but is never known directly; all that we can comprehend is the way objects appear in our mind. Through our senses: sight, hearing, smell, taste, touch, we experience the external world. Then our brain brilliantly, in a split second, takes all of these images received, and without us noticing, puts the entire data together and presents its own picture of the so-called reality from what is out there.

For instance, when we look at a plant, the light reflected from the plant shapes an image of the plant on our retina. Then, the photo-sensitive cells in the retina release electrons, setting off electro-chemical impulses that travel through the optic nerve to the visual cortex of our brain. The data endures a complicated procedure that then discerns patterns, colors, motion, and shapes, which the brain puts together as information received into cohesive position and makes its own version of the outside world. Eventually, an image of the plant shows up in our consciousness. The issue of concern is that how neural activities bring about conscious experience is an extremely difficult question to answer, since we have no idea how an image appears in our mind since it does occur, as we have the conscious experience of seeing a plant.

Conscious exposure on one hand generates an abysmally enigmatic circumstance. On the other hand, a fairly able-bodied world of materialism must be for real so that we can explain how it is that conscious events relate and interact with non-conscious physical incidents, and why we are not able to describe how physical phenomena gives rise to conscious experience. An ever present and ubiquitous consciousness can play a significant role in relatively clarifying most of the events taking place in our world. The irony is that we endure the body-mind experience, but cannot materialize consciousness, and it's not possible to describe dilemmas of phenomenal experience denoting physical realization. It seems consciousness is going to remain a mystery in the near future, or within the realm of infinity.

Images in the Mind

Parallel activities happen with the other human senses. The strings of a vibrating violin constitute pressure waves in the air. These waves stir up tiny hairs inside the inner ear, which then send electrical impulses to our brain. The same with vision; data received are analyzed and cleverly assembled, activating our experience for hearing music. For smelling, chemical molecules originating from the skin of a rose trigger receptors in the nose, leading to the experience of smelling a rose. And similarly, cells in the skin forward messages to the brain that guide to experiences of touch, pressure, texture, grain, and affection.

In short, all that I perceive—all that I see, hear, taste, touch and smell—has been reconstructed from sensory data. I think I am perceiving the world around me, but all that I am directly aware of are the colors, shapes, sounds, and smells that appear in the mind.

"Every man's world picture is and always remains a construct of his mind, and cannot be proved to have any other existence." Erwin Schrödinger

Our perception of the world has the very convincing appearance of being "out there" around us, but it is no more "out there" than are our nightly dreams. In our dreams we are aware of sights, sounds, and sensations happening around us. We are aware of our bodies. We think and reason. We feel fear, anger, pleasure, and love. We experience other people as separate individuals, speaking and interacting with us. The dream appears to be happening "out there" in the world around us. Only when we awaken do we realize that it was all just a dream—a creation in the mind.

When we say, "it was all just a dream," we are referring to the fact that the experience was not based on physical reality. It was created from memories, hopes, fears, and other factors. In the waking state, our image of the world is based on sensory information drawn from our physical surroundings. This gives our waking experience a consistency and sense of reality not found in dreams. But the truth is, it is as much a creation of our minds as are our dreams (Erwin Schrödinger).

Therefore, all we know is what actually stems out of experience. We become in tune with the picture the brain draws, in which the brain maneuvers so rapidly that we cannot know what took place. For instance, the color green; in realty, there is no color green out there. When light of certain frequency is reflected from the physical world, which then is experienced in our mind, or consciousness, call it as you wish, we then see the color green. Colors are seen in particular shades after they are dealt with, or manipulated by, the brain. Colors are not in the material world; they are only wavelength and reflections. Colors are utterly the products of our mind. It is believed that consciousness is the field of all possibilities; in other words, consciousness makes anything possible. It is the foundation of our experience. "Everything that is experienced is perceived by mind, made by mind, and ruled by mind" (Buddha).

The Greek philosopher Demetrious, 400 BC, was the first person who used the term atom, meaning indivisible.

Demetrious thought that if one takes a piece of matter and divides it, and continues to do so, one will consequently arrive to a point where one could not divide it any more. This fundamental unit was what Democritus called an atom. He believed all matters consist of atoms; atoms are bits of matter too extremely small to be seen. There is an empty space between atoms. Atoms are solid, as they have no internal structure. Atoms of various substances are different in size, form, and weight.

Then, approximately one hundred years later, scientists discovered the atom is made of subatomic particles, which recently modern science found out those particles do not exist, they are just potentials for our experiences, as consciousness there, or better said: there is not a thing there.

"Matter as we know it, exist only in our mind" (Max Plank).

It seems the tables have turned, and contrary to calling idealists superstitious, it is clear that the materialistic view has scientifically been proven wrong, but no one has the guts to admit that matter as we know it does not exist, and everything that we call matter comes from something that is not materially based. Most contemporary scientists, and noticeably philosophers, now believe the essential nature of the universe is not physical. They also say that nature is a discontinuation, where there are gaps, suggesting on-and-off events.

Deepak Chopra said: "There is a field of possibilities, a field of pure potentialities, if not God, call it what you want. The immense potentiality of all that was, and all that is, and all there will be, if not God, then what?"

Science says there exists a field of non-local correlation, since everything is connected to everything else; there is a field of creativity, there are quantum leaps of opportunities promising miracles, and rightly so. It has now more than ever become clear that we are an undeniable part of the universal consciousness.

Rumi, the great Persian philosopher and poet, said: "You are not just a drop of the ocean, you are the mighty ocean in the drop." It is so surprising that our feelings, emotions, hopes, dreams, imaginations, thoughtfulness, insight, free will, freedom, often creativity like miracles, and millions of other things are done through our "neurons" that we cannot see. But then, some callously minded individuals are still denying an omnipotent God, that is beyond space, time, and infinitely so big to be detected by human nervous system. Not reckoning with such infinity enlightening and intelligent force, is extremely unscientific, and non-philosophical, in which science and philosophy are potently equipped to answer most of "whys" and "how's" of the world.

Einstein added that "Science without religion is lame, and religion without science is blind."

Steven Hawking said, "It would be very difficult to explain why the universe would have begun in just this way, except as the act of God who created beings like us."

Double slit experiment

One of the most noticeable experiments in physics is the double slit experiment. It uniquely shows that the strange behavior of the little particles of matter also have something of a wave position. The experiment manifests that every act of observing a particle has a dramatic effect on its observer. It shows that what we know as particles, such as electrons, exhibit both combined characteristics of particles and characteristics of waves. That's the illustrious wave particle duality of quantum mechanics.

It denotes that the act of observing, of measuring, a quantum system has a deep effect on the system. Strangely enough, as if the particles knew they are being looked at, they manage not to get caught in the performance of bizarre quantum pranks. The question of exactly how that happens constitutes the measurement problem of quantum mechanics. The double slit experiment reveals the principle limitation of the observer's ability to foresee the experiment's result. Richard Feyman called it "a phenomenon which is impossible to explain in any classical way, and which has in it the heart of quantum mechanics in reality, it contains the only mystery of quantum mechanics.

- "Everything we call real is made of things that cannot be regarded as real" (Niels Bohr).
- "Those who are not shocked when they first come across quantum theory cannot possibly have understood it" (Niels Bohr).
- "If you are not completely confused by quantum mechanics, you do not understand it" (John Wheeler).
- "If [quantum theory] is correct, it signifies the end of physics as a science" (Albert Einstein).
- "I do not like [quantum mechanics], and I am sorry I ever had anything to do with it" (Erwin Schrödinger).
- "Quantum mechanics makes absolutely no sense" (Roger Penrose).
- "It is safe to say that nobody understands quantum mechanics" (Richard Feynman).

And, in a little more detail, from Richard Feynman:

I am going to tell you what nature behaves like. If you will simply admit that maybe she does behave like this, you will find her a delightful, entrancing thing. Do not keep saying to yourself, if you can possibly avoid it, 'but how can it be like that?' because you will get 'down the drain,' into a blind alley from which nobody has yet escaped. Nobody knows how it can be like that.

Here's a rather more optimistic,

In two slit interferences, quantum mechanics cannot determine which slit the electron went through."

This statement reflects not the poverty of quantum mechanics, but its richness.

In classical mechanics, an electron must have a position — it must pass through one slit or the other.

In quantum mechanics an electron might have a position, but there is an infinitely rich variety of other possibilities as well.

It is no failure of our instruments that they cannot measure what does not exist.

The observe effect

Observer effect may refer to the Hawthorne effect, a form of reactivity in which subjects modify an aspect of their behavior in response to their knowing that they are being studied. Same goes for the "Heisenbug" effect of computer programming, where a software bug seems to disappear or alter its behavior when one attempts to study it.

What is the Heisenberg effect?

In quantum mechanics, the uncertainty principle (also known as Heisenberg's uncertainty principle) is any of a variety of mathematical inequalities asserting a fundamental limit to the precision with which certain pairs of physical properties of a particle, known as complementary variables, such as position x and ...

Do particles behave differently when observed?

When a quantum "observer" is watching, quantum mechanics states that particles can also behave as waves. In other words, when under observation, electrons are being "forced" to behave like particles and not like waves. Thus the mere act of observation affects the experimental findings.

What is Heisenberg most known for?

He developed new theories in quantum mechanics about the behavior of electrons that agreed with the results of previous experiments.

Heisenberg is most famous for his "uncertainty principle," which explains the impossibility of knowing exactly where something is and how fast it is moving.

In science, the term observer effect means that the act of observing will influence the phenomenon being observed. For example, for us to "see" an electron, a photon must first interact with it, and this interaction will change the path of that electron.

The Heisenberg uncertainty principle states that it is impossible to know simultaneously the exact position and momentum of a particle. That is, the more exactly the position is determined, the less known the momentum, and vice versa. This principle is not a statement about the limits of technology, but a fundamental limit on what can be known about a particle at any given moment. This uncertainty arises because the act of measuring affects the object being measured. The only way to measure the position of something is using light, but, on the subatomic scale, the interaction of the light with the object inevitably changes the object's position and its direction of travel.

With the advent of new technology modern science is able to dig deeper into the mysteries of universe. It is no brainer as it is now very clear, what is taking place in the unseen world is drastically different from what for so long had occupied the classical physicist's mind stating, what we see, is what we get. where modern science has proved many people wrong saying that: what you see is not what you get. And it is the unseen world which rules the physical world. Now more than ever the evidence of a magnificent creator is much more apparent to scientific community. Since prominent physicists, philosophers and scholarly minded individuals are now aware of quantum consciousness.

The views on new paradigm shift from a world known as objectively real which existed as a separate entity, and not connected to us has altered toward creationism. The question is if there is a God behind the existence? And the quantum world says yes, if not, how could quantum physic describe possibilities which can substantiate actual experience of events taking place in our world. None locality, cosmic awareness, and downward causation are the properties of consciousness, where no matter can behave non-local, since the quantum soup is entirely about energy oriented information and awareness. One cannot model life based on reductionists mentality, where life can be simulated in laboratory and become jubilated just because some short sighted scientists are able to manage a self-replicating molecule. One cannot reproduce life from a self-replicating molecule. "Life can only be produced from a down-ward causation." (Amit Go swami)

Paul Davis said, "The secret of life won't be cooked up in a chemistry lab."

Paul Davies

Life's origins may only be explained through a study of its unique management of information.

"Even the simplest bacterium is incomparably more complicated than any chemical brew ever studied."

The origin of life is one of the great outstanding mysteries of science. How did a non-living mixture of molecules transform themselves into a living organism? What sort of mechanism might be responsible?

A century and a half ago, Charles Darwin produced a convincing explanation for how life on Earth evolved from simple microbes to the complexity of the biosphere today, but he pointedly left out how life got started in the first place. "One might as well speculate about the origin of matter," he quipped. But that did not stop generations of scientists from investigating the puzzle.

The problem is, whatever took place happened billions of years ago, and all traces long ago vanished—indeed, we may never have a blow-by-blow account of the process. Nevertheless, we may still be able to answer the simpler question of whether life's origin was a freak series of events that happened only once, or an almost inevitable outcome of intrinsically life-friendly laws. On that answer hinges the question of whether we are alone in the universe or whether our galaxy and others are teeming with life.

Most research into life's murky origin has been carried out by chemists. They've tried a variety of approaches in their attempts to recreate the first steps on the road to life, but little progress has been made. Perhaps that is no surprise, given life's stupendous complexity. Even the simplest bacterium is incomparably more complicated than any chemical brew ever studied.

But a more fundamental obstacle stands in the way of attempts to cook up life in the chemistry lab. The language of chemistry simply does not mesh with that of biology. Chemistry is about substances and how they react, whereas biology appeals to concepts such as information and organization. Informational narratives permeate biology. DNA is described as a genetic database, containing instructions on how to build an organism. The genetic code has to be transcribed and translated before it can act. If we cast the problem of life's origin in computer jargon, attempts at chemical synthesis focus exclusively on the hardware, the chemical substrate of life, but ignore the software, the informational aspect. To explain how life began, we need to understand how its unique management of information came about.

In the 1940s, the mathematician John von Neumann compared life to a mechanical constructor and set out the logical structure required for a self-reproducing automaton to replicate both its hardware and software. But Von Neumann's analysis remained a theoretical curiosity. Now a new perspective has emerged from the work of engineers, mathematicians, and computer scientists, studying the way in which information flows through complex systems, such as communication networks with feedback loops, logic modules, and control processes. What is clear from their work is that the dynamics of information flow displays generic features that are independent of the specific hardware supporting the information.

Information theory has been extensively applied to biological systems at many levels from genomes to ecosystems, but rarely to the problem of how life actually began.

Doing so opens up an entirely new perspective on the problem. Rather than the answer being buried in some baffling chemical transformation, the key to life's origin lies instead with a transformation in the organization of information flow. Paul Davis. When an atom is broken down, quarks and electrons are discovered. Within these founded particles subsist pure energy that cannot be physically measured. Quantum science has concocted this energy as its exclusive intelligence, which replies with no common sense approach. Quantum physics knows that everything in our universe is managed with the same note through a grand, unified, indestructible force. But human curiosity does not stop there.

We question: what is existence? What is consciousness? What is our awareness of the universe, or the existence? We cannot be certain of any answer that has been rendered so far. What we know is the universe exists, and also we are aware that we exist." But both knowings are contextually puzzling. Scientists tell us that about 74 percent of the universe is made of dark energy, and also made of 22 percent of dark matter, of which only 4 percent is visible matter.

What is dark energy? What is dark matter according to Hubble site discoveries?

So what is dark energy? Well, the simple answer is that we don't know. It seems to contradict many of our understandings about the way the universe works.

We all know that light waves, also called radiation, carry energy. You feel that energy the moment you step outside on a hot summer day.

Einstein's famous equation, E = mc2, teaches us that matter and energy are interchangeable; merely different forms of the same thing. We have a giant example of that in our sky: The Sun. The Sun is powered by the conversion of mass to energy.

Something from nothing.

Could dark energy show a link between the physics of the very small and the physics of the large? Energy is supposed to have a source—either matter or radiation. The notion here is that space, even when devoid of all matter and radiation, has a residual energy. That "energy of space," when considered on a cosmic scale, leads to a force that increases the expansion of the universe.

Perhaps dark energy results from weird behavior on scales smaller than atoms. The physics of the very small, called quantum mechanics, allows energy and matter to appear out of nothingness, although only for the tiniest instant. The constant brief appearance and disappearance of matter could be giving energy to otherwise empty space.

It could be that dark energy creates a new, fundamental force in the universe, something that only starts to show an effect when the universe reaches a certain size. Scientific theories allow for the possibility of such forces. The force might even be temporary, causing the universe to accelerate for some billions of years before it weakens and essentially disappears.

Or perhaps the answer lies within another long-standing unsolved problem, how to reconcile the physics of the large with the physics of the very small. Einstein's theory of gravity, called general relativity, can explain everything from the movements of planets to the physics of black holes, but it simply doesn't seem to apply on the scale of the particles that make up atoms. To predict how particles will behave, we need the theory of quantum mechanics. Quantum mechanics explains the way particles function, but it simply doesn't apply on any scale larger than an atom. The elusive solution for combining the two theories might yield a natural explanation for dark energy.

Stranger and Stranger

Most of the universe seems to consist of nothing we can see. Dark energy and dark matter, detectable only because of their effect on the visible matter around them, make up most of the universe. Illustrated by Hubble site discovery.

It seems rather odd that we have no solid concept about what makes up 74 percent of the universe. It's as we had pioneered all the land on planet Earth and not ever in all our search found an ocean. But currently that we've grasped sight of the waves, we want to conceive what this colossal, peculiar and potent entity really is.

The idiosyncrasy (peculiarity, eccentricity, strangeness, quirkiness) of dark energy is exciting. It indicates to scientists that there is a discrepancy in our understanding that requires to be addressed, signaling the way toward an unexplored territory of physics. We see the cite (evidence) that the cosmos may be arranged enormously different than we previously thought. Dark energy both signals that we still have a great deal to cultivate, and warns us that we stand ready for another great hop in our comprehension of the universe.

We are aware of this: Since space is prevalent, this dark energy force is ubiquitous, and its outcome multiplies as space grows. Comparably, gravity's force is mightier when things are close together and tenuous (weak), when they are far apart. Because gravity is becoming weaker with the augmentation(enlargement) of space.

Therefore, some of the questions modern science has not been able to answer are: What is the universe? What is existence? Are they separate? What is consciousness? What is our awareness of consciousness? What is our awareness of existence? And so on. What we supposedly know is that the universe exists, and we are aware that we exist, even though we do not know where we come from and we do not know who we are, why we are here, and where we are heading.

Scientists tell us that 74 percent of the universe is arcane (mystic) force called dark energy, which Einstein pointed out as "cosmological constant" so scientists think it is the cause for expanding the universe quicker than the speed of light. It seems that galaxies move apart from each other, and as the speed of the movement of galaxies from each other increases more and more, spaces are split and further expand. Scientists believe that the "cosmic horizon" of outer space is presently forty-seven to forty-eight billion years away from where we are. Scientists also tell us that the remaining stuff, the 22 percent that is called dark matter is not atomic, which means it doesn't reflect light; it can neither emit nor absorb light. But it holds entire galaxies through the gravitational force; it is just not possible to interact with it.

Hence, 74 percent of the universe is dark energy, and 22 percent dark matter, which leaves 4 percent of atomic force. And then science reveals that 99 percent of this said 4 percent atomic force is hydrogen and helium that hasn't yet formed into stars. The remaining effect is .01 percent, which is apparently the visible universe from which 99 percent of .01 percent is not seen, which is intergalactic interstellar dust. Then figure that billions and billions of galaxies within galaxies, each with billions and billions of planets forming indefinite universes are constituted only within .01 percent that is atomic. This evidences what we so far comprehend and depend on, hoping the gravitational forces do not collapse for guarantying what exists, not to exclude humanity.

Scientists have realized that atoms are particles, particles are waves, and waves are possibilities that exist in what we know as nothingness. Therefore, past the emergence of molecules, when science arrives at the subatomic realms and then beyond, what they see is nothing; but then again, if the nature of our existence is nothing, where is consciousness? And what is consciousness? What is the biological nature of consciousness, if any? Starting with self, we cannot locate any one, any ghost or any shadow inside, no matter how advanced our magnifiers are or how sophisticated our scientific tools are, such as MRI, CT scan, laser beams, or x-rays machines, and using any other advanced radiation machine to detect the observing-self is just not possible. It seems the observer is delusional, since we cannot find who is doing the hundreds, if not thousands, of things that we daily do, but no one is to be found within us, or inside our brain. No matter how deep we look into every cell, every neuron, or any other part of our body, it is not going to happen. It is all about feelings, all about sensation. If we can feel our presence, feel our breath, our thoughts, that must be the observing self. And if we can feel the universe, that is what supposedly exists; which the sages, and scholarly minded people say has always existed beyond space and time.

Now how true that is, it is one's prerogative to convincingly accept or reject.

The observing self is not about thoughts, emotions, and feelings, but more an awareness entity. One knows when thinking and feeling because there is an awareness, but can we make sense of being aware? Yes, only by noticing the effects of being aware of self and the atmosphere around us. We change due to the human emotional roller coaster, due growing up, and as we mature, we often have to take a variety of positions in life. As our thoughts and feelings change, we deal with different roles in our lives. But the observing self does not alter; it seems the observing self does not change, but sees and experiences.

It makes you aware of your conduct, which is the result of your thinking self, your emotional self, your cultural self. The observing self does not judge, does not take responsibly, does not produce any thoughts. It surreptitiously observes without being seen. The wise, the saints, gurus, and the godly philosophers of the world have been insisting on a cognized universe all along, even before there ever was a brain or a body created, before you and I and everyone else started with a single cell, then multiplied, and replicated fifty times, arriving at about three trillion cells or more, making what we know as humans. Cosmic consciousness has always been the layout for existence in our world and is the reason we can experience and feel our identity, and have a sense of administrative control over the mind. Consciousness is the potential for experiencing our awareness of existence, and is prior to subject/object split.

Top of Form

Quantum physic is in line with the philosophy of science. It states that there is no actual world of electrons, photons, quarks, or any other subatomic entity that we might encounter in the future. There is only delineation (description) of the world that uses these terms and it works in explaining what one observes.

The traditional scientific inquiry, basically the "Newtonian world," is to learn about things as if they exist independently of the observer. It works well in the visible world where cause and effect, time and space, seem to be the nervous system of scientific experimentation—until we are faced with studying the quantum world of the very small. It is here, where the traditional ideas of causality, time, and space breakdown, where the observer's effect or consciousness plays a conspicuous (remarkable, prominent) role.

It is by way of observation that the quantum world arrives. Before observation, the quantum realm exists for mathematical assessments, acknowledged as probability waves. Once an observation happens, this situation collapses into something that can only be known in quantum terms. When one has the experience, one then perceives and gets into cognitive mode, where personal interactivity materializes looking at the universe. It is then the subject/object split substantiates.

The dynamics behind such subject/object split is of significance, since no one knows why and how should such transition takes place, giving the observer an illusion of the external world. The outside world impacts our senses; we become aware of our environment via the nervous system and our brain. We experience and become familiar with our surroundings. Yes, and as we experience, perceive, and analyze, the subject/object split occurs. This entire interchangeability happens with infinite speed, and so quick that no transformation of the subject/object split is ever noticed either by the naked eye or other senses, only to remind us of magic.

What so far is known is that our experiences, our creations, sketches, observations, and all that we are involved with, happens in consciousness, but there is no scientific corroboration (verification) of consciousness, since it cannot be seen by our senses, it can only be felt via awareness; for instance, one being conscious of oneself in one's mind. Consciousness observes, measures, evaluates; it verifies, but it cannot be observed or measured. All of scientific confirmation of consciousness is deduced. It is based on inference, which means a guess or opinion that comes from information that one has. The sole linear experience of consciousness is self-awareness within awareness.

Bear in mind that electrons and other subatomic entities are remarkably diminutive (infinitesimal, tiny), and they also have extremely low mass. They move extremely fast, and due to the Heisenberg uncertainty principle, their precise position is absolutely undetectable. We can solely approximate their position to within a confident uncertainty. Hence, not being able to know the exact position renders it impossible to watch them. With a mass so low, even the smallest interplay (synergy, interaction) with them by another electron or photon will send them flying off so that no one can observe them, and we're now left with a worse understanding of their EXACT location.

Due to the Heisenberg uncertainty principle (HUP), it is impossible to exactly locate electrons and quarks and other subatomic particles. Scientists only know where electrons are likely to be, but never where they actually are positioned. Electrons can exist in multistate, at the same time—things are extremely strange at the quantum level.

Bear in mind that the internet, laser beam, broadband, GPS, computer, fiber optic, are all the result of quantum theory. And yes, it is counterintuitive, but it is what it is. It is difficult to believe the activities at the atomic level. They use electron cloud models of atoms as a probability field to recognize their whereabouts. No one, including physicists, scientists, or anyone else, has seen a subatomic particle.

As Deepak Chopra says, there is no such thing as particle, it is space time event into consciousness. Therefore, in answering who are we? Again as Deepak Chopra says, "We are qualia matrix/ a continuum of probabilities in transcendent infinite field of possibilities." Deepak also believes we are luminous stardust with self-awareness.

UNREALISTIC SCIENTIFIC BELIEFS

Science is based on the observation of facts and measurements. This renders many scientists to posit that science is the most reliable way of knowing the truth. What is misunderstood is that the empirical analogy driven from direct observation, or what we know as a description of empirical facts, are basically descriptions of modes of human perception formed by the human nervous system and not through an assessment of reality. What occurs in each and every scientific endeavor happens after subject/object split. Therefore, there is no such thing as non-duality, it simply cannot be obtained. There is no observer-sovereign or self-governed reality.

What exists before the subject/object split is called qualia, which is defined as "the internal and subjective component of sense perceptions, arising from stimulation of the senses by phenomena." Qualia as a capable matrix subsists in marrow (core) consciousness before the subject/object split. Qualia's ghostly characteristics are sensation, images, feelings, thoughts, and emotions.

Heisenberg said, "What is observed is not nature itself, but nature exposed to our method of questioning."

And John Wheeler said, "Every particle, every field of force even the space time continuum itself-derives its function, its meaning, its very existence, entirely from apparatus elicited, concepts to questions we ask-this is a participatory universe."

Observation, scientific outcomes, comprehension, awareness, theories, space, time, events, and what we as human beings can meaningfully grasp, entire worldly activities and beyond, are all in the consciousness. Whatever we perceive, and what is hidden in the womb of nature waiting to be discovered and born, are the offspring of consciousness. Without mindful awareness, no theories can be coagulated. Without consciousness, no experience is ever possible. It has always been there with no interruption.

And as Deepak Chopra said, "Science cannot explain consciousness, but consciousness can conceive and construct the scientific method. How do we get the body experience even though we are not in the body?"

Our experiences of reality occur after subject/object split. Other organisms do not share the same experience as their reality. Hence, perceptual experiences differ as different species' (genus, breed, phylum) representation of mode of observation are varied. Relative to humans, spiders see ultraviolet and green; honey bees see ultraviolet, blue, and yellow. Reptiles see some colors and infrared. Birds see five to seven colors, mammals (cats and dogs) see two colors, but weakly. Most fish also see two colors. Rabbits and rats see two colors, blue and green. Squirrels see blue and yellow. Primates (apes and chimps, African monkeys) see as humans. Bats utilize echolocation to maneuver and find food in the dark. To echolocate, bats send out sound waves from their mouth or nose. When the sound waves impact an object, they generate echoes. The echo bounces off the object and returns to the bat's ear.

Chameleons have a distinguishing visual system that empowers them to observe their atmosphere in almost 360 degrees (180 degrees horizontally and +/-90 degrees vertically). They activate it in two ways. The first is with anatomical specializations that enable the eyes to spin freely. The next is the chameleon's ability to switch between monocular and binocular vision, meaning they can see objects with either eye independently, or with both eyes at the same time. The chameleon's eyeball works on different axes.

Dolphins have expanded the ability to utilize echo-location, often known as sonar, to assist them in observing better underwater. Scientists believe this competency probably evolved gradually over time. Echolocation permits dolphins to "see" by interpreting the echoes of sound waves that bounce off of objects near them in time.

The awkwardness for physicists, and many scientists, occurs in the world of quantum mechanics, where seeing means conscious observation, denoting that consciousness and the quantum world are inseparable. It seems that quantum activities and consciousness can never be quantifiable, materialized as thoughts, or arrived at as an object of thought.

The Buddhist states this unknowability by saying, "You can't bite your own teeth and can't taste your own tongue." And in the Bible, in Exodus 33:20, it is expressed by God telling Moses, "You cannot see my face, for no one can see me and live."

Nagarjuna said, "There is no runner beside the action of running and that outside of running there is no runner."

It would be easier for a scientist to meditate on the interaction of things, seeing the world not separately but as a unit, and not to cultivate the thing in itself. Scientists would agree there are no such things as persistence subatomic particles, and comparatively, a Buddhist would believe there is no persistent self. Neither scientist nor Buddhists contextually negate facts; they are not nihilist (atheists). Both scientists and Buddhists say it is a world of interactivities, where not much can be said on consciousness and the fundamental stuff of the universe.

But we need to think in quantum terms, since observation seems to be the essence of what we can drive at. Since particles move or run from point A to point B and when the observation is halted, both runner and the running cease to exist, as the particles return in manifesting probabilities, as they do not persist in time.

Scientists also need to know that all natural phenomena are governed by a vital life force outside the realm of physical and chemical laws. To believe that all natural phenomena, including the process of life, are governed by physical and chemical laws is not savvy, since any physical or chemical mechanism would prove futile if exhausted of the universal vital life force.

The fact is we live in an awakened, orderly universe, which is why any scientific formula, not excluding physical and chemical agendas or other scientific endeavors, respond to mathematics, geometry, and so on, which are the nucleus of most scientific research. Otherwise, no precise scientific discovery can be materialized in our laboratories. If not so, then no adequate assessment can ever be achieved, and no proper laws can be invented. We should expect going haywire in a DISORDERLY and CHAOTIC universe where no proper rules can be obtained, as law and order make no sense and issues such as discipline, meaning, responsibility, logic, objectivity, preciseness in conclusion, expectation, and hope, are out of the window.

"Subatomic particles do not exist but rather show 'tendencies to exist', and atomic events do not occur with certainty at definite times and in definite ways, but rather show 'tendencies to occur'" (Fritjof Capra).

SOUL HUNTERS: THE ENEMIES OF GOD

"The function of prayer is not to influence God, but rather to change the nature of the one who prays"

– Soren Kierkegaard

"I would never die for my beliefs because I might be wrong"

– Bertrand Russell

In a perilous world, the sacred Baha'i house of worship (Baha'is), chaitya/Buddhist temples/monastery (abbots, lamas, monks, Buddhists), church buildings, particularity Catholic nuns and priests, the Hof (Germanic pagans), Hindu temple (puja), synagogue (rabbi), mosque (sheikh, mullahs), and other organized sanctuaries are meant for people to assemble and venerate God. People seek refuge in them for repenting of their sins and to rescue their souls from the toxically cultured world, but often with no avail, as to the contrary, many of these revered places of worship are so sadly abusive, often by the officeholders, men and women of the so-called godly obedient, in which some trustees have become the very menace that we should be warned against.

It seems the offenders, the men and women of God, set up booby traps triggered by the believers visiting certain inappropriate places of worship where the naïvely minded flock to their moral and spiritual death, as if they have surrendered to satanic rituals, taking away the decency of what they stand for, and for most victims, permanently depriving them of the God they once believed in.

Many holy predators who preach the almighty God annihilate what we believe and hope for by taking advantage of the innocents, as the culprits, and the so-called priests, nuns, sheikhs, mullahs, rabbis, abbots, and other supposed saints, inappropriately infringe and prey on, killing the very religious spirit of their helpless victims as they impose on the target's sovereignty, sabotaging believers' souls.

They wickedly dehumanize their victims through rape and molestation and by other demonic misconducts. They veil themselves behind God to cover their beastly behaviors to get away scot-free. Then, rest assured, millions would doubt God when aware of such atrocities done by allegedly (erroneous testimony, supposedly, purportedly) religious role models and teachers of faith. And also, they have so naively downsized the scope of the infinite God to their likings, for satisfying their own selfish and wacky (ludicrous) agendas, aiming at filling up their pocket for the wrong reasons.

They have no brain malleability (plasticity), and without vast brain intelligence, as they manufacture a manmade God to fit their own agendas they are shortsighted and mentally incompetent to contrive reason for proving God.

The so-called theoreticians of faith are not able to separate facts from fiction and to substantiate logic from what is obsolete and does not make any sense. These hocus-pocus activities are happening in the twenty-first century, which is meant to be the era of civility of mind and manner and the age of the enlightenment.

They hence misdirect the populace and embolden some to question the existence of the all-powerful God. And further, because of the inability and abusive character of the agents to whom they so wrongly represent God, it leads in making the believer's position questionable and exacerbates the non-believer's views on God. Criteria, as such, should remind us of how shallow so many people's beliefs are in knowing God, and as Friedrich Nietzsche said, "God is dead, and we have killed him."

Humanity ought to become awakened to the infinitely resourceful God, the true God, the most loving, the omnipotent, the omni-present God that is by nature infinitely compassionate; a God that does not in any way call for protection by the religious extremists and terrorists who kill and maim innocent people.

They believe in the very same God, just with a different name or disparate (distinct) denomination; a God that can be felt in hearing our prayers and pleas, since the glorious Almighty has endowed humanity with senses and thought frequencies enabling us to maneuver in a conscientiously based universe.

Not a thing can ever go unnoticed; cosmic frequencies are ubiquitously aware and in tune with all that happens in our mind and zealously (relentlessly) grasps what is precisely taking place in the so-called physical world.

NOTHINGNESS

> A universe that came from nothing in the big bang will disappear into nothing at the big crunch. Its glorious few zillion years of existence not even a memory.
>
> –Paul Davies

First, why is there anything at all, or something at all? This question becomes clearer when put in comparative form: why is there something rather than nothing? Some doubt whether we can ask this question because there being nothing is not an option. "What exactly is nothing? What would nothing be?" We analogize nothing with the idea of empty space, in which we can conceptualize nothing.

"The body is made up of atoms and subatomic particles that are moving at lightning speed around huge empty spaces and the body gives off fluctuations of energy and information in a huge void, so essentially your body is proportionately as void as intergalactic space, made out of nothing, but the nothing is actually the source of information and energy" (Deepak Chopra).

We ponder on this contentious issue whether things are created from something, or perhaps are made out of nothing. But then, the proper question should be addressed as: Is nothingness impregnated with an infinite number of things or not? And if not, then existence, and quintillions of scientific discoveries which scientists and scholars have divulged and employed, should mean fiction, and no more.

Our inventions have stemmed from nothingness and been transmitted into actuality from the unknown, in which we either have already concocted, or hope to excogitate (devise, design), in the future. And if yes, then we should tirelessly dig into nothingness to further get closer to the truth, and not let what is explicitly clear become a conundrum of a scientific and philosophical argument.

If our notion of space is as a particular type of relation between objects, the removal of all objects (everything) should leave nothing, including their interactions. We can easily be misled by the language of there being nothing at all, leading to the notion that nothing has no being or existence. Nothing might be a harbinger to the big bang. But this idea is also a misconception—though one widely held by many who believe the universe came about out of nothingness, for instance an Archimedean (void) variation (fluctuation.)

A vacuum oscillation is itself not nothing "but is a sea of prowess (conscious aptitude) energy endowed with vibrant structure and subject to imperative physical laws." Further, if nothingness in the void should mean "nothing," then there wouldn't be any possible state of affairs. But this could not be, since from "nothingness" is the actuality from which things come about.

Let's further delve into nothingness in which some of the so-called scientific community believe: it all came out of nothing, where nothingness is perhaps the suspect and from which life has originated.

We are conducive to perceiving and defining nothingness according to available human resources and competency. The term nothingness can be alarmingly deceptive, since what we know as nothing is actually everything. But since nothingness is incomprehensible to us at certain times, not discovering and realizing how, when, where, or by whom, nothing is going to give birth to our next scientific breakthroughs. Then we are deluded into believing nothingness as literally meaning immaterial and barren to us, which is based on our limited senses.

The consensus should be in accepting nothingness as the holy grail of creativity, and where the real potential lays for things we persist on to decode and eventually conquer. And if not, then we have acted shortsightedly in all of which we have discovered and hope to invent. We are faced with no choice but to delve into the reality of nothing and realize there is no such thing as a void.

Hence, it would make sense to switch and replace the word nothingness for the words the unknown. An advanced space digger telescope can reveal a world of magic to the eye, where human senses can only dream about, and certainly see as absence of matter and emptiness without a colossal scientific magnifier.

And if the most advanced telescope available to man could only ascertain some of the facts, then this should only mean we must strive for even better technology to make human dreams reality and closer than expected.

To say life came out of nothing is honestly an insult to reason, since literally it would mean God is in charge of the womb of what we know and grant as emptiness, which in contrary is filled with propitious (auspicious, favorable, benevolent) prospects that gave birth to all there is and all of which there will ever be.

Through the eyes of quantum physics, which represents the world of the unseen, renowned physicist Niels Bohr says (and many of his colleagues accept), "Atomic uncertainty is truly intrinsic to nature: the rules of clock might apply to familiar objects such as snooker balls, but when it comes to atoms and quarks, string theory, and other subatomic particles, the rules are those of roulette." Many scientists believe these subatomic particles are being thrown around by an unseen ocean of microscopic forces.

It is therefore apparent that we must adhere to the bounds of our senses to acquaint and comply with the world outside of us. As humans, we cannot reconnaissance with what is beyond our ability and knowledge to decipher. This should not mean that there is no magic in the air, or perhaps we need to quit searching for miracles. The history of evolution should validate the human mind that progresses into dynamic stages of enlightenment where boundaries are graciously torn and miracle-like discoveries become norms.

Bear in mind that one of the basic concepts in new Existentialism is nothingness. It includes the whole being, and being comes out of nothingness. According to this philosophy, being and nothingness are the same. The latter causes fear, and the former causes amazement. Fear is event-based on discovery in which man sees all existents standing on the basis of non-existence.

Our curiosity into the realms of speculation and probabilities is fostered and potentially backed up by hidden agenda conveyed into the unknown, ready to be exploited and burst into reality. Of course it is inclined to action by passion, human drive, time consumed, and keen enough to feel and detect the maturity and the magnificent moment of delivery. That is encouraged with hope, perseverance, and bearing hardship through many trials and errors; and then occasionally bull's-eyed into stepping stones for other miracle-like disclosures and sometimes a huge leap into successful challenges where our struggle in bettering human life pays off generously.

Paul Davies argues that one need not appeal to God to account for the big bang. Its cause, he suggests, is found within the cosmic system itself. Originally a vacuum lacking space-time dimensions, the universe "found itself in an excited vacuum state," a "ferment of quantum activity, teeming (producing) with virtual particles and full of complex interactions" (Davies 1984 191–2), which, subject to a cosmic repulsive force, resulted in an immense increase in energy. Subsequent explosions from this collapsing vacuum released the energy in this vacuum, reinvigorating the cosmic inflation and setting the scenario for the subsequent expansion of the universe.

But what is the origin of this increase in energy that eventually made the big bang possible? Davies's response is that the law of conservation of energy (that the total quantity of energy in the universe remains fixed despite transfer from one form to another), which now applies to our universe, did not apply to the initial expansion.

Cosmic repulsion in the vacuum caused the energy to increase from zero to an enormous amount. This great explosion released energy, from which all matter emerged.

Consequently, he contends, since the conclusion of the kalām argument is false, one of the premises of the argument—in all likelihood, the first—is false. Craig responds that if the vacuum has energy, the question arises concerning the origin of the vacuum and its energy. Merely pushing the question of the beginning of the universe back to some primordial quantum vacuum (nothingness) does not escape the question of what brought this vacuum laden with energy into existence.

A quantum vacuum is not nothing (as in Newtonian physics), but is a sea of continually forming and dissolving particles that borrow energy from the vacuum for their brief existence. A vacuum is thus far from nothing, and vacuum fluctuations do not constitute an exception to the principle enunciated in premise 1 (Craig, in Craig and Smith 1993: 143–4). Hence, he concludes, the appeal to a vacuum as the initial state is misleading.

Further, if the universe has a beginning, what is the cause of that beginning? This is the question that is addressed by the Avicenna's kalām cosmological argument, given its essence that everything that begins to exist has a cause.

Some are under the wrong impression that their kind of visage (image) and bounded interpretation of the so-called nothingness has no cause. But then the renowned British theoretical physicist Stephen Hawking says God did not create the universe, gravity did, and the big bang was an unavoidable consequence of the laws of physics.

In his book The Grand Design, Professor Hawking gets overexcited with pride, just human nature, as our good professor writes: "Because there is a law such as gravity, the universe can and will create itself from nothing. Spontaneous creation is the reason there is something rather than nothing, why the universe exists, why we exist. It is not necessary to invoke God to light the blue touch paper and set the universe going."

The first and foremost question should be, by gravity, does Mr. Hawking mean an energy-driven entity that is propelled by an energy-driven universe that also motivates electromagnetic forces and manifests light and heavy atomic forces; also associates with infinite numbers of other imperative phenomenon necessary to operate constructively for arriving at its objectives, orchestrated by the mind of God? Or does he mean gravity should replace God and for humanity to revere gravity as the reason for our existence?

If the latter, then it cannot be overlooked by any savvy and healthy mind to question how an unintelligent entity without any purpose-driven consciousness, absolutely without will and determination, utterly lacking common sense, could create and sustain a colossally intelligent and rational-minded environment and a magnificent cosmos fueled by order, while superbly managing to reach its destiny.

No sarcasm is intended, but I wonder if Professor's Hawking's findings should remind humanity of the dark ages when the so-called apostles encouraged people to believe and worship gods made of a variety of manufactured materials as the real cause for their demise and happiness. There is a classic saying, "Tragedy plus time equals comedy." Mark Twain wrote, "It's easier to fool people than to convince them they have been fooled."

Chew on this, and see if reason can digest such a callous matter; Mr. Hawking was somehow contaminated with many dreams believing that about fourteen billion years ago (when life roughly began, so say scientists), gravity created itself from nothing. One needs to question if must-have resources (crucial ingredients, the primordial soup) could have played a definite and significant role prior to either creating the first bio-cell or in dealing with prerequisite atmosphere for giving birth to the force of gravity. Millions, if not billons, of variables must be assumed as constant and utterly of no use but for gravity to pop out of nowhere to perhaps give some credibility to Mr. Hawking's insight.

Professor Hawking behaved just like another "reductionist," Blaise Pascal, who said that somehow we live in a bubble where laws of our universe can be reduced in manifesting gravity as the actual reason for the entire existence.

"All things have sprung from nothing and are borne toward infinity. Who can follow out astonishment career, the author of these wonders and he alone comprehend them" (Blaise Pascal).

In the remainder of How the Universe Got Its Spots, which is unbearably beautiful in both intellectual elegance and stylistic splendor, Levin goes on to explore questions of quantum relativity and free will, death and black holes, space time and Wonderland, and more. Complement it with Levin on science, free will, and the human spirit, then revisit Alan Lightman on how dark energy explains why we exist and treat yourself to this poetic primer on the universe written in the 1,000 most common words in the English language.

INFINITY

The skeptics refer to infinity as if there is actually such a decisive number as infinity active in mathematical realms, not realizing it is just a figure of speech since an integer, or fractional tally (count) as infinity does not exist in any true sense, and hence one should further investigate boundlessness. But some people still argue there is no beginning, nor is there an end.

Some argue there is neither a beginning nor an end to existence.

Al-Ghāzāli (1058–1111) argued that everything that begins to exist requires a cause of its beginning. The world is composed of temporal phenomena preceded by other temporally ordered phenomena. Since such a series of temporal phenomena cannot continue to infinity because an actual infinite is impossible, the world must have had a beginning and a cause of its existence; namely, God (Craig 1979 part 1).

Let's further discuss infinity. Craig concluded that an actual infinite cannot exist.

A beginning less temporal series of events is an actual infinite.

Therefore, a beginning less temporal series of events cannot exist.

The incorrect assumption, and the main suspect, is the subject of infinity.

And Max Tegmark, on the subject of infinity, wrote that infinity is a beautiful concept—and is also ruining physics. Infinity doesn't exist; the impossibility of an actual infinite.

A rubber band can't be stretched indefinitely because although it seems smooth and continuous, that's merely a convenient approximation. It's really made of atoms, and if you stretch it too far, it snaps. If we similarly retire the idea that space itself is an infinitely stretchy continuum, then a big snap of sorts stops inflation from producing an infinitely big space and the measure problem goes away. Without the infinitely small, inflation can't make the infinitely big, so you get rid of both infinities in one fell swoop—together with many other problems plaguing modern physics, such as infinitely dense black hole singularities and infinities popping up when we try to quantize gravity.

In the past, many venerable mathematicians were skeptical of infinity and the continuum. The legendary Carl Friedrich Gauss denied that anything infinite really exists, saying, "Infinity is merely a way of speaking," and, "I protest against the use of infinite magnitude as something completed, which is never permissible in mathematics." In the past century, however, infinity has become mathematically mainstream, and most physicists and mathematicians have become so enamored with infinity that they rarely question it. Why? Basically, because infinity is an extremely convenient approximation for which we haven't discovered convenient alternatives.

Consider, for example, the air in front of you. Keeping track of the positions and speeds of octillions of atoms would be hopelessly complicated. But if you ignore the fact that air is made of atoms and instead approximate it as a continuum—a smooth substance that has a density, pressure, and velocity at each point—you'll find that this idealized air obeys a beautifully simple equation explaining almost everything we care about: how to build airplanes, how we hear them with sound waves, how to make weather forecasts, and so forth. Yet despite all that convenience, air, of course, isn't truly continuous. I think it's the same way for space, time, and all the other building blocks of our physical world. He carries on to say that We Don't Need the Infinite.

Let's face it: Despite their seductive allure, we have no direct observational evidence for either the infinitely big or the infinitely small. We speak of infinite volumes with infinitely many planets, but our observable universe contains only about 1,089 objects (mostly photons). If space is a true continuum, then to describe even something as simple as the distance between two points requires an infinite amount of information, specified by a number with infinitely many decimal places. In practice, we physicists have never managed to measure anything to more than about seventeen decimal places. Yet real numbers, with their infinitely many decimals, have infested almost every nook and cranny of physics, from the strengths of electromagnetic fields to the wave functions of quantum mechanics. We describe even a single bit of quantum information (qubit) using two real numbers involving infinitely many decimals.

Not only do we lack evidence for the infinite, but we don't need the infinite to do physics. Our best computer simulations, accurately describing everything from the formation of galaxies to tomorrow's weather to the masses of elementary particles, use only finite computer resources by treating everything as finite. So if we can do without infinity to figure out what happens next, surely nature can, too—in a way that's more deep and elegant than the hacks we use for our computer simulations.

Our challenge as physicists is to discover this elegant way and the infinity-free equations describing it—the true laws of physics. To start this search in earnest, we need to question infinity. I'm betting that we also need to let go of it; infinity doesn't exist.

Famous mathematicians such as L. E. J. Brouwer, Per Martin-Löf, Errett Bishop, Ludwig Wittgenstein, Henri Poincare, Carl Friedrich Gauss and Leopold Kronecker didn't believe infinity existed. Many others, such as Bertrand Russell, doubted the existence of infinity in various forms and fought against the axioms of the mainstream mathematical community that were in flux at that time.

The most compelling argument to admit that infinity does exist comes from the Axioms (a fundamental rule, doctrine) of Mathematics, namely the Axiom of Infinity, which in plain English states: "Mathematical objects infinite in size, exist." Many prominent scientists and scholarly minded mathematicians believe no infinity should exist in the axiom of mathematics, or physics, which tightly depends on mathematics to present savvy results of their work.

And I say that mathematics, physics, and kindred (cognate, related) scientific experiences must deal with real numbers and are derived from a true state of being; which, by the way, can only be obtained from a disciplined universe for reaching reliable findings, since no scientific theory of any kind can be formulated in a chaotic world without orderly conduct. Further, infinity is nothing more than an assumption, where mathematics and related fields must eventually give in to finite assessment for a trustworthy conclusion. In the physical world, it would be hilarious to believe in an effect without a cause, since any serious scientific research must cultivate the beginning and the asymptotic (end) result for their research, where no open-ended outcome, or infinity-related concept, can be convincing.

Astrophysicist Janna Levin on free will and whether the universe is infinite or finite, in letters to her mother, writes,

"The simpler the insight, the more profound the conclusion."

By Maria Popova

In 1998, while on the cusp of becoming one of the most Significant theoretical cosmologists of our time, mathematician-turned-astrophysicist Janna Levin left her post at Berkeley and moved across the Atlantic for a prestigious position at Cambridge University. During the year and a half there, she had the time and space to contemplate the question that would eventually become the epicenter of her career—whether the universe is infinite or finite. What began as a series of letters to her mother, Sandy, eventually became an unusual diary of Levin's "social exile as a roaming scientist," and was finally published as How the Universe Got Its Spots: Diary of a Finite Time in a Finite Space (public library)— a most unusual and absorbing account of the paradoxes of finitude.

"I'm writing to you because I know you're curious but afraid to ask," Levin offers in the opening letter— a "you" that instantly becomes as much her mother as the person Virginia Woolf memorably termed "the common reader." From there, she springboards into remarkably intelligent yet inviting explorations of some of the biggest questions that the universe poses—questions most of us contemplate, sometimes consciously but mostly not, just by virtue of being sentient participants in the chaos and enchantment of existence.

A 1617 depiction of the notion of non-space, long before the concept of vacuum existed, found in Michael Benson's book Cosmographic, is a visual history of understanding the universe.

In an entry from September 3, 1998, Levin fleshes out her ideas on infinity and writes with exquisite Sagan-esque sensitivity to the poetics of science:

For a long time, I believed the universe was infinite. Which is to say, I just never questioned this assumption that the universe was infinite. But if I had given the question more attention, maybe I would have realized sooner. The universe is the three-dimensional space we live in and the time we watch pass on our clocks. It is our north and south, our east and west, our up and down. Our past and future. As far as the eye can see there appears to be no bound to our three spatial dimensions and we have no expectation for an end to time. The universe is inhabited by giant clusters of galaxies, each galaxy a conglomerate of a billion or a trillion stars.

The Milky Way, our galaxy, has an unfathomably dense core of millions of stars with beautiful arms, a skeleton of stars, spiraling out from this core. The earth lives out in the sparsely populated arms orbiting the sun, an ordinary star, with our planetary companions. Our humble solar system. Here we are. A small planet, an ordinary star, a huge cosmos. But we're alive and we're sentient. Pooling our efforts and passing our secrets from generation to generation, we've lifted ourselves off this blue and green water-soaked rock to throw our vision far beyond the limitations of our eyes.

The universe is full of galaxies and their stars. Probably, hopefully, there is other life out there and background light and maybe some ripples in space. There are bright objects and dark objects. Things we can see and things we can't. Things we know about and things we don't. All of it. This glut of ingredients could carry on in every direction forever. Never ending. Just when you think you've seen the last of them, there's another galaxy and beyond that one another infinite number of galaxies.

Illustration from Thomas Wright's visionary 1750 treatise 'An Original Theory,' found in Michael Benson's book Cosmographic, a visual history of understanding the universe

But having painted this bewitching backdrop for our intuitive beliefs, Levin sublimates the poet to the scientist, pointing out that however alluring these intuitions may feel, they are nonetheless ungrounded in empirical fact:

No infinity has ever been observed in nature. Nor is infinity tolerated in a scientific theory—except we keep assuming the universe itself is infinite.

It wouldn't be so bad if Einstein hadn't taught us better. And here the ideas collide, so I'll just pour them out unfiltered. Space is not just an abstract notion but a mutable, evolving field. It can begin and end, be born and die. Space is curved, it is a geometry, and our experience of gravity, the pull of the earth and our orbit around the sun, is just a free fall along the curves in space. From this huge insight people realized the universe must be expanding. The space between the galaxies is actually stretching even if the galaxies themselves were otherwise to stay put. The universe is growing, aging. And if it's expanding today, it must have been smaller once, in the sense that everything was once closer together, so close that everything was on top of each other, essentially in the same place, and before that it must not have been at all.

The universe had a beginning. There was once nothing and now there is something. What sways me even more, if an ultimate theory of everything is found, a theory beyond Einstein's, then gravity and matter and energy are all ultimately different expressions of the same thing. We're all intrinsically of the same substance. The fabric of the universe is just a coherent weave from the same threads that make our bodies. How much more absurd it becomes to believe that the universe, space and time could possibly be infinite when all of us are finite.

A decade and a half later, Alan Light man would come to write with a similar scientific poeticism about why we long for permanence in a universe defined by constant change. But however poetic the premise, Levin brings a mathematician's precision to her "reasons for believing the universe is finite, unpopular as they are in some scientific crowds."

In another entry twelve days later, she writes:

Infinity is a demented concept…

Infinity is a limit and is not a proper number. No matter how big a number you think of, I can add 1 to it and make it that much bigger. The number of numbers is infinite. I could never recite the infinite numbers, since I only have a finite lifetime. But I can imagine it as a hypothetical possibility, as the inevitable limit of a never-ending sequence. The limit goes the other way, too, since I can consider the infinitely small, the infinitesimal. No matter how small you try to divide the number 1, I can divide it smaller still. While I could again imagine doing this forever, I can never do this in practice. But I can understand infinity abstractly and so accept it for what it is.

Pointing out that all titans of science — including Galileo, Aristotle, and Cantor — were besotted with the notion of infinity at some point, "each visiting the idea for a time and then abandoning the pursuit," Levin notes that we can neither accept nor dismiss infinity on the basis of popular opinion alone.

In early October, she writes:

Where in the hierarchy of infinity would an infinite universe lie? An infinite universe can host an infinite amount of stuff and an infinite number of events. An infinite number of planets. An infinite number of people on those planets. Surely there must be another planet so very nearly like the earth as to be indistinguishable, in fact an infinite number of them, each with a variety of inhabitants, an infinite number of which must be infinitely close to this set of inhabitants. Another you, another me. Or there'd be another you out there with a slightly different life and a different set of siblings, parents, and offspring. This is hard to believe. Is it arrogance or logic that makes me believe this is wrong? There's just one me, one you. The universe cannot be infinite.

I welcome the infinite in mathematics, where … it is not absurd nor demented. But I'd be pretty shaken to find the infinite in nature. I don't feel robbed living my days in the physical with its tender admission of the finite. I still get to live with the infinite possibilities of mathematics, if only in my head.

Illustration by Lisbeth Zwerger for 'Alice in Wonderland.' Click image for more.

Understanding the infinite—both as a mathematical possibility and an impossibility of the physical universe—might be more a matter of coming to terms with infinite simplicity than with infinite complexity.

Characteristics of matter

There are basically three kinds of characteristics of matter.

Some nonbelievers relate to matter as the real cause for existence, and do not accept any idea-driven spirit or energy-oriented life creation or design to ever be possible, as if matter is not energy-driven. Regardless of what state matter is in, solid, liquid or gas, all matter is energy-driven. Therefore, one should research the quality and the essence of matter not only in the physical world, but certainly excavate (dig, burrow, and root) into the subatomic realm.

"In all my research I have never come across matter. To me the term matter implies a bundle of energy which is given form by an intelligent spirit" (Max Planck).

Matter is made up of atoms. Depending on the sort of matter, the characteristics may differ. Solids have certain shape and volume but cannot be pressed. Likewise, liquids have definite volume but no distinct shape. Liquids cannot be compressed either. Gases are made up of random atoms with very high energy and have neither definite shape or volume. But gases can be compressed. Hence, it depends on which type of matter is available and what kind of characteristics are needed for an exclusive purpose.

Atoms possess weight, mass, volume, and density. All atoms unstoppably move. The more energy that is applied to a group of atoms, the more they move.

Atoms in a lower energetic state do not move much; they stay in place and palpitate (pulsate, vibrate.) Atoms in such a position make solid matter. Solids consist of fixed mass, weight, density, and volume.

Mass is the body (quantity) of matter in any object, while weight is the pull of gravity on the mass of that object. Volume is a measure of how much is physically there, and of space the object occupies or captures, while density is a description of how the mass takes up that space. Objects with higher solidity (density) have a lot of mass in a small amount of space.

Atoms that are more energetic and, hence, move more freely, are in a liquid state. Liquids also have a fixed mass, weight, volume, and density. Particles in a liquid can flow freely past one another rather than being stuck in a single position. While solids do not change shape easily, liquids can conform instantly to the shape of their container. Atoms in elevated energetic state (e.g., gases), can not only alter their shape, but also their volume, because the particles have sufficient energy to extensively separate from one another while flowing.

However, scientists have learned that atoms are not the smallest particles in nature. Despite their microscopic size, a number of much smaller particles exist, known as subatomic particles. In reality, it is these subatomic particles that form the building blocks of our world, like protons, neutrons, electrons, and quarks, or destroy it, such as alpha and beta particles. And since quantum physic deals with the world of subatomic particles and with much smaller units, like quartz, can better attest to the fact that no tangible substances are manifested in a state, as they notice the effect of energy-driven environment where frequencies are pulsating.

What the human eye sees as matter is actually energy-driven entities, since various kinds of matter are made of atoms, and atoms in liquid and gases are constantly in motion, imbued with high energy. Atoms in solid matter are in a low energy state; they stay in one place and pulsate. Hence, matter cannot be the reason behind creating life, since atoms in matter are constantly moving. Matter is unstable and in transition; matter is destructible. No matter is ever permanent.

"All matter originates and exists only by virtue of a force... We must assume behind this force the existence of a conscious and intelligent Mind. This Mind is the matrix of all matter" (Max Planck).

Perhaps Professor Hawking saw matter-like substances as not energy-driven, which would be very odd. Then, the question should be how dubious, irrational, amply questionable, unintelligent, insensible, unconscionable, volatile (inconsistent), and perishable matter could create life-bearing intelligence in some state, manifesting extreme "knowledge" beyond belief.

Professor Hawking believed gravity is responsible for creating existence.

"In Stephen Hawking's new book The Grand Design, he says that because of the law of gravity, the universe can and will create itself out of nothing. But isn't that gravity being a module (subroutine, function) of mass, as per Einstein. How can one have gravity before mass and therefore how can gravity explain mass?"

Dr. Kaku: In Stephen's new book, he says that the Theory of Everything that Einstein spent 30 years of his life chasing, is known as string theory (or its latest incarnation, M-theory).

In string theory, we have a multiverse of universes. Think of our universe as the surface of a soap bubble, which is expanding. We live on the skin of this bubble. But string theory predicts that there should be other bubbles out there, which can collide with other bubbles or even sprout or bud baby bubbles, as in a bubble bath.

But how can an entire universe come out of nothing? This apparently violates the conservation of matter and energy. But there is a simple answer.

Matter, of course, has positive energy. But gravity has negative energy. (For example, you have to add energy to the earth in order to tear it away from the sun. Once separated far from the solar system, the earth then has zero gravitational energy. But this means that the original solar system had negative energy.)

If you do the math, you find out that the sum total of matter in the universe can cancel against the sum total of negative gravitational energy, yielding a universe with zero (or close to zero) net matter/energy. So, in some sense, universes are for free. It does not take net matter and energy to create entire universes. In this way, in the bubble bath, bubbles can collide, create baby bubbles, or simple pop into existence from nothing.

This gives us a startling picture of the big bang, that our universe was born perhaps from the collision of two universes (the big splat theory), or sprouted from a parent universe, or simply popped into existence out of nothing. So universes are being created all the time. (But Hawking goes one step farther and says that therefore here is no need of God, since God is not necessary to create the universe. I wouldn't go that far.

"Because there is a law such as gravity, the universe can and will create itself from nothing," he writes. "Spontaneous creation is the reason there is something rather than nothing, why the universe exists, why we exist."

"It is not necessary to invoke God to light the blue touch paper and set the universe going."

In the forthcoming book, published on 9 September, Hawking says that M-theory, a form of string theory, will achieve this goal: "M-theory is the unified theory Einstein was hoping to find," he theorizes.

"The fact that we human beings – who are ourselves mere collections of fundamental particles of nature – have been able to come this close to an understanding of the laws governing us and our universe is a great triumph."

Hawking says the first blow to Newton's belief that the universe could not have arisen from chaos was the observation in 1992 of a planet orbiting a star other than our Sun. "That makes the coincidences of our planetary conditions – the single sun, the lucky combination of Earth-sun distance and solar mass – far less remarkable, and far less compelling as evidence that the Earth was carefully designed just to please us human beings," he writes.

Hawking had previously appeared to accept the role of God in the creation of the universe. Writing in his bestseller A Brief History of Time in 1988, he said: "If we discover a complete theory, it would be the ultimate triumph of human reason – for then we should know the mind of God."

As essential as gravity is, just like other fundamental forces in nature, like electromagnetic, strong and weak atomic forces are derivatives and all are the reflection of the majestic power of God which, perhaps because of gravity, as Hawking puts it, "the universe can create itself from nothing." But it is the magnificent maestro (the majestically eminent) and undeniably superb programmer of the entire cosmos and beyond that manipulates and controls everything with awesome order and discipline more than anyone can imagine.

And of course, we mustn't exclude these imperative energy-driven forces, such as gravity, strong and weak atomic forces, along with electromagnetic forces, as they play a remarkable role to prevent nature from falling apart.

"As a man who has devoted his whole life to many research about atoms this much: There is no matter as such. All matter originates and exists only by virtue of a force which brings the particle of an atom to vibration and holds this most minute solar system of the atom together. We must assume behind this force the existence of a conscious and intelligent mind. This mind is the matrix of all matter" (Max Planck).

Nothing Is Solid & Everything Is Energy – Scientists Explain the World of Quantum Physics

This is what the most prominent scientists are saying about an energy-driven universe.

It is presently clear that the world of quantum physics is an uncanny (spooky, unearthly) one. It sheds light on the truth about our world in ways that were not known before, since it disputes the contemporary scaffold (supporting structure) of customary lore (learning, information, knowledge.) This is what Niels Bohr, a multiple Nobel Prize-winning Danish physicist, who has made a meaningful bequest (endowment) to comprehending quantum theory and atomic structure, is saying quote "if quantum mechanics hasn't profoundly shocked you, you haven't understood it yet. Everything we call real is made of things that cannot be regarded as real." The bottom line is that: all of which we have thought about so far as our material world, is absolutely not material, and in the true sense is far from what we grasp as the physical world.

At the beginning of the nineteenth century, physicist's sought into the connection between the structure of matter and the energy. Further, the understanding that a physical, Newtonian world which regarded matter as the kernel of science was dropped; the scientific community realized that matter is nothing but an illusion, as they concluded that everything in our universe is made out of energy. "Despite the unrivaled empirical success of quantum theory, the very suggestion that it may be literally true as a description of nature is still greeted with cynicism, incomprehension and even anger" (T. Folger, "Quantum Shmantum," Discover 22:37-43, 2001).

Quantum physicists contrived that physical atoms are made up the mass of spinning air, liquid, etc., that pulls things into its center known as turbulence, vortices or whirlpool. The energy that are constantly spinning and vibrating, each one glimmering exclusively unique energy signature. Hence, if we see ourselves and figure out what we are, we are in reality made of vibrating energy beaming our own unique energy perception. This is fact, and is what quantum physics has consecutively revealed to us, again and again. We are much more than what we see ourselves to be. We should start to see ourselves in the manner of light and vibrating immortal souls, temporary inhibited by mortal bodies.

If one watches the composition of an atom through a microscope one would observe a small, undetectable, tornado-like vortex (whirlpool) with a boundlessly small energy vortices known as quarks and photons, which they make up the structure of the atom. And if one further focuses in closer and closer on the edifice of the atom, one would see nothing; one would see a physical void. Informing us that the atom has no physical structure, we have no physical structure, as physical things, in fact, don't have any physical building! As strange as it is, but it is now authenticated that atoms are made out of invisible energy, not tactile (palpable, tangible) matter. "get over it, and accept the inarguable conclusion, the universe is immaterial-mental and spiritual" (Professor of Physics and Astronomy at Johns Hopkins University Richard Conn Henry, The Mental Universe).

It's quite puzzling, isn't it? Our experience state that our reality is constructed of physical material things, and that we live in an independently existing, an objective one. The idea that the universe is not a symposium (conclave, assembly) of physical parts, as argued by Newtonian physics, and alternatively comes from a holistic participatory of immaterial energy waves, stemming from the work of Albert Einstein, Max Planck, and Werner Heisenberg, among other scholarly minded scientists and philosophers.

The Role of Consciousness in Quantum Mechanics

What does it mean that our physical material reality isn't really physical at all? It could mean a number of things, and concepts such as this cannot be explored if scientists remain within the boundaries of the only perceived world existing; the world we see. As Nikola Tesla supposedly said, "The day science begins to study non-physical phenomena, it will make more progress in one decade than in all the previous centuries of its existence."

Fortunately, many scientists have already taken the leap and have already questioned the meaning and implications of what we've discovered with quantum physics. One of these potential revelations is that the observer creates the reality.

As observers, we are personally involved with the creation of our own reality. Physicists are being forced to admit that the universe is a "mental" construction. Pioneering physicist Sir James Jeans wrote: "The stream of knowledge is heading toward a non-mechanical reality; the universe begins to look more like a great thought than like a great machine. Mind no longer appears to be an accidental intruder into the realm of matter, we ought to rather hail it as the creator and governor of the realm of matter (R. C. Henry, "The Mental Universe"; Nature 436:29, 2005).

One great example that illustrates the role of consciousness within the physical material world (which we know not to be so physical) is the double slit experiment. This experiment has been used multiple times to explore the role of consciousness in shaping the nature of physical reality.

A double-slit optical system was used to test the possible role of consciousness in the collapse of the quantum wave-function. The ratio of the interference pattern's double-slit spectral power to its single-slit spectral power was predicted to decrease when attention was focused toward the double-slit as compared to away from it. The study found that factors associated with consciousness, such as meditation, experience, electro-cortical markers of focused attention and psychological factors such as openness and absorption, significantly correlated in predicted ways with perturbations in the double-slit interference pattern. There are many scientific studies that prove consciousness can effect and change our physical material world.

What's The Significance?

The significance of this information is for us to wake up and realize that we are all energy, radiating our own unique energy signature. Feelings, thoughts, and emotions play a vital role; quantum physics helps us see the significance of how we all feel. If all of us are in a peaceful, loving state inside, it will no doubt impact the external world around us and influence how others feel as well.

"If you want to know the secrets of the universe, think in terms of energy, frequency and vibration." – Nikola Tesla.

Studies have shown that positive emotions and operating from a place of peace within oneself can lead to a very different experience for the person emitting those emotions and for those around them. At our subatomic level, does the vibrational frequency change the manifestation of physical reality? If so, in what way? We know that when an atom changes its state, it absorbs or emits electromagnetic frequencies, which are responsible for changing its state. Do different states of emotion, perception, and feelings result in different electromagnetic frequencies? Yes! This has been proven.

Random chance:

"Quantum mechanics is certainly imposing. But an inner voice tells me that it is not yet the real thing. The theory says a lot, but does not really bring us any closer to the secret of the 'old one.' I, at any rate, am convinced that He does not throw dice." Albert Einstein

Einstein is so right; God does not throw dice. As far as progression in quantum physics, the world has come a long way since Einstein.

We are what we learn. But the essence of who we are, and what we do, all that exists, is what the Chinese call "chi," which is the fuel that drives what we know as life.

GRAVITY

How vital is gravity really? Well let's put it this way: life would not be possible without it. An average person perhaps does not think about gravity as a physicist or any other related professional does, yet gravity affects us all, and because of gravity, we do not fly up into space when we feel like jumping up. It is gravity that pulls us down; hence, we fall down and not up. And gravity is why objects crash down to the floor. This mysterious force is the reason we are bound to Earth, enabling us to live as we do.

No one can honestly claim where this mysterious force comes from except that without it, life would not be possible. We discern from Isaac Newton's gravitation law that objects in the universe exert a force of attraction on each other. This interconnectivity is based on the mass of any two objects and the distance between them. The greater the mass of the two objects and the closer the distance between them, the more powerful the pull of the gravitational forces they impose on each other.

We also know that gravity can work in a complicated system with several objects. For instance, in our own solar system, not only does the Sun influence gravity on all the planets, holding them in their orbits, but reciprocally, each planet exerts a force of gravity on the Sun, as well as all the other planets with varying degrees based on the mass and distance between the bodies. This not only includes our solar system, but is also true for beyond just our solar system. The fact is that every object with mass in the universe pulls every other object that has mass—again, the attractions have varying degrees based on mass and distance.

In the theory of relativity, Albert Einstein described how gravity is more than just a force: it is a curvature in the space-time continuum. That sounds like science fiction, but simply put, the mass of an object makes the space around it bend and curve. This is often shown as a heavy ball sitting on a rubber sheet, and other smaller balls fall in towards the heavier object because the rubber sheet is warped from the heavy ball's weight. In actuality, we can't directly see curvature of the space, but we can discover it in the motions of objects. Any object caught in another celestial body's gravity is affected, since the space it is moving through is bent or curved toward the object.

A phenomenon known as "gravitational lensing" can enable us to detect the effects of gravity on light. A large galaxy or cluster of them can also cause an otherwise straight beam of light to curve, circling it, creating a lensing effect.

This is what scientists are saying: "But these effects – where there are basically curves, hills and valleys in space — occur for reasons we can't fully really explain. Besides being a characteristic of space, gravity is also a force (but it is the weakest of the four forces), and it might be a particle, too. Some scientists have proposed particles called gravitons cause objects to be attracted to one another. But gravitons have never actually been observed. Another idea is that gravitational waves are generated when an object is accelerated by an external force, but these waves have never been directly detected, either."

The scientist further acclaim that

"Our understanding of gravity breaks down at both the very small and the very big: at the level of atoms and molecules, gravity just stops working. And we can't describe the insides of black holes and the moment of the big bang without the math completely falling apart. The problem is that our understanding of both particle physics and the geometry of gravity is incomplete."

"Having gone from basically philosophical understandings of why things fall to mathematical descriptions of how things accelerate down inclines from Galileo, to Kepler's equations describing planetary motion to Newton's formulation of the Laws of Physics, to Einstein's formulations of relativity, we've been building and building a more comprehensive view of gravity. But we're still not complete," said Dr. Pamela Gay. "We know that there still needs to be some way to unite quantum mechanics and gravity and actually be able to write down equations that describe the centers of black holes and the earliest moments of the Universe. But we're not there yet."

ORDER AND MATHEMATICS

Order plays an extremely vital role in our lives, without which, we simply wouldn't be able to reach our objectives and would become vulnerable to chaotic atmosphere. Scientists, mathematicians, innovative minds, and other scholarly oriented inventors who create premier discoveries know that the nucleus of most scientific novelties (something new, invention) and technological undertakings is mathematics. And that mathematics undeniably dictates order, without which, no accurate assessment is ever possible.

Walter Bradley said, "An orderly universe is described by mathematics." And Heraclitus said, "There is a stability in the Universe because of the orderly and balanced process of change, the same measure coming out as going in, as if reality were a huge fire that inhaled and exhaled equal amounts."

A disorderly universe with muddled (disorganized) conduct, without any disciplinary measures and in acting lawlessly random, cannot be measured or correctly assessed to produce reliably precise results for dependable scientific discoveries.

This should make those who believe we are the product of random chance, the result of a helter-skelter universe, to think twice and know the only alternative to an intelligently designed and orderly universe is to accept being blindly propelled with no purpose, and to ignore that "no genius and bright product can ever be produced by obtuse, dull and ingenious force."

We ought to be reminded of this ingeniously potent force that has flawlessly directed towards its destiny for more than fourteen billion years, and perhaps for trillions of years to come; call it God, Allah, the Creator, or whatever you wish.

The conscientious universe is robustly alive. It is active in its ever evolutionary track for ever so long; otherwise, it would have been extinguished and exterminated in its very preliminary stages, and not lasting as long as it has. It is still heralding, without any hesitation or in every maneuvering hasty, exercising and exhibiting the very essence of existence and balance with awesome power and might.

Nicolas Copernicus wrote: "The universe has been wrought (carefully formed, shaped) for us by a supremely good and orderly creator."

The universe had a beginning

We should clear our mind from insensible views deficient of reasoning power, in this case, specifying if our extremely complex universe had a beginning or not. It is rather difficult to renounce years of cultural conditioning that we are still mulling (pondering, cogitating), often without any merit. It is not easy for millions to discard such idea that "in the beginning, God created heaven and earth," and so no. Yes, of course an intelligent designer is responsible for creating our universe, and not excluding the entire cosmos. But it ought not to be stated as grossly as acknowledged without the merit it so justly deserves.

Many schools of thought have traditionally assumed that the universe had no origin, and some believed otherwise.

Abrahamian's faith of Judaism, Christianity, and Islam also believed in a beginning and the end. Hence, the burden of proof can become as meandering and puzzling as the subject matter itself, if one is not clairvoyant (able to see beyond the range of ordinary perception) and enlightened enough to defend the truth as thoroughly as possible.

In primeval times, the ancients either fatuously (foolishly, inanely) or wisely believed that gods made the universe out of eternal mushy water that had been there forever. And from Plato to Einstein, the scientific view was that our universe has simply existed before anything else, therefore lessening the burden of scientific proof on the origin of the universe, since paranormal was rather cumbersome for relative understanding and not attuned with time parameter.

In his book Show Me God, George Smoot (head of the NASA COBE satellite team that discovered cosmic "seeds") says, "Until the late 1910s, humans were as ignorant of cosmic origins as they had ever been. Those who didn't take Genesis (birth, inception, and onset) literally had no reason to believe there had been a beginning."

Adduce (notes, evidence, invoke) for a beginning

Einstein's general theory of relativity declared the universe's expansion. Expansion marked a beginning, and a beginning implied a Beginner.

The evidence became undeniable, however, when Edwin Powell Hubble utilized the largest telescope of his time to display that all the galaxies are precipitately (impetuously, rushing) going away from us, and in which there was an exact, linear relationship between the galaxies' distance and their velocity, as Einstein's equations foresaw.

Profusion (abundance, wealth) of Helium.

Later scientific findings carried on to strengthen the big bang concept, as Fred Hoyle humorously first called it. While Hoyle was insisting on proving his "steady state theory of an everlasting universe," he instead validates that only an incredibly hot, condensed origin for the universe could elucidate (explain, clarify) the reason for the plentifullness of helium in the universe.

An external job

The great quest of science is to find the cause for every effect. But as we trace the cause-effect chain back through time, we come to a scientifically perplexing moment at the beginning where cause-effect relationships simply stop. This denotes the theory of creation out of nothing, the emergence out of nothing, a universe that is theological and correlated with monism religions (Judaism, Christianity, and Islam), since they all teach creation ex nihilo (creation out of nothing).

As Einstein stated: space, time, and matter are inextricably interconnected. The development of the universe is not because of galaxies whirling out into a larger void, but of space itself elongating and carrying galaxies along for the ride. This means that if our journey toward the end of time ends with disappearance of matter, then time and space must disappear too. Logic tells us that causes must precede their effects. So what reasoning other than the cause of our universe being placed outside of it is there, when there is no time before the beginning?

This God could not be contained by the universe. King Solomon prayed: "The heavens, even the highest heaven, cannot contain you. How much less this temple I have built!" (1 Kings 8:27 (link is external)). Naturally, the idea of monist varied much from the image of physical gods accepted by ancients, where so many gods were worshiped, not excluding the ocean gods, earth gods, sky gods, sun gods, moon gods, star gods, animal-headed gods, and many goddesses, etc.

Monism is theology that delves into metaphysical views, where there are no decisive divisions other than a unified set of laws underlining God and nature. This is in contrast to dualism, which believes that there are two kinds of essences, and from pluralism, which maintains there are many kinds of meaning and materials.

The word monism is based on the idea of "monad," derived from the Greek monos, which means "single with having no subcategory, or any division. Monism is subject to different contexts within metaphysics, God, epistemology (distinguishes justified beliefs from opinion), morality and ethics, philosophy of the mind and existence, and so on.

But it always means oneness contesting dualism in body and soul, in matter and spirit (an energy-driven concept), object and subject, matter and force, where monism refutes and denies any distinction and persists on conceptual unity in a higher realm. The attempt is to eliminate the dichotomy (bisection, cutting in two, halving) of body and mind.

And today, if science points to a Creator who must be separate from the physical universe, then pantheistic ideas of God appear to be as misconstrued as polytheistic ones. The Eastern notion of a Star Wars God, a God who is a mere "Force" that is one with or part of the universe, is seriously challenged by modern cosmology.

A Creator outside of time

Nothing that is confined to time could have created the cosmos. The Creator must have existed before the beginning of time, and from a God perspective, God exists in our past, present, and future simultaneously.

Some have accepted a beginning, but they have described it as a random event, drafting a similarity between the origin of the universe and quantum events. Quantum theory states that even though space seems to be empty, in reality it is filled with virtual particle pairs that appear and fluctuate for extremely short periods of time. Our universe might have come into being via such a quantum vibration.

Fred Hoyle states, "The physical properties of the vacuum would still be needed and this would be something." The space in our universe is called a "false vacuum" since in actuality, it has properties that make it much more than nothingness—it is not an empty space as we assess it.

Besides, what we grasp as empty space stems from our limited senses that are only applicable to the visible world. Unless we're utilizing sophisticated telescopes and an up-to-date magnifier, we would be completely estranged from subatomic life and the quantum world.

Physicist Robert Gange states that relating to quantum physics, any universe that lasts for more than a Planck time (10-43 seconds) demands more than an arbitrary notion and a chance to describe it. Gange believes that quantum physics refers not only to an outside sustainer, but also to an outside initiator.

Physicists say that our universe is an astonishingly fine-tuned environment, and they are very interested to know how it happened to be this way.

Most scientists agree on the critical density of the universe; that it expands at a precise rate, just right for the building of galaxies, rather than ending in a premature collapse or a too-quick scattering (dispersion, refraction) and must have a flawless conductor. Physicists assent that the augmentation rate at the beginning had to be fine-tuned to one part in 10 to the 60th power; that's 1 with 60 zeros after it, a level of accuracy that they call "insane."

Stephen Hawking referred to this critical balance when he said, "The odds against a universe like ours emerging out of something like the big bang are enormous." Hawking also acknowledged the ratio between the masses of the proton and the electron as one of many critical numbers precisely met in nature. "The remarkable fact," he said, "is that the values of these numbers seem to have been very finely adjusted to make possible the development of life."

An incredible fine-tuning for life's advantage challenges natural explanation. After British astrophysicist Fred Hoyle calculated the probabilities that carbon would have exactly the same resonance by accident, he claimed that his atheism was greatly shaken, adding, "A common sense interpretation of the facts suggests that a super intellect has monkeyed with physics."

Fine-tuning undeniably pertains to each of nature's four fundamental forces that are so precisely harmonized that the ratios between them cannot differ without crushing the possibility of life. If the strong nuclear force were slightly weaker, the universe would only end up with hydrogen; if a nuance (slight degree) stronger, the universe would be depleted of hydrogen (and, of course, without stars). Stronger or weaker electromagnetic forces or a different value for the gravitational constant would also end in a universe with no stars.

Physicist Edward Kolb of the Fermi National Accelerator Laboratory stated, "It turns out that 'constants of nature,' such as the strength of gravity, have exactly the values that allow stars and planets to form .... The universe, it seems, is fine-tuned to let life and consciousness flower." Science, he declares, may never be capable of telling us why this is the case. The breathtaking convergence of quantum mechanics theory, microscopic world theory, general relativity, elementary particle theory, our theory of the universe as a whole in which the ideas involved, are speculative. This area of research is still an interesting brawl where the power of imagination is as imperative as careful calculation and surveillance.

Quantum mechanics is the most principled theory about the microscopic world. This precise, mighty, profound, and most attractive theory educates us that the world of the tiny is extremely varied from the world of our day-to-day experience. One remarkable difference is that infinitesimal (tiny, microscopic) things have opaque (vague, obscure) properties.

The Heisenberg uncertainty principle illustrates this shadowy situation by declaring that one cannot modulate (harmonize, attune) and measure a particle's position and speed at the same time as accurately as one desires. To size one very solicitously (carefully) will dislocate the measurement of the other, which disappoints the lector (reader), with the result that the particle has a specific position and velocity, but scientists are unable to measure it.

A more truthful statement of the fact denotes the uncertainty principle presents that a particle does not have a particular situation or velocity. The scientific measuring shows that scientist and the particle coincidently (collectively) generate unclear position or velocity.

It seems magic is truly orchestrating the invisible world of subatomic particles, as scientists name nothingness the vacuum and where the vacuum has ghostly properties. They admit particles and antiparticle spring into existence and disappear again. The physicists attest they must act so fast because they cannot directly see them, and because they are invisible, they call it a vacuum. By now, the scientists know that the quantum things appear and vanish, pop in and out of existence.

General relativity is the most Grass-Rooty theory concerning the whole universe; about gravitation, and about space and time. Einstein reminded us that these things inextricably entwine. Even though general relativity is not a quantum theory, scientists believe that every theory at its foundation has to be a quantum theory.

ENTROPY

The second law of thermodynamics (physics that deals with the mechanical action or relation of heat, electromagnetism, microphysics, mechanics, and quantum mechanics) states that the amount of energy in a system that is available to work is dwindling (diminishing.) Entropy rises as available energy lessens, which interprets that the innate proclivity (inclination) of things is to move toward chaos, not order, and accessible energy needed for moiling (working) is lost as heat in the process. Asymptotically (eventually, ultimately) the universe will run down, and everything will end because all the energy that is available will be more or less evenly allotted (allocated, distributed) so no work can be fulfilled and life can no longer exist.

This is how all things are naturally going to end up. Every living entity will eventually die, and nonliving things wear out and become destroyed. But the universe is not endlessly old because the universe is operating feasibly and without disturbance. The universe would have been exhausted of usable energy if the universe were infinitely old. An infinite universe with no beginning essentially would require infinite usable energy, which, according to the laws of entropy, is not possible. Therefore, the universe must have a beginning. And because the universe had a beginning, it cannot be of infinite size.

Because motion, time, and space are undeniably interweaved, it would demand an infinite amount of time to become infinite in size. Since the universe had a beginning, it couldn't have had an endless amount of time to expand; hence, it is finite in size. No endless regression events are possible, since that would mean the universe was infinitely old. And again, if the universe is already in a state of unusable energy, then it would have been infinitely old, which is not the case.

If any regression analysis has to stop at some certain point, any mathematical or any math-derivative agendas need to start with a beginning and sensibly calculate the progression until the end to have a reliable result. Any event, for that matter, must have an initial position and then an expiration date. I wonder why regression events that must have stopped at some infancy point for the universe to initiate should be difficult to comprehend in which reasoning at that specific point beyond space and time certainly demands an UNCAUSED CAUSE, the omnipotent and the omnipresent God.

One might still say that is supernatural to believe in an uncaused cause. But then again, one should ask oneself, if the subatomic particles at the quantum level cannot be tested, since they too quickly appear and disappear, it seems the particles are being influenced as soon as the examiner physicist, or any related quantum scientist, tries to calculate the event. If that is not supernatural, I do not know what it is. Because in the natural world at the Newtonian level, and the visible world everything can be tested, examined, and derived with an adequate result.

We should not forget that the human nervous system can only relate to vibrating frequencies of the visible world, as many individuals so strangely deny what they cannot not fathom. It should resonate to the inquisitive mind that the uncaused cause of the universe has to be infinitely bigger in size and span than the universe that it caused into existence. Other than that, we have the uncaused cause manifesting into existence something greater than or equivalent to itself.

Any entity or event that is inseparable from the universe cannot create itself into existence, because anything that is natural to the universe is part of it. This is not as uncanny as some people may think, since there must be an uncaused cause outside of space and time that has brought life into being, but certainly not subjected to the laws of the universe.

Pascal's wager is an argument in philosophy devised by the seventeenth-century French philosopher, mathematician, and physicist Blaise Pascal (1623–62).[1] It posits that humans bet with their lives that God either exists or does not.

Pascal argues that a rational person should live as though God exists and seek to believe in God. If God does not actually exist, such a person will have only a finite loss (some pleasures, luxury, etc.), whereas they stand to receive infinite gains (as represented by eternity in Heaven) and avoid infinite losses (eternity in Hell).

DEMOCRACY AND JUSTICE

People do not have to die to live, struggling for employment, food, shelter, fighting for the very basic necessities of life to keep them afloat, as billions are horrified as they face devastating condition just to survive. This is not how living should be. There are serious flaws in the allocation of resources and grave wrongdoing in how humanity needs to be treated. Since it seems justice is managed via force and by the power of gun, I wonder if God has anything to do with it?

The voices of justice must resonate with friend and foe; it must awaken the ignorant and the cruel. It is mandatory, and utterly not optional for the deprived and the righteous to be heard. In a democratic society, justice, heard loud and clear, not suffocated, is the only tool available that can expose and chastise the evils of the uncivilized, and the callous behaviors of the reprobate (a person who behaves in a morally wrong way.) As Reinhold Niebuhr says, "Man's capacity for justice makes democracy possible, but man's inclination to injustice makes democracy necessary."

It is of moral imperative to deny an oligarchical democracy, where the rest are tricked into believing they live in a democratic state and they do not. People must demand constructive change to prevent further corporate takeover, since corporate imperialists have no loyalty to either people or the state of the republic.

We are not delusional when we hear a painstaking cry for help—or are we? That is when we lose courage and behave with numb indifference to inequities for the wrong reasons, which keeps so many acting sub-human and away from doing what is right. And as Benjamin Franklin said, "Justice will not be served until those who are unaffected are as outraged as those who are."

Justice must be done in a timely manner to prevent genocide. Fair play must halt displacement of inhabitants from their homeland and stop further devastation in global warming, where a toxic and destructive atmosphere is literally killing human-beings for the sake of greed and hoarding money. Global policies must become in tune with movements already implemented towards one nation under God, since revolutionized technology and speed-of-light communication is making phrases such as this by Marshal McLuhan undeniably true: the world that has been "shrunk" by modern advances in communications. McLuhan likened the vast network of communications systems to one extended central nervous system, ultimately linking everyone in the world.

It is so undeniably true that dynamic communications, and the so fluent socio-cultural, socio-economic, and international political interactivities, cannot be obstructed by the walls of nationalism and prejudices anymore. It is quite difficult to turn conscionable people into robots, as if they ought to be controlled by remotes, striving to keep so many silent to undergo mental and spiritual sabotage.

It is time to wake up and notice the decisive difference in shifting priorities awaiting mankind. As Martin Luther King Jr. said, "An injustice anywhere is a threat everywhere." Globally, atrocious behavior must be noticed and dealt with.

WORK AND PRODUCTIVITY

Acting accordingly productive is the gist of living. Any consciously intelligent member of society should know that idleness and shirking can make one's sovereign position weak and vulnerable to dependency on others. There is no guaranty that wrong and morbid behavior is requested from the needy to satisfy the provider's demand. In exchange for receiving funds, as willful solicitation is often expected in return, an unproductive and jobless individual can be open to all sorts of vileness just to maintain one's basic needs for survival.

Managing short-term budgeting, and planning long-term financial activities—saving, wisely overseeing, and controlling one's financial status—are the keys for staying economically independent. The capitalist economy is systematic and very disciplined; it is cruel, and does not budge to any incompetency or sluggishness. Karma believes "what goes around, comes around," and this is true in every literal sense in dealing with balancing one's income and expenditures.

Once the victim of a monetary system and vile bankruptcy, there are no immunities but awaiting the tragic consequences of homelessness and dependency on other financially able bodies to either help, or not.

This scenario is not only true on an individual basis, but also ominous when exercised on a larger scale, when people are collectively unemployed. An unproductive nation redundantly looks for philanthropy from other powerful and productive nations, and their mercy.

Behaving lazily and not being productively active, not managing time, and in acting nonchalant, easily quitting, and not challenging the odds, or acting incompetent and not persevering enough to fight back against tough times will surely invite a systematically dire culture of creeping normalcy where the inhabitant's destructive behavior can become the norm. Concentrate all your thoughts upon the work at hand. The sun's rays do not burn until brought to a focus (Alexander Graham Bell).

When losing golden opportunities and repeatedly making wrong decisions, one can lose self-confidence and the value of independency, and end up hoping for survival. Productivity is not accidental. It is certainly the result of a commitment to excellence and hard work, savvy thoughts, bright planning, and concentrated effort in which one can muster magnificent creativity. But we ought to realize it is faulty to measure productivity checking one's BlackBerry over dinner and in obsessive behaviors with one's gadgets.

THE SUBCONSCIOUS MIND

As the science of psychology and psychiatric behaviors advances, we become even more consciously alert. Your subconscious mind is a second, hidden mind that exists within you. It does translate and acts upon the predominating thoughts that reside within the conscious mind. It objectifies circumstances and positions and identifies with the images that impact us from within.

Perceive your subliminal mind as tremendously fertile soil, an infinite agricultural ground that produces any seed you plant in it. One's habits, beliefs, and thoughts are implanted, and seeds are constantly sown till the day one expires. Just as grape seeds generate grapes, and walnut seeds produce walnuts, lemon seeds generate lemons, and wheat seeds produce wheat, the nature of your thoughts will affect you without you even being aware. You will reap what you sow; this is a fact.

It is also known that we are the products of our environment. So, it makes much sense to establish a constructive atmosphere and productive upbringing not to jeopardize our position where toxic thoughts and misconducts are cultured and normalized. It is also hugely important to educate people, since we play the role of gardeners, which for most should mean we are responsible for planting wisely so that all kind of seeds are not manifested into our subconscious mind.

As gardeners that tend to the soil of our unconscious mind, we need to meditate on what enters into our mind; as they say, garbage in, garbage out. The subliminal doesn't prejudice, judge, delete, or censor. It will stress success, plenty, and good health just as simply as shortcomings, scarcity, defeat, ill health, distress, and misfortunes do. Your subconscious mind imprints what is marked with feeling and repetition, whether these thoughts are positive or negative. It does not assess things as your conscious mind does.

This is why it is very crucial to know what you are thinking. Your subconscious mind is subjective. It does not think or reason on its own. It solely takes orders it captures from the conscious mind. It is fertile ground in which the seeds of our thoughts germinate and are cultivated. Your conscious mind commands, and your subconscious mind obeys. One has the prerogatives and should be able to wisely choose, especially if one has the blessing of having a decent environment and the opportunity of a good and prosperous upbringing.

Synchronicity

Once you understand that your subconscious will bring you what you need or desire, and you begin working daily to project thoughts and images of what you want, seeming chance events will start happening to you. To the untrained mind, synchronicity appears to be coincidence or luck, but it is neither. It is simply the operation of the forces you have set into motion with your thoughts. This powerful inner collaborator, working with your conscious mind, will bring to you the people and circumstances you require to achieve your goals.

We are all part of the greater whole.

Modern physics sees the universe as a vast, inseparable web of dynamic activity. Not only is the universe alive and constantly changing, but everything in the universe affects everything else. At its most primary level, the universe seems to be whole and undifferentiated, a fathomless sea of energy that permeates every object and every act. It is all one. Scientists are now confirming what mystics and seers have been telling us for thousands of years: we are not separate from, but part of, one greater whole.

We now know that everything in the universe is made up of energy. Everything from the items in your home, to the events that happen to you, and even our thoughts, are made up of vibrations of energy. This means our thoughts are made of the exact same substance as the building blocks of the universe. Knowing this, we can use it to our advantage.

In the past, it might have seemed unbelievable that we could create our reality through this process. But now we know how to do it, and why it works. Since our thoughts are energy, it only makes sense that repeated images, affirmations, deeply held beliefs, fears, dreams, and desires would have an effect on our own reality by vibrating within the larger fabric of reality. In fact, if we are all linked, how could it be otherwise?

The subconscious mind is something that has a huge effect on every action, but is constantly overlooked. Instead, the focus is often on our conscious mind, which contains the critical thought function of our brains. The subconscious is the powerful layer underneath. It encompasses the awareness of all things the conscious mind cannot recognize. Once the subconscious is tapped into, this remarkable part of the brain plays many different roles in your everyday life.

The Memory Bank

Your subconscious mind is similar to a huge memory bank. Its faculty (capability, competency) is virtually (almost entirely, pretty well) unlimited. It perennially (infinitely) stores everything that ever occurs to you. By the time you reach the age of 21, you've already permanently stored more than one hundred times the contents of the entire Encyclopedia Britannica. Under hypnosis, older people can often remember, with perfect lucidity, events from sixty years before. Your unconscious memory is just about perfect. It is your conscious memory that is suspect.

The function of your subconscious mind is to store and retrieve data. Its objective is to make certain that you respond precisely the way you are programmed. Your subconscious mind makes whatever you utter and do fit a pattern consistent with your self-thought. It is your "Master Program."

The Obedient Servant

Your subconscious mind is subjective. It does not think or reason independently. It merely obeys the commands it perceives from your conscious mind. Your conscious mind can be thought of as the gardener planting seeds. Your subconscious mind can be thought of as the garden, or fertile soil, in which the seeds germinate. Your conscious mind orders and your subconscious mind obeys. Your subconscious mind is an unquestioning servant. It works 24/7 to make your behavior fit a pattern coherent with your emotionalized thoughts, desires, and hopes.

Your subconscious mind cultivates either blossoming flowers or a wasteland of weeds in the nursery (botanical garden) of your life. Whichever you plant is based on the mental equivalents you create.

The Preserver of Balance

Your subconscious mind has what is called a homeostatic impulse. It keeps your body temperature at 98.6 degrees Fahrenheit. It keeps you breathing regularly and keeps your heart beating at a certain rate.

Your autonomic nervous system maintains a balance among the hundreds of chemicals in your billions of cells. Your entire physical machine functions in complete harmony—most of the time.

Your subconscious mind also practices homeostasis in your mental realm. It keeps you thinking and acting in a manner consistent with what you have done and said in the past.

The Comfort Zone

All your habits of thinking and acting are stored in your subconscious mind. It has memorized all your comfort zones and it works to keep you in them.

Your subconscious mind makes you feel emotionally and physically uncomfortable whenever you attempt to do anything new or different. It goes against changing any of your already set patterns of behavior.

You can feel your subconscious pulling you back toward your comfort zone each time you try something new and challenging. Even thinking about doing something different from what you're accustomed to will cause you feel tense and uneasy.

One of the biggest habits of successful people is always stretching themselves or pushing themselves out of their comfort zones. They know that smugness (self-satisfaction, complacency) is the great enemy of creativity and future possibilities.

MODERNISM VS. TRADITIONALISM

Humanity is facing a fundamental and often difficult matter that has permeated into every aspect of our lives, and apparently with little competency to resolve. Modernism is facing off to overcome traditionalism, which is making life convoluted (twisty, winding) and difficult. Global inhabitants, particularly developing countries, are caught between decisive transition from traditionalism to modernism, not because they want to, but because they have to.

It is the almost daily advances in technology that have increased information and knowledge that has resulted in modernism, and dynamic worldly communication encompassing cultural, social, economic, and scientific discoveries make it a blessing.

But it's also discouraging, since the old beliefs and new trends of thought do routinely clash, and sometimes for the worst. Like giving birth to religious extremism, terrorism, and enacting dictatorial regimes that hinder modernity for maintaining the status quo to halt progress.

Advances in technology and science are inevitable. It is the womb of nature that is impregnated with piercing ideas and faithful inventions sought by miraculous minds relentlessly endeavoring and searching for new discoveries that are inundated (overwhelming) and revolutionizing contemporary status to enhance human lives, and in making further advances to modernize our position for better living.

We dig into the unknown looking for answers, searching to satisfy our curiosity, hoping for the pursuit of happiness, to quench our thirst for mindboggling questions such as why are we here, where did we come from, and where are we going? What is our purpose for living, and is there a God? And if yes to this last question, why so much pain and suffering?

There are hundreds if not thousands of other imperative inquiries that are basically interrelated with historical human science (anthropology, biology, medicine, sociology, astrology, space, ecology, etc.), digging into cultural morality, spiritual, philosophical, and scientific inquisitions, and more. They substantiate direction and hope to fulfill generations' urges for good living that might one day make millions of enigmatic positions and unanswered questionings transparent and amazingly clear.

It shouldn't be a hesitancy in knowing that freedom, democracy, liberty, human rights, and the pursuit of happiness are keys to creating a flourishing atmosphere promising human progress. They need to be incited and free from limitation, dictatorial anxiety, and a policing environment.

The culprits are inclined to unwaveringly safeguard unabsorbent and unnecessary traditions, as they are not in accord with time parameters and modernism, since they often carry dark ages mentality that impedes greatness into the future.

But modernism should certainly be accompanied by making big attempts to inspire citizens' progressive attitude to gain knowledge and to maintain social security for better living.

It's time for free education, free medical care, free housing, and free transportation, and most definitely employment for everyone so that people can be relatively free of stressful financial uncertainties which make millions bereft (barren, utterly lacking) of the ability to devote time and energy to magnify production and become a better member of society.

It is savvy to realize that some schools of thought and socioeconomic, socio-cultural entities are by nature more advanced than others.

For instance, institutions that practice social-democratic systems and prioritize social security first and then manifest democracy, like Scandinavian societies, such as Denmark, Finland Norway, Sweden, Iceland, and to some degree Germany and France, Canada, and others that are social democracies. They are countries that value equality, trust, and public welfare services, as they are well-adjusted for furthering human accomplishments and civility of mind and manner. They are adequately positioned, as they first attend to basic human needs and then value democracy, as freedom should be considered a sacred and inseparable part of humanity, but not abused.

Freedom and good behavior do complement each other, and one without the other invites a crime-infested society, often with nasty outcomes. Democracy first, and then social security second, has unleashed so much violence and inexorable (uninviting, austere, harsh) individualism, truly actuating survival of the fittest behavior and everyone to his own attitude, resulting in impetuous (marked by force and violence action, impulsive) decision-making and defaults that make it almost impossible to give meaning to peaceful coexistence and human rights.

It is noteworthy to know this system of democracy-social, which most capitalist systems practice, has unleashed excitement in violence and often destructive actions that encourage smell-blood conduct that is for sure provoked by Hollywood and more recently, politics. Bollywood, savagely digital video games, deadly sports and competitions, and other "entertainment" fallacies have globally caused havoc, especially among younger generations that are extremely chaotic, criminal, and inhumane.

It seems they are people with no conscience, and I am afraid so-called professionals deliberately promote criminal behaviors, endorsing destructive programs and extremely violent movies and distasteful television agendas, satellites, and other mischievous social medias that are utterly barbaric.

"Because one cannot exercise true democracy in a violent society." If one is bereft in training and education, and not able to experience a civil society, one is much more inclined to act immorally and criminally when unemployed and hungry, when one's loved one is sick or terminally ill without having access to professional medical help, or without housing assistance, where so many have to end up living on the street and homeless.

I believe those institutions that practice democratic-social rather than socio-democratic are literally facing agendas that are backward, and not in favor of the majority of their citizens—but they are making living extremely luxurious for the very few, which gravitates towards lopsidedness in almost every aspect of our lives since perhaps they inadvertently are encouraging a menacing atmosphere that most definitely demands a police state.

I am afraid democracy-social has also caused a serious dilemma, especially in developing nations, since they are often faced with dictatorial governments and fascist regimes that do not believe in fair allocation of resources, resulting in extreme income inequality, while the ruling elites also reject freedom and democracy, and even if they exhibit some, it is definitely cosmetic, and not at all authentic.

RESPECT, RETURN THE FAVOR

Yes, it is true that some individuals might behave kinder than others, tolerate undesirable conduct, and perhaps insightfully bear inconsiderate actions. Even put up with impetuous, cruel, and hasty behavior. Whatever the case may be, the point is that we all have a boiling point that will sooner or later erupt if we are pushed to our limits.

Many take acts of love and kindness for granted, giving no thanks and without returning the favor. When one is continuously sacrificing and is constantly there to give so much of oneself, but not being appreciated, it will gradually but surely influence one's subconscious mind, which can eventually surface, making the caregiver exhibit harsh retaliation in one way or another.

Expecting nothing in return is because of one's devotion, act of kindness, and goodness of heart that should not be taken advantage of. When one is careless for so long towards one's benefactor, and retorts (to say in reply) nonchalantly, one can unexpectedly face violence from the very same person that has ceaselessly assisted him or her in their time of need.

When it comes to human emotions, time is of the essence; true feelings and emotions do not occur abruptly. They gradually mature and progress; they can be subtle, and not alerting.

If others are neither emotionally intelligent nor sensitive enough to appreciate one's ceaseless support and good deeds, or perhaps are acting with complicity or not wanting to reciprocate, then be smart and terminate the unjustified one-way relationship before it erupts like a volcano, making damage beyond repair.

For instance, in a marriage where the marital covenant is at stake, both parties need to sincerely comply by the rules of marriage that encourage the couples to appreciate each other and to sacrifice within their means for keeping the sanctity of the marriage intact.

We ought to be reminded that no matter how much one is in love or is willing to sacrifice, if the significant other cannot mutually favor and render sincere love in return, then in the name of good will and decency, one should not persist in taking advantage of the significant other; it will sooner or later backfire.

If not able to constructively deal with one's egotistical conduct, then bail out softly before resentment can brew to a point of no return with irreparable damage. Remember, even a mother's unconditional love has its limit.

It is of paramount importance that you always return the favor. We sometimes might not be able to respond financially, but it is always possible to render kindness, either with words or actions. Many of us take things for granted, forgetting that no matter how much of a saint one really is, or how much of a good character one might be, we are not perfect. What I mean is, we all do have a threshold, a breaking point that can cause anyone to behave adversely and in negative ways. One should try to overcome one's selfishness and believe in the decency of a fair give-and-take relationship where compassion, balance, and appreciation is truly served.

"We are what we repeatedly do. Excellence, then, is not an act, but a habit" – Aristotle

The secret is to do what is mindful and virtuous, where bad habits cannot eventually tear us apart.

CREEPILY MANEUVERING

When people are kept illiterate by design, they easily succumb to fallacies of the ruling system as they acquiesce (submit, give in) to dishonest politicians that are in cahoots with business elites determined to preserve the status quo. Prerogative gentries (privileged class) are entitled to receive the best, while the underprivileged and financially repressed are restlessly engaged in an unbearable lifestyle, worrying about their next meal and a roof over their head, and how to deal with irreparable health problems they encounter.

That is exactly why no weight is put on the miracle of learning for the deprived by the powerful, coupled with keeping people busy with a difficult life, which results in ill conditioning for the poor and jeopardizes their position, making it impossible for them to grow, despite much insane positivism and obsolete affirmations that supposedly are meant to motivate the hopeless and help the destitute.

The suppressors are well aware that literacy, knowledge, and information awakens people to question more and ask why. In which all answer should apparently lead to bizarre sociocultural and socioeconomic plans meant to cultivate the worst in people and to bind them to the psychology of work while facilitating millions with the conditional techniques to make them one-track-minded in maximizing productions for the rich elites and to act docile (amenable, obedient) and robot-like in taking orders.

It should remind one of Pacific salmon, which are motivated to lay their eggs and are determined to breed after an arduous journey struggling upstream, which makes them exhausted. And sometimes amid the ferocious storm, that is the very reason for their death.

And if they are not caught by fishermen and other predators, like bears and eagles, or do not get trapped behind dams and large waterfalls before breeding, they are very lucky, since so many cannot make it to fulfill their mission, what they are destined to do.

NATURE OR NURTURE?

Which one of these is the responsible party: our genes or our environment?

Is it our genes and our biology that is responsible for our behavior and who we really are? Or could it be the environment and the way we are raised that is the main and decisive factor in how we are shaped?

Genes are defined as "a specific sequence of nucleotides in DNA or RNA (messengers) that is located on a chromosome which is the functional unit of inheritance controlling the transmission and expression of one or more traits by specifying the structure or a particular polypeptide and especially a protein or controlling the function of other genetic material."

In layman terms, we can say that nature is the bottom line, and the very reason for our behavior. It is a deterministic factor to the code of codes and how we are driven to be, because we are predisposition, preprogrammed, and there is nothing that we can do about it. Therefore, we are predestined to be who we really are. Or is it the environment and how we are nurtured and fostered that plays the real decisive factor, and a huge role in identifying who we really are that shapes our true personality and character?

Scholars of biology, philosophy, the environment, anthropology, sociology, psychology, neurology, psychiatry, nutrition, physiology, economy, and many other social, cultural, mental, and behavioral sciences have wrestled with this perplexing human issue for many years now. The overall assessment and the truth behind this very crucial point is that "it is virtually not possible to understand and to comprehend how human biology would be able to function outside of the context of the environment."

To believe genes are things that cannot be changed, since they are rooted in our very biology and they are to determine our fate and manifest what kind of personality we become, is a very detrimental and hazardous view that has polluted many people's minds, leaving horrifying side effects and is an extremely irresponsible way to deal with this crucial human quandary (dilemma).

Obviously, believing in the gene argument and the hypothesis as being the only fateful factor in shaping our behavior and character, and in denoting who we really are, permits the luxury—and the irresponsibility—of not adequately dealing with this damaging idea. To leave out the historical, environmental, social, political, economic, and many other variables and educational factors that are responsible in shaping our personalities, our behavioral mishaps, or good characters, is to unjustly deny anyone his or her true potentiated identity for the better, as most probably so many deprived individuals could become much more progressive and improved people if they were not exhausted from living in an improper atmosphere and depleted from decisive educational agendas that could spur and motivate millions toward the right direction.

Tell me if violent Hollywood movies and violent video games and so many other electronic conditioning gadgets are not deliberately designed and programed to shape people's minds and to emotionally disconnect people and cultures, which certainly brainwash future generation to become zombie-like, as many do the most inhuman behaviors, regardless of what type of genes or traits they carry or have been born with. Would we still be in this violently messy society as we literally are, where, for example, so many mass shootings occur in schools, high schools, colleges and universities, killing and injuring innocent people? And ironically, these centers are designed to literate students for the best they can be. Or other mass shootings that redundantly happen in public gatherings, shopping malls, and many entertainment places, where people are supposed to unwind and relax from exhaustive daily workloads and have a good time. Hundreds of other crime-infested neighborhoods are dealt with as remote islands, where no hope for recovery and improvement is ever mustered to prevent or mitigate further atrocities relating to social and economic disasters.

Tell me if hate-mongering movies, and the most distasteful sexual programs and scenarios, have anything to do with our thoughts and conduct as human beings, as the human brain cannot tell the difference, particularly for the most naïve (ingenious mind, deficient in worldly wisdom), and perhaps mentally disturbed, between films onscreen and films playing in the mind.

And yes, of course it is good to pray for peace, health, happiness, liberty, human rights, and justice for all. for the sake of goodness, and for the love of God, let's not turn a blind eye and play these utterly double-standard and misleading games on people's psyches, taking them for fools. That would eventually lure them into the corner to give in to these subtle and creeping misdeeds. I am sure you, the culprits, know that living is easy with eyes closed. For the love of God, open your eyes! Humanity is on the verge of annihilation because of your greed for wealth and power.

Promoting a genetically predispositioned argument and predestined nature as an absolute, and expecting no progress in genetically programmed human beings, is a diabolical and premeditate folly that gives a green light to those who justify their lies and deplorable acts in any society. It should remind us of eugenics, where the idea was to create an environment where variables were to be controlled for the production of good offspring, to improve and control such variables as health, beauty, intelligence, aptitude, strength, and other outstanding and desirable factors that would have been complimentary to their prejudiced and discriminatory notions.

I say discriminatory because there are enough resources to gratify every born child with the best possible outcome.

ESSENTIALLY REQUIRED

Do not be fooled into acting foolishly arrogant or in behaving cocky and irrational. These inept behaviors do not comply with the spirit of goodness and what is right. Use your mental, spiritual, moral, physical strength, and your financial strength to progressively leverage and extend help to the deprived and those in need, the destitute. Acting otherwise will put you in a stranglehold to one day suffocate you.

Being blessed and endowed with so much wealth, prosperity, and power is a premeditated and predestined trust in you, expecting you to be fair in the just allocation of resources and not to bondage mankind. It is all about making it or breaking it. Remember, nothing is meant to be with no purpose; it is a universe amazingly well-designed, superbly constructed to reach its objective and goals.

We are lucky to be part of it, at this particularly wonderful phase; given a choice and the freedom to be constructive or to behave destructively, to annihilate it all. And since it is no longer a hypothesis but a fact that the weapons of mass destruction are now as real as wisdom is beyond value.

IF I WAS GOD

I am glad that God is God, and I am not, as God is a God of infinite patience, the most compassionate with infinite forgiveness, infinite resourcefulness, infinite justice, infinite effluence of good, the most benevolence, the most merciful, infinitely prevalent, infinitely graceful, the Proprietor of all there is, the most graceful, the Fiduciary of time, space, and beyond.

I say the most patient because no one but God can tolerate the evils of man. And yes, survival of the fittest is very much alive in the animal kingdom, as beasts kill and devour beasts, as by nature they are baneful (harmful) serving their instinct (non-taught, biological capabilities) to survive. It is a jungle out there, but so is here, a crime-ridden atmosphere; only with one difference. What the beasts go through is mandatory, while so many of us choose harmful behaviors and violence although they are not compulsory, but optional.

Then again, the so-called "animal man" with some instinctual traits is confident with mind power and created with a brain that is potentiated to one-day reach the entire universe. Man is credited with intelligence, goodwill, consciousness, and as one is entrusted with wisdom, self-awareness, sacred feelings, righteous emotions, and is also a moral being with the likelihood of acting in the image of God. That is why the "animal man," with some instincts, is as well-named a human-being.

One ought to acknowledge and know that man's instinctual conduct for living is to stay alive for manifesting its heavenly qualities, to produce good deeds, to work hard and shine, to ascend and be the best that one can be. To sacrifice when one hears a cry for help, and to negate the unjust, to encourage happiness and discourage sadness, to be considered, to tolerate others, and assist the less fortunate, to denounce fascism, to believe in freedom, democracy, dignity, and human rights. To let freedom of thought, freedom of speech, freedom of expression, freedom of religion, and freedom of assembly thrive. To believe in collective cooperation, to believe in a world with no boundaries and walls, to practice in good faith, to live and let live; otherwise, why should anyone be different than a beast?

I am sure the all-knowing God has taken those reverence merits (values) into account when God created human beings, and perhaps God has taken those profound properties in man for granted. But God is being betrayed in return, and with no sign of remorse from mankind that it is doing the infinite wrong. I wish humans would have not been entrusted with ultimate generosity and kindness, and had not been taken for granted to act in his image.

I wish human creatures were born with intelligence, and not a clean slate at birth. I wish we were wise and knew enough from the day we were born, from the very beginning, to discern right from wrong so that perhaps infinite wrongs and perpetuated crimes could have been avoided or relatively mitigated. But that would have been against the evolutionary nature of the entire universe, which is gradually perfected and awakened, as everything is bound to incrementally advance, reaching its potentiated trace and maturity. So basically that thought is futile and out of the question.

The other alternative is to be born with a thumb-like horn, realizing that unless one would wise up as one grows and perseveres to ripen to the height of humanity in acquiring education, knowledge, integrity, wisdom, intelligence, empathy, caring, hard work, sacrifice, and being a productive member of society, then one's horn would not diminish as one grows, but it would get larger. Which of course would raise a red flag for the rest as a clear sign to watch out and be aware of the beast-like personality that one carries.

This not only motivates the horn-bearer to diligently try for bettering oneself so that one's horn would eventually vanish, as one can gradually become the best that one can be, since no one likes to become finger-pointed and shunned regardless of one's gender and ethnicity or any other personal trait; but warns those improved, the wise and civilized, to keep away from troubling souls. To stay away from those impregnated with stupidity and violence as signified by the height of their horn, aiming at correcting a violent society infested with offenders.

It could be that atrocities occur because not every victim is an expert psychologist, psychiatrist, or a professional sociologist, to relatively detect insane characters, to perhaps avoid trouble, and certainly before is too late.

This alternative also has its flaws, because it cannot work in uncivilized nations where no commitments are made to grassroots change of the backward conditions, where people's pride is suffocated and no funds are available for training, skill, and education, and the entire society is dominated by illiteracy, where the power of force, hypocrisy, and violence is the key to advancement, and it can be a blessing to have a long horn and rough attitude to overpower others. This is where behaving inhumanely and approaching the peak of savagery for one's own interest and pleasure is the key to success. Furthermore, it would take away the dignity from the one born with horn, as it simulates and lowers a human's position to beasts.

The other option would be to professionally (exhibiting conscientious and ethical standard) facilitate newborns in highly standard centers for the first three to four years of their lives, which are extremely crucial in shaping their personality, accommodated by the state for upgrading the children with the most viable learning assistance through every decisive educational training and health field study possible, to the expected result. It is also extremely imperative that children have access to parental love while under professional care, to avoid negative emotional side effects that are bound to occur if babies are deprived of parental love.

This scenario demands skillful devotees that are willing to exercise every humane ingredient possible to also boost the motherly love and parental care that any child needs to prosper, which seems a bit utopian, because it is bound to time and very far in the future, when people are advanced in their thoughts and the overall society has the emotional intelligence to accept the visionary expression, "From each according to his ability, to each according to his needs," a slogan popularized by Karl Marx in his 1875 Critique of the Gotha Program. The principle refers to free access and distribution of goods, capital, and services.

After all is said and done, not only are we the product of our genes, but also the product of our environment, in which a productive atmosphere demands constructive plans, and certainly adequate funding to properly spend on decisive matters, not to exclude professional and adept management to oversee the upbringing of the children, especially in poverty-stricken areas where people are much more at risk for destructive behaviors, where there is no light at the end of the tunnel.

I am afraid it has become a testosterone-driven world where aggression, bullying, and brute force works, as no civility of mind and manner matters, as millions are taking advantage of God's blessing and infinite patience as he watches the devil's work in most of us, but still renders a chance until judgment day or punishes the culprits without letting the transgressor (violator) connect the crime that one commits to one's later punishment while living.

We should realize that God has ushered the way and has endowed humanity with a mind, a brain that can think and create miracles, a will to freely choose and ask why, and a spirit to challenge the unjust. While knowing that God's interference in any and all that we choose to do should contradict free will and is despotic, that is why it is left up to the victims to fight back and constantly pressure the evils of our time and say no to the unfair and unethical practices of the few, curse like mighty and belligerent souls.

It is critically vital to question the empire of wealth and influence, the rich elites, that have unfairly accumulated the entire wealth of the globe, since modern moguls have denied opportunity to billions and have decided to let their horns grow and ram into all that is just, violating the basic principle of humanity, which is to not let innocent people die for the sake of accumulating enormous wealth in the hands of the few.

The key is fair allocation of resources, where a family-oriented society would be competent enough to adequately survive and not become so stressed-out and pressured to go through unbearable family violence, to become dispersed and broken into a single family parenthood, or utterly destroyed, which the end result would be a chaotic society having rampant crimes without the possibility of an argument or evidence in affirmation.

And for the after-death reward, or demise, reason should dictate those guilty as charged, or those with good deeds won't burn in Hell or drink wine in Heaven, but inevitably ought to expect either grace or ills of some sort, other than being incinerated in Pandemonium (the capital of Hell) or land in the vicinity of milk and honey, surrounded by beautiful girls and handsome men, accompanied by soothing music, breathtaking dancers, along with exotic birds surrounded in a majestic atmosphere.

Logic dictates that justice should be accordingly swift, and within precise measure. And of course, the expression that says "innocent until proven guilty" is out of the question, since the ever-present God already knows the accused and can utterly identify the perpetrator. Other than that, fear of Hell and Heaven, in all honesty, seems bogus and beyond my mind, as it is denied to those charlatans that blindly claim they have talked to the Almighty and know of the judgement day. They naively claim they are aware of the punishment mechanisms God carries to chastise us in Hell, or prize us in Paradise.

One thing that I am certain of is: what comes around, goes around, as a multiplier of castigations (punishment) should face those exploiters in which their demonic conduct wrongly effects so many innocent human beings that burns them like wildfire as they are boycotted from having the least opportunity in this lifetime. I also know, and so should you, we were born from dust, and to dust we shall return, and should excitingly await our soul to depart to higher realms for a new beginning, perhaps a being not inhibited with imperfections, but a higher spirit in a higher realm.

We all should expect some type of positive or negative response after death. It is infinitely far from reasoning and savviness of mind to accept vanity in a universe that not a single cause is without its merit, since everything is so precisely calculated. The irrefutable fact is that what we do not see controls what we see, and also oversees human conduct.

In entropy there is a principle that says: unless there is a greater control over a process, either a complex chemical reaction or anything else, the process generates chaos; and as big as our universe is, it certainly demands a higher force to control and keep the universe, the entire cosmos and beyond, orderly; which should warn us that there is judicious and epiphenomenon (indirect) control in everything.

IT IS NOT WHAT IT IS

Life goes on, and perplexingly enough, we often disappointedly wonder, and justly so question, why thousands of unfair, gloomy, and painstaking situations are materialized, and are kept vague, not identifying the actual source of suffering for so many, making the inquisitors believe "it is what it is" and this is how living works while controlling people's minds by the very advanced technology of thoughts and startling (staggering, astonishing) psychological and psychiatric maneuvers.

These are well-executed through dubious media and bogus delivery instruments of greed and immorality to preserve the status quo for the handful of bloodthirsty corporate sharks, since the perpetrators relentlessly fuel their oligopoly system by spilling millions of the innocents' blood without mercy. The corporate media, through never-ending electronic illusions, merges fact and fiction until it is perceived indiscernible and not clear, entrapping people's minds into believing the worst.

In the meanwhile, the victims are busy fighting manufactured racial and ethnic tension, struggling with an extreme disparaging social and economically classified society, and with the very troubling income inequality. They're also impacted by a toxic ecological system, putting up with violence inside our borders and outside, and bearing the devastating consequences of unjust, and unfair competition that is the gist of a free enterprise system.

The invisible hand of the market is to balance supply and demand, but only a few have monopolized the world economy by humongous trusts, cartels, bank holding companies, and through global financial intuitions where domestic and small businesses, middle, and the working class do not stand a chance to thrive.

People are not even immune from consuming basic food to stay alive, since billions can utterly not afford organic and wholesome produce and meat, so they have no choice but to eat poisonous junk foods that are infested with chemicals and preservatives and a host of other malignant agents deemed to kill consumers for the sake of generating billions of dollars of profit for the empires of wealth and power.

It seems the air, food, and water are purposely infected, surreptitiously planned to exterminate inhabitants of the overpopulated world, also causing thousands of other atrocious conducts done by the global corporates without any impunity. It should remind one of the expression that says "pick your poison"; either die from hunger, or die from taking food that is supposed to nourish people.

Transnational corporations and their cronies brainwash so many that it is normal to put up with this globally caused hell, and it is ok to live at your own risk with a pandemic-oriented culture of insanity causing humanity irrefutable troubles; after all, so they say, this is the price we pay for our freedom, as they muddy sacred words such as human rights, liberty, and the pursuit of happiness, literally done under a capitalist culture that ironically tries to export freedom and democracy. Civilized and proud nations need to rethink new ways to catapult beliefs that have quick-sanded so many hardworking people without any hope for recovery. Progressive mechanisms of governing can replace the outdated approach to many of a nation's irresolvable dilemmas and gridlocks. The truth is that it is not what it is, and I wonder if God has anything to do with it.

EVOLUTION VS. REVOLUTION

According to the dictionary, some of the definitions for revolution are A) a sudden, radical, or complete change. B) a fundamental change in political organization, the overthrow or renunciation of one government or ruler and substitution of another by the governed. C) activity or movement designed to effect fundamental changes in the socio-economic situation. D) a fundamental change in the way of thinking about or visualizing something, a change of paradigm. E) a changeover in use of preference, or technology of thoughts.

Revolution also means: the action by celestial body of going around in an orbit or elliptical course; also apparent movement of such a body round the earth. The time, taken by a celestial body to make a complete round in its orbit, the rotation of a celestial body on its axis: completion a course (as of years); the period made by the regular succession of a measure of time or by a succession of similar events, motion of any figure about a center or axis.

Evolution, according to the dictionary, means a process of change in a certain direction: Unfolding, the action or an instance of forming and giving something off: Emission, furthermore, a process of continuous change from a lower, simpler, or worse to a higher, more complex, or better state: Growth. A process of gradual and relatively peaceful social, political, and economic advance, the process of working out or developing, something evolved.

Human beings, by nature, are bound to what their genes are made of and influenced by the environment they live and are raised in. Relatively speaking, there are basically four scenarios that can impact our wellbeing or demise; as in good judgement one cannot say that genes and DNA are the sole reason to who we really are and the only cause for people's character buildup.

Many inherit excellent and healthy genes that significantly affect their physical, emotional, and mental attributes, as they are endowed with intelligence, high IQs, compassion, and other decisive humanly factors. And the environment they are born to is also constructively productive and magnificently fruitful, where negative variables often stand no chance to detour someone's promising fate and enhanced position.

Then, we have those with good genetic characters and attractive human properties, but they are, I am afraid, born into an environment that is not suitable for anyone's upbringing, which can most definitely affect their personality and significantly reduce their ability for success, preventing what great deeds they could have probably accomplish.

The third situation is when one is born chromosomally disadvantaged, but are fortunate to be born into an impeccable (flawless), witty environment with tremendous opportunity to grow.

The fourth condition is the worst, when one is born with unfavorable genes, chromosomes that are not auspiciously oriented (a specific sequences of nucleotides), and born into a destructive and unpleasant atmosphere as well, which is cause for one's ugly fate, as they can have a gloomy multiplier effect on one's life.

Sadly, millions globally suffer from grave income inequality and are stricken with utter poverty, which denies them any opportunity to progress since the monetary system persistently drives to widen the gap between the haves and the have nots. The system deepens social and economic gaps, alienating billions from each other and self, disassociating billions from a meaningful life.

It alienates us from family, from work; it removes so many from body, mind, and soul, ending in acting robot-like. We have become zombies, as if a supernatural power has entered billions to behave will-less, speechless, only capable of automatic movement directed at producing zillions for the rich elites and the corporate bosses; only to glorifying the gone-mad empires and for the actual wealth-producers, to be humiliated and discarded when out of use. The system so cleverly manages such atrocities by linking it to our fate, and subtly enculturing that it is how God's plans work. Imagine what can culminate if the environment is fundamentally altered for the better, where the atmosphere is not as toxic as it is designed to be and everyone gets a chance to grow no matter what genes one carries.

The corporate capitalists and the oligopoly system of ruling that comprises roughly 5 percent of the Earth's population hold and control more than 90 percent of the international resources and the entire wealth of nations without any mercy. Humongous private enterprises rule governments and the world by force and through evasive, clandestine, and not so legitimate conduct that is so puzzling it should certainly raise eyebrows.

Evolution relates to the historical development of a biological group (as a race or species): phylogeny, development of a new biological group, speciation, a theory that the various types of animals and plants have their origin in other preexisting types and that the distinguishable differences are due to modifications in successive generations; the extraction of a mathematical root, a process in which the whole universe is a progression of interrelated phenomena. Both revolution and evolution have historical trademarks, and the footprints for either evolution or revolution can be traced from millions of years ago.

The truth is that evolution, in its real sense, encompasses time, steady transition, and requires maturity, where no revolution is possible without evolutionary process for reaching animated revolt.

To be specific, sociopolitical and socioeconomic changes definitely demand a cultural revolution that is bound to gradually gain knowledge and information, where the overall society would be ripened enough and ready to tolerate the explosive nature of the revolution, to acknowledge and align themselves to the new condition, since decisive issues are expected to proactively be gauged with a different yardstick, to become as promising and helpful as possible to quench people's thirst for gaining dynamic results.

The evolutionary process is basically continuous, where the incremental changes constantly happen and gradually resume the higher stages of development. No existence or any phenomena can escape this scientifically natural and realistic fact, since its reality is ingrained in the very nature of the universe itself. The footprint of evolution is prevalent and can historically be traced where it is deemed necessary.

Every nuance of natural and social sciences, and in what we see and known as the tangible world, needs to deal with the evolutionary process of things—unless we want to believe in the world of magic, where superstition can rule us and things burst out of nowhere. Socioeconomic, sociopolitical, and cultural manifestations of events are no exception to the evolutionary facts, and ought to be taken seriously and heavily valued.

No matter what stages of evolutionary process we are in, taken from the dark ages to contemporary societies, there will always be the exploiters and their victims. Name any system you wish, no perfect society is ever going to materialize to forcefully but effectively deal with unjustified and unfair situations of mankind since the mechanism of greed, self-interest, and thirst for power can undeniably mushroom in any so-called progressive situation. This can prevent accessing an ideal utopian environment. The good news is that relatively speaking, gradual evolutionary changes for the better are often possible, which definitely calls for relentless objections and criticism of the governing bodies and the crooks in charge through intelligently constructive means and by constantly holding authority's feet to the fire, demanding fair play.

It is very crucial to know that fundamental requirements for a civil society are literacy, higher education, information, wisdom, preserving knowledge, insightful leadership, modernization, up-to-date infrastructure, training and skills, and the most imperative, money well spent on these decisive issues that are all key ingredients for any talented society to demand an ideal prospective for better living.

An educated and informed society can significantly disrupt the culprit's peace of mind and disturb their tranquility, where the powerful elites must not be unleashed to abuse their power that is rendered to them by the people. The governed should take the livelihood away from the public enemies that intend to keep the master-slave relationship intact.

Bear in mind, when we historically refer to social and political revolutions, we are reminded of bloodshed and huge sacrifices without much improved change—often, changes for the worse. What is gained from most revolutions are temporary excitement and rabblerousing, where violence is inevitable, since most of failed revolutions would have been successful if only they could have occurred in a timely manner, as thoughtfulness and socio-cultural progress in any nation is of utmost importance.

WHERE IS GOD?

God is the silent voice within you, behind every nuance of existence. God is beyond the infinite universe; God is not matter, as positivism doctrine and other beliefs as such so naively utter, "I must see God to believe it." God is the silent pulsation and the rhythmic throbbing you experience, making you feel alive. God is the unseen thoughts and invisible memories one cannot see, but experiences the effects of, and is literally impossible to live without. God is in every breath you take to keep you animated.

God is the oxygen circulating through your body; God is your faith. God is your good conscience, your kind behavior. God is the cosmic energy that permeates all beings and percolates everything in existence. If God could be seen, then God would have descended to our physical level. God is the infinite Spirit beyond the mind of the universe, and we are so lucky to be the proprietor of a single drop of this holy soul.

One feels God when being enlightened, considered, compassionate, and when in love; you sense God when you empathize and feel pity for others in need. It is when one is strengthened with faith and acts hopeful despite difficulties, and self-sacrifices, forgives, and believes in piety and patience. One feels the presence of God when one is philanthropically active, and notices God when one passionately tries to save lives.

Your ingenuity, intelligence, and talent, your dreams and desires, seeking truth, fighting for freedom, democracy, equity, justice, and peace, are all reflections of God within you. It is only then that you feel God as one sees no choice but to practice one's higher self, where the spirit of goodness directs you to do no evil and become pleasantly righteous in all that you do. It is when you are in a realm engulfed with the spirit of the almighty God, the omnipotent, omniscient, and omnipresent Father, that you are accorded with infinite silence of the almighty God within you.

Do not fall into the trap in the world of the blind leading the blind, as some people stand their dogmatic ground like an empty walnut shell with no kernel and claim: why believe in something one cannot see? This pushes them to the brink of behaving in a delusional way in their belief and deprived of any adequate reasoning; it makes them obscure and despondent. They do not realize that "ideas are the origin and cause to all matters, since thought are energy driven, and because matter disappears, as matter is never stable to rely on."

Some so unduly try to mimic and build artificial human brains in laboratories, practically a vain attempt, not knowing their effort will be futile. Our human brain comes with a super complex software called the mind that is inseparable from the cosmic programming potentiated to conquer the universe, and is linked to cosmic energy that has rendered sanctuary to mankind and enabled humanity to reach the heavens above.

It is an EXTRATERRESTRIAL and a metaphysical domain that rejects making brain hardware manufactured by mortals that is beyond our limited senses. It is the world of unseen that surreptitiously maneuvers, the quantum world, the world of string theory, and the world of subatomic particles, where even the most complex telescopes and advanced magnifiers are not as efficient as they need to be to reveal the magic that lies in the heavens above, as its magnanimity should be appreciated.

The prevalent sacred energy, the electromagnetic forces, the gravity, and the small and big atomic forces that are so potent and not visible, which we take for granted, are the work of the unseen energy that fuels everything we do via internet, cells, digital gadgets, computers, TV and satellite, radar, and so many other things such as x-rays, scans, MRI, and other medical technology that is influenced by the undetected energy, making our living healthier and much easier.

It is all about the unperceived world that orchestrates and rules the world we see; it is all about the almighty God, that some credulously choose not to see.

"Rejoice with those who rejoice" is paired with "mourn with those who mourn" in Rom. 12:15. Even more interesting is what follows in v.16, "Live in harmony with one another. Do not be proud ... Do not be conceited ...

Be careful to do what is right in the eyes of everyone" (v. 17) ... "If it is possible, as far as it depends on you, live at peace with everyone" (v. 18).

Atheists, infinity, and evolution

Referencing atheists' claims on evolutionary perspectives, it shouldn't be odd to identify with motion and grasp the meaning of any evolutionary work, defined as "a process of change in a certain direction as also applicable to Darwinian account of the origin of species." We then should know that evolution and motion are correlated, and evolution without motion will literally lose its significance and conceptualized meaning.

No evolutionary process can be defined without a starting point, a departure that can lead to its destiny, or a task well done and completed.

If so, it is only common sense to know the first requirement for motion is to have an origin, a starting point; infinity translates as having no inception and without an end. As so many nonbelievers adamantly believe in evolution as a scientific fact, it should only serve them futilely, since they cannot learn that evolution must have a beginning and an expiration date, where a complete course of event is substantiated, no matter how long the duration or the complexity of the situation.

It is a conflict of interest with huge discrepancy to believe in evolution and in the meantime accept infinity and a life with no origin, because an infinite existence cannot objectify an end and should only mean having no purpose; otherwise, if rational, we should expect life with having a start and an end.

And if the message is to understand evolution based on matter, then we must understand that where there is matter, there is motion, and where there is motion, then time and space are certainly involved. If so, then having an origin, a departing point, and in reaching a designated destiny for objectifying a purposeful deed is not far from reason, as it should make much sense. No sensible analogies can occur in believing otherwise.

GLOBALIZATION AND THE DISHARMONY OF THOUGHTS

In our contemporary world, even the farthest dwellers of the planet are unquestionably affected by global political, cultural, and financial interactivities, where the conglomerate (cartel, trust, consortium) news media is leveraged to influence so many through modern telecommunication and technological innovations.

Today's generation possess advanced industries that can unfold superb thoughts and brilliant activities. We are able to disclose helpful breakthroughs and information via dynamic ways of communication. Technology has made the globe much smaller, as billions of people can share and enjoy the exchange of ideas, access plenty of information, become enlightened on vital issues, and learn about other cultures. Education can certainly play a key role in differentiating fact from fiction, to identify with progressive ways of life, and to speed up partaking with those who truly value freedom and human rights.

It is a blessing that many social media empower people to discern lethal ideologies from constructive outlooks and enable us to distinguish dark ages thoughts from revolutionary concepts that are potentiated with robust plans and animated programs to make a better world possible. Further education gives meaning to the expression that "knowledge is power" because related socio-cultural cognizance should certainly make us aware of taking sides with those who value humanity and what it stands for, rather than blindly aligning with static beliefs and backward traditions that literally squander so many lives as we speak. With astonishing headways in science and great technological novelties (inventions), enormous military and puissant (powerful) policing, along with massive accumulation of wealth and influence beyond anyone's imagination, the wealthy empires can positively resolve many prolonged iniquitous (sinister) sagas beholding humanity. Imperial corporations can halt consolidated attacks from fiendish (perversely diabolical) Jihads and put an end to the prolonged purgatory state of mind that has disturbed world peace and tranquility. So many diversified groups and guilds have yielded to subtle fear, from small-scale business meetings to large enterprise assemblies.

People worry in every important gathering and affluent community, in government entities, even at places of worship, in national and international airports, as millions of innocent travelers become nervous not knowing where terrorists have designated their next targets, and when or how terrorists are going to strike again and again, blasting themselves off and exploding other harmless human beings to pieces.

They can stop religious extremist's sporadic attacks and their fragmented inhumane terrorist behaviors at will. The mighty powerful are illusions that ordinary people who, unlike the super-rich, have no protection against sinful terrorism, and other wicked misconduct can live in a bubble impervious from harms, since the powerful elites act so indifferently to people's sufferings and very fragile situations they endure. Many believe that wars give birth to advance civilizations, which fools them into spreading their wings too far, where they do not belong, and the very reason to losing it all.

Albert Einstein said, "The pioneers of a warless world are the [youth] who refuse military Service." Charles Sumner noted, "Give me the money that has been spent in war and I will clothe every man, woman, and child in an attire of which kings and queens will be proud. I will build a schoolhouse in every valley over the whole earth. I will crown every hillside with a place of worship consecrated to Peace."

And Eve Merria so eloquently said, "I dream of giving birth to a child who will ask, Mother, what is war?"

President Thomas Jefferson said, I recoil with horror at the ferociousness of man. Will Nations never devise a more rational umpire of? Differences than force? Are there no means of Coercing? Injustice more gratifying to our nature? Than a waste of the blood? Of thousands and of the Labor of millions of our fellow creatures?

CAPITALISTS AND CULTURE

The effect of capitalists' transgressions is so structurally designed that has fundamentally influence on our way of life, where our thought process has deliberately been molded to accept our own demise without noticing the culprit's surreptitious behaviors and ugly intent. The significance of capitalists' cultural and social interactions epitomizes class differentiation, since its fundamental belief system is blatantly biased but intricately formatted in the fabric of many societies without its horrifying maneuvers being identified and clearly detected. And because of the corporate capitalists dominating the economic and political system, basic liberty and human rights are already being eroded, which can further lead to a fascist and dictatorial state of governing to further uphold the exploitive and backward system intact.

It is a shame seeing too often that wealth and money, prestige, influence, rank, and fame, dictate morality, virtues, dignity, integrity, etiquette, manners, and other humane principles; since even believing in God is washed out and has become an inseparable part of propaganda and spiritual offense. Every word is carefully tailored, and what is grasped as right or wrong is meant to prolong the nature of the beast and to conserve the status quo, as the entire culture is set up to save the rich oligopolistic regime at any cost while constraining progressive thought.

Its settings and cultural layout are overwhelmingly poisoned, but they are acknowledged as norms and are fluently communicated among the ordinary man's belief system that has adversely effected so many for the wrong reasons. People subconsciously relate to cultural linguists and are entrapped in a host of premeditated agendas planned to keep them apart and under control.

For instance, when deprived, and the working class are not sexually monogamous, they sure are demonized as whores and finger-pointed to as misfits and prostitutes, but when the super-rich are promiscuous and sexually active they are known as celebrities, titled as the rich and the famous. We ought to know better since the superbly rich are God's chosen people, with luck, that are blessed with prosperity and extreme fortune. And when tycoons forfeit billions, they are the victims of an economy gone bad, and hence need to be saved by taxpayers' hard-earned money. But when a nobody, an ordinary dude, diligently tries but cannot find job, again due to an economy that is gone wrong, and takes a loaf of bread, or cannot pay his bills, then he is a thief, an outcast that must be sternly punished and incarcerated. And if anyone dares to complain, they are then labeled with being "a rebel with no cause," or lazy, a vagabond (hobo, derelict, bum, drifter), and is slapped with being a failure and a non-productive member of society.

Is it not obvious that the making of financially destitute people, which by the way, count for extremely large numbers, should constitute a toxic environment that can certainly feed into producing wretched and hostile members of society. Many not only are a threat to themselves but to others, since they are exhausted from having the basic training and education to equip them enough for a better future.

The poor have to live on everyday prayers to survive, since the system has made sure the working and the middle class are insecure so that the corporate rich can play with people's fate and keep them as vulnerable as possible, leaving them no choice but to obey the capitalist bosses for their minimal subsistence. And because the deprived masses, the indigents, are unsafe and not adequately guarded against life's financial, social, and political hazards, many are bound to risk their shady position doing wrong for making the bare minimum to function. Then, of course, they have to bear the utmost of punishments, and with no professional help available to represent them justly, they may pay with losing their lives or facing a long imprisonment time.

On the other hand, when the super-rich risk in doing wrong and they get caught, there are always topnotch lawyers and other decisive avenues available to free them with only a slap on the hand. This reminds us that when justice is trampled, humanity shall mean nothing other than beastly conduct. It is time to deny the expression that says "it is what it is" because accepting it is what it is will denote the spirit of a nation, and who we really are as moral and civilized inhabitants. There is a saying that if you have integrity, nothing else matters; and if you don't have integrity, nothing else matters. people should not let the system take away their integrity, which is the essence of one acting as a human being.

It is not a lie that extreme income inequality, class differentiation, stark poverty, social and economic insecurity, nationalism, wars of aggression, ethnic cleansing, genocides, forced migration, overpopulation, misallocation of resources, unemployment, inflation, recession, economic depression, stagnation, deceptive economic practices, unfair and wrongful competition, monopoly, policing the world, race for atomic and other horrific weapons, climate change, extremism, toxic food industries, conspiratorial pharmaceutical corporations, financial industrial complex and corporate hegemony, jihadists, Armageddon nonsense, religious enmity and other faith-based encounters, homemade and international terrorism, fear, distress and anxiety, cause high statistical-oriented violence.

Parochialism (radicalism, sectarian), individualism, apartheid (economic and political discrimination), racism, prejudice behaviors, sexism, gender inequality, xenophobia, misogyny, family violence, troubling addictions, prostitution, sex, drugs, alcoholism, homicide, suicide, loneliness, homelessness, unheard of mental and physical illnesses, illiteracy, bankruptcy, and a host of other ills have so sadly become the fate of humanity. They are the hallmarks of the capitalist system that values money over human lives and dignity, as so many malefactions (evil deeds, crime) are conducive to its culture and malignant nature of this ferocious system.

These cruel and bitter situations urgently call for a dynamic and constructive response to make a better world possible, because positive changes should significantly affect the status quo to avoid global destruction that can potentiate everyone's demise, since its troubling signs should already be crystal clear for every enlightened and inquisitive mind to further cultivate the next progressive socioeconomic stages in the most advanced and civilized nations and to gradually permeate and trickle down into developing countries, because we all certainly are in this mess together.

EMOTIONAL DISCORD

Anger and fear are very challenging issues for us all. We resort to our animal nature when we are angry. We also become anxious, nervous, and worried when fearful. It is not an easy task to control these very damaging emotions. Anger can build up gradually if things do not go our way, or with having a one-track mind acting dogmatic and opinionated. A variety of reasons could stir up an outburst and make us do the unthinkable.

To name a few: ignorance, jealousy, greed, selfishness, or feeling resentment towards others when one is financially deprived. And the inferiority complex that is felt when one sees those with superiority complex rules the day.

Often feelings of being alienated, having negative thoughts and emotions, a sense of being a nobody despite hard work and extreme effort that one makes to reach one's objectives, but one is not even able to make a decent living for oneself and loved ones can surely have an adverse effect on many people. These troubling situations can ruin our health, and our social and spiritual wellbeing. Sometimes they're so destructive they need immediate medical and psychological attention.

We can become frustrated and distressed when we are unable to correctly assess our financial position, and miscalculate the actual capacity for undertaking an endeavor that becomes almost impossible to successfully manage. And when lacking crucial resources imperative to finish the task can fail us, it surely then makes one the victim of tremendous pressure and causes too much stress. A troubled marriage and a host of related issues with family violence can utterly destroy our peace and tranquility, no matter how rich or poor one really is. And when in fear, we can panic and become distressed and behave strangely, especially when one's life or loved one's life is threatened. Our fear can also be economically based when we lose jobs, as our livelihood becomes threatened and we no longer have the means to comfortably support ourselves.

Bear in mind also that we live in a crime-infested society forcing us to constantly be watchful, and in fear of losing our lives or in getting maimed, which can deny us the basic serenity of mind, depriving citizens from having peace and making so many vulnerable to anxiety and nervous breakdown. We have been preyed on in the most civilized nations by wealthy, influential, and powerful elites, since they utterly control viable resources where they mismanage funds for their own livelihood but render citizens with wrong information and deprive so many from having basic knowledge and training. As millions cannot afford proper education, they are left out from improving their miserable condition. People are so engaged in making a living it has forced them not to care for what is actually taking place, and therefore not participating to stop troubles facing them, which sometimes affect the ordinary man the most.

To resolve our conflicts in a truly civilized manner, not letting violence get the best of us, we need to know that we are the product of our environment. Practically and diligently, try to bring about a dynamic and a do-good culture. We need to encourage humanity that seems it is forgotten, to persist on the welfare of the majority and all the people; we should not let the powerful elites furnish an environment conducive only to their interest. We cannot expect those that are cocooned in so much comfort and possess extreme fortune and fame to give a damn about others in need.

Until troubles reach us all with no mercy or a way to escape it, knowing divided we fall, our ignorance will clear the way to be easily conquered. We should have the audacity to challenge norms and our cultural limitations, to become globally savvy, and enlightened, and possessing a fine personality to accept everyone with no prejudices, and as a first-class citizen of the world. We should not believe in boundaries, and actively interact with other nations and cultures. Not acting in vengeance, either in our private and family lives or in our social life, but in a peaceful manner acting wisely. We should be able to control and to manage our emotions, particularly our anger and our fears.

Wise people persist on reaching a stage where no violence of any sort could take place. That is possible only if we invest more in our brain to raise our knowledge and information for collective bargaining and everyone's livelihood, and not in manipulating others by their lack of education and through fear and anxiety keep people divided and colonize them for taking their valuable resources, annexing (sequestering, taking by force, expropriate, usurp) what belongs to them.

DOES THE SOUL EXIST?

Recent scientific theory notices life's spiritual parameter. This refers to the reality of the soul, among many other affiliated and vital issues in our lives. Religions relentlessly remind us about its existence, questioning how do we know if souls really exist? A series of new scientific experiments shed light on this primordial spiritual question.

The question of the soul is raised with the idea of a future life and our belief in the next realm of existence. It is an animated and subtle issue that permeates our thought; it cannot be reflected upon via scientific analysis, which since has created skeptics that misunderstand such potent energy. The enlightened are relentlessly curious, wanting to know about its manifestation independent from our physical body. The human soul, like our mind, is not visible, and is as important if not exceedingly more tempting to evoke our curiosity. Our mind, although not perceived through tactile sense, does play a very significant role in our mental and cognitive activities. Only the effects are known, and the evidence is substantiated in our undertaking of tasks.

Yet, some physicists and scientists cannot fathom or accord insightfully with a spiritual dimension of life. Mr. Steven Hawking stated, "We're just the action of carbon and proteins which protein is made of amino-acid that is the building block in our life. And when amino-acid, and other molecules such as salt and water are mixed the soup responsible for creating life happens. He further stated we can make life with lifeless molecules, since a molecule began to replicate itself from the raw material of nature.

Mr. Hawking goes on to say that we are a wonderful biological machine produced through biological evolution, in which evolution is a process that is powerful enough to produce a species from previous species, as the strongest of them all will survive a process called the survival of the fittest, which in the long run will morph into other species, and that is how life began. Mr. Hawking carries on to say life is a process of chain reaction inside a wonderful biological machine that can infinitely carry on if some grave disaster does not happen, as DNA can replicate itself, where amino acid and other molecules can actually assemble themselves. Mr. Hawking and others explain that we live a while and die … and the universe? It too has no purpose with no meaning. He goes on to utter that it is all planned and worked out with no need for spirit. The irony is planned by who, if the plan has already been laid out?

One should respect the scientific analogy that Mr. Hawking and others are pondering on, but in the meanwhile, let's not forget they are only indicating a viable mechanical process taking place in nature that is exhausted of any dynamic life force, which does not explain the impetus behind, as he puts it, the "wonderful biological machine." Mr. Hawking seemed not to know so obviously that nothing cannot create something.

And let's assume that life began about four billion years ago, starting with a single cell that replicated itself and became what we currently are through the intricacies of the evolutionary process. Then the question is how their claim could ever be validated if the precise raw material and the careful conditional environment that could have been comprised of millions of variables, if not billons, would have not been present, since I am certain that life did not originate in a bubble.

How could such evolutionary advancement ever take place or be accredited with the absence of a very potent and intelligent energy source, and occur without a sacred spirit or a ubiquitous soul? If so, seeing a dead man walking in a science fiction movie should not raise any eyebrow and be seen as fact. Overwhelming scientific discoveries are literally available that attest to cosmic energy that is clearly shown in an infinite number of species, making life in its entirety possible.

I am afraid Mr. Hawking acquainted the cause of such astonishing animated energy to the force of gravity, which he thought is responsible for all there is, But then, we can only wish it would have been that easy to extrapolate a definite conclusion on an unanimated thing to represent vigorous life-bearing reality, since it should alert us not to expand on emblematic lab work experiments and avoid stretching them as authenticated facts.

For such a puzzling and complexly intelligent entity as the cause of life, a phenomenon full of vigor with infinite intricacies is clearly beyond anyone's imagination to empirically identify with. Mr. Hawking's findings should only be delivered as hypothesis, and no further than speculation.

A new theory of everything demands an insightfully convincing theory rather than a materialistic model that denies the tutelage of the enigmatic soul that can only denote unripe knowledge and yet callous wisdom in acknowledging truth. Neuroscience, I am afraid, is constrained only to lab work as it tries to decode the material brain but is distracted from realizing the intricacy of the definitive human mind and insightfully exhausted from knowing the transcendent soul.

Scientific views have deselected the soul as an object of human belief and reduced it to a psychological idea that forms our cognition from the perceptible natural world. This believes delivery of "life" and "death" are no more than the common notion of "biological life" and "biological death."

The active assumption is simply that the laws of chemistry and physics, and all that exists, are just dust orbiting the core of the universe. This unreasonably equates the energy-driven cosmos as lifeless, which is contrary to the colloquial scientific view that everything is purposefully programed to collectively fulfill its destiny. Nature and bio-centric agendas are energy-driven and cooperatively spearheaded to fulfill its destiny.

The physical world relates to our limited senses, and constraints of the human nervous system, which has led many in making serious flaws for assessing the reality of our lives. This should remind us of great spiritual thinkers and philosophers who tirelessly pursued to find the link between the human mind and the conscious universe, and often with much more convincing outcomes than what science has to say.

It is no longer dubious that consciousness is the core of the animated, and makes sense on the reality of the cosmos. Even though the contemporary scientific paradigm is based on the credence that the world has an objective observer-independent existence, real trial suggests antithetical, since a great number think life is just the activity of atoms and particles that spin around for a while and then dissipate into nothingness. But if we add life force to the equation, we can elaborate on some of the major puzzles of science, including the uncertainty principle, the wrangling and tweaking (enhancement) of the laws that shape our universe.

Let's contemplate on the famous "two-slit experiment," and the observer effect phenomenon. Since it elaborates on when one watches a particle enter through the holes, it maneuvers like a bullet, passing through one slit or the other. But when no one observes the particle, it exhibits the action of a wave and can pass through both slits simultaneously. Likewise, experiments tell us that undetected particles exist only as waves of probability, as the great Nobel laureate Max Born proved in 1926. They're statistical predictions—nothing but a likely consequence. Until observed, they have no real existence; they only do when the mind sets the framework in place, and they can be thought of as having duration or a position in space. Experiments make it unavoidably clear that even mere knowledge in the experimenter's mind is good enough to flip-flop possibility to reality. Many scientists believe the observer-dependent behavior not only is applicable in the subatomic world, but showed that "quantum strange" also happens in the human-scale world.

In referencing whether humans and other living creatures actually have souls, over two hundred years ago Kant pointed out:

Everything we experience – including all the colors, sensations and objects we perceive – are nothing but representations in our mind. Space and time are simply the mind's tools for putting it all together.

Will Durant wrote: "The hope of another life gives us courage to meet our own death, and to bear with the death of our loved ones; we are twice armed if we fight with faith."

We should be reminded that the human mind and soul are not visible and materially oriented, but the effects are known and can be experienced, since without having a "sound mind," a worthy living is not possible. Our mind is also believed to be a derivative of our physical brain. If so, why should the human soul that is irrefutably ingratiated with our powerful emotions and feelings be any different from a non-visible mind?

And why are scientists and other scholarly minded individuals not able to verify and identify the real substance behind referencing human thoughts and the essence of our ideas and where they come from? They bombard us every second, and no one has an inkling on how ideas are manufactured or formed and what they are made of, and consciousness is nowhere to be found in our brain, since the most prominent scientists do not have the slightest clue where consciousness is located in our brain.

The answer is that consciousness is non-local; it is universally vast, prevalent in every fiber of existence, either animated or not, where unanimated matter is only coagulated condense energy that pulsates at a lower rate, and not as actively vibrating as animated entities that throb at a higher grade.

Perhaps scientists expect to find the human soul in laboratories. I believe there should not be any ambiguity in the by-productivity of human soul, because we need to ask: who or what is it that cries when unhappy and pressured? What and who is it that laughs with joy when happy and vibrant? What and who is it that hopes and desires; gets nervous, panics, becomes frightened and desperately seeks to be free, is in search of progress, and diligently tries to be somebody? Acts heartened and captivatingly courageous for the right reasons? The human soul.

What becomes sad when it faces injustice? Feels pity and becomes depressed when others are in need of food and shelter? What feels stranded, frustrated, and lost when deprived of love, like a dead man walking? What envies? What is rejuvenated when in love, wanting to conquer the world? What jumps to its death to save an innocent life? What hates to be alone and can get alarmingly belligerent and dangerous? What acts manic and behaves insanely? What acts wisely, seeks logic, acts greedy, acts cool, has purpose, seeks happiness, attracts love and repulses fear, adores to be praised, and seeks human rights and freedom, and wants to belong? The human soul.

The human soul reasons; it chooses, gets curious, is judgmental, has willpower, manifests consciousness, conveys intelligence and constitutes the most strengthened forces to challenge nature. It perseveres and to breed, and wants to make sure of life continuum for others to come and the next generation to be. It is like being hypnotized and programmed without our consent and interference; it seems it is on autopilot as it is preprogramed and predestined.

It might sound farfetched, but we should keep digging until one day, humanity can perhaps catch up with its soul-searching idea where spiritual endeavors and undertaking are prioritized, rather than our quest for so much materialism and pride. And also because we are geared into putting up with so much egregious disparity, taking our very soul hostage, trying to make a living just to survive, leaving no time for any soul-searching. Our spirit belongs to higher dimensions; we should realize that and let it connect to the infinite power of the universe, where it belongs.

If so, it is only then when humanity can reach its true essence. But this is not an easy task, because our mind and spirit are caged and fettered to fit the present standard of living, which is caught in the web of uncertainty and materialism. It sure makes it difficult to quench our thirst for seeking true love and let our soul evolve into aesthetic living to objectify happiness; to enrich the way we live, which can potentiate the image of God in man and for humanity to reach higher realms, if given a chance.

Floating man, flying man or man suspended in air by Avicenna (Ibn Sina, d. 1037) refers to the existence of the soul. The argument is used to argue for the knowledge by presence. The argument is that the subject is suspended in midair in which he can reflect on his own without any help from sense perception and is deprived of assistance from any material body.

According to Avicenna, we cannot deny the consciousness of the self. His argument is as follows: Let's imagine a fully developed and perfectly shaped person, but with his vision disguised from perceiving all external objects—suspended in the air, and not protected by any perceptible current of the air that supports him. His limbs are apart and kept out of contact with one another so they do not feel each other. Then let the subject consider whether he would confirm the existence of his self. Avicenna argues that the "floating man" would ratify (approve) his own existence, although not affirming the reality of any of his limbs or his bowels, inner organs, kidney, heart, or brain, or any external thing. That indeed, he would affirm the existence of this self. Ibn Sina believes that inner awareness is utterly independent of sensory experiences.

This argument depends on a contemplative thought experiment. We have to imagine a man who, by accident, arrives into existence cultivated (developed) and fully formed, depleted of having any relation with sensory experience of the world or of his own body to ameliorate (make better), making him aware of his position. There is utterly no physical contact with the outer world. According to Avicenna, this subject is, however, essentially conscious of himself. His argument is that the self is not coherently (consistently) a substance, and there is no subjectivity, as Avicenna tries to prove the existence of the soul, or "Nafs." That is completely independent of sensory interactivities.

Descartes's Cogito and Avicenna's Floating Man

Before the French philosopher Descartes (1596–1650) referred to the existence of the conscious self as a cusp (turning point) point in epistemology, utilizing the phrase "Cogito ergo sum," the eleventh-century Tajik-Persian philosopher Avicenna had pointed out the existence of consciousness in the flying man argument. Thus, long before Descartes, Avicenna had accomplished an argument for the existence of knowledge by presence without necessitating for the existence of the body.

Both Avicenna and Descartes accepted that the soul and self are something other than sense data. Also, Avicenna believed that there is logically no relationship between the self and the body. He believed there is no logical dependency between them. We live in two worlds; the physical world, which the human body must respond to for survival, and the immaterial realm, in which our mind, the subconscious, and if you prefer the spirit or the soul, maneuvers, as only the effects are seen as our thoughts and ideas materialize, often creating physical wonders where matter substantiates.

Criticism

Adamson says, "The weakness in the argument is that, even if the flying man would be self-aware, the thought experiment does not prove that the soul is something distinct from the body. One could argue that the self-awareness is seated in the brain. In this case, in being self-aware the flying man is only aware because of his brain that is doing the experiencing, not because of a distinct soul. He just doesn't realize that the self-awareness is a property of his nervous system."

Mr. Adamson misses that what we know as the nervous system, is the "self," which is the property of consciousness. One should be savvy-minded enough to know: The nervous system is the consciously oriented self, since the apparatus of the nervous system is not seen, only the effects are noticed.

INCORPOREAL GOD

> "Is man merely a mistake of God's? Or God merely a mistake of man's?"
>
> – Friedrich Nietzsche

And I say, neither, since what has sought God is so far shallow; and what has assessed man is not adequate.

Not knowing the whole truth. No one can claim if either one has made a mistake or not. "I can control my passions and emotions if I can understand their nature" – Spinoza

We live in an age of information and intelligence, an era that defies superstition and hocus-pocus maneuvers that are based on lies and charlatanism. If a rational dialogue is intended, subjects like incorporeal (having no material body or form) God, existence, consciousness, mind, subliminal mind (unconscious mind), morality, spiritualty, philosophy, science, the universe, cosmos, soul, metaphysics, and the like, should not be toyed with. Also, issues such as monetary and fiscal policies, extreme income inequality, racism and apartheid behavior, neo-colonialism (the economic and political policies by which great power indirectly maintain or extend its influence over other areas or people), feminism, corporate capitalists, climate change, wars of aggression, and threat of atomic war, should constructively be dealt with. This list is definitely not to undermine vital social issues like gun control, police brutality, human trafficking, immigration, unscrupulously powerful lobbyists, abortion, violence, drugs, police brutality, single parenthood, prostitution, pedophilia, unjustified incarceration, capital punishment, overpopulation, and so forth that are in need of urgent attention.

Such subjects are complex and can often be vulnerable to ambiguity and shortsightedness. This should alert one to avoid being derailed from what makes sense and is wise, and to dispose of what lacks logic, or is vain and does not make sense.

The subject of existence and God urge meditative minds, as they are intricate by nature and are solely possible through the recognition of circumstantial evidence. They can be astonishing when they are knowledgeably discerned through inference and with clear-sightedness.

Anyone in their right mind should not claim seeing God or physically speaking to God, because the almighty God is not limited in space and time as we mortals are, and since no messages fall from the sky and/or from an incorporeal God above except snow, rain, drizzle, and perhaps asteroids (planetary bodies) that every billion years or so strike planet Earth with devastating effect. That is why dinosaurs vanished, and meteorites (comets, falling star, fireball, meteor) reach the surface of Earth without being completely vaporized.

What prophets of God can claim are they offer mind-bending revelations and genius, are superbly intelligent, magnificently talented, with amazing wisdom and creativity, since prophets possess incredible IQ that was bestowed upon them to lead humanity to the light at the end of the tunnel, helping them with meaning to get out of the dark ages, and often from desperate and chaotic situations? Prophets were sages that so wisely paid attention to circumstantial evidence of what our universe divulged that at the twenty-first century it's what quantum mechanics has discovered to talk about the world of the unseen.

Quantum physics and the realm of the subatomic particles sees the universe not as a pharmaceutical entity, as Newtonian physicists or as atheist scientists have thought of, solely acknowledging the physical world. Instead, the universe is imbued with spirit, the invisible energy that manages what we see, where matter is inconspicuously vibrating as condensed energy. So we ought to know we are an inseparable part of this infinitely vast universe where the sky is not the limit. Making the expression of you are what you believe very true, where reprogramming one's thoughts is the key to changing one's life. Popsugar: "If an egg is broken by an outside force life ends. If an egg is broken by an inside force, then life begins. Great things always begin from inside." And that inside force is what absolutely controls and manages life in its entirety.

The [invisible] field is what solely manages the visible world.

Albert Einstein said: "The [invisible] Field is the Sole Governing Agency of the Particle." We are often baffled by phenomena and the state of affairs in our life, desperately wanting to alter our destiny. We desire to get all we wish out of life. But the fact is, the way we counter our environmental stimuli determines our fate. Our shortcomings are within. Wonderful and positive things in our life occur when this limitation is broken by the unseen field of energy within us.

Beneath what is deciphered as thoughts, mindfulness, conscious, subconscious, spirit, and soul are but subtle energy that drives us to be who we are. Most of all, it is the subconscious mind that is mostly responsible for how one reacts to the outside world, from which our nervous system and senses of seeing, hearing, tasting, smelling, and touching receive stimuli and capture information. Our conscious mind can be credited with logical manifestation and having 5 to 10 percent decisiveness in how we respond to the external environment.

Seemingly, every cell in one's body is affected by every single perception that one has, as if billions of cells do have their own central processing unit in which they all so amazingly work with extreme discipline and cooperation, comprising a very intricate system. Being an integrated part of the universal energy, the human brain acts as a mediator, or a transmitter, which proclaims vibrations, leadership, and path to one's cells. But then who is behind one's choosing the stations that are in tune with millions of everyday broadcasting thoughts?

It is not a mystery anymore that just thinking about something makes our brain release chemical neurotransmitter messengers that communicate with our nervous system and even part of itself.

This makes the role of neurotransmitters extremely essential, since they control our happiness, sadness, or being stressed, as well as digestion and other hormonal bodily functions.

Interestingly enough, we ought to know even our base energy-oriented thoughts are very relevant to "epigenetics." It is now scientifically proved that our environment, and how we interpret the occurrences in our lives, and how we respond to them, directly impacts the behaviors of our genes. They control biology, as it is not so much about self-actuating genes, as it was thought before. Genes can turn themselves off and on to decisively influence our personality and who we really are. The headway in biology realizes that when we change the way we think and alter our perceptions or beliefs, we relate entirely different messages to our cells and can reprogram and revamp cells' meaning and their expression. It is believed that each and every cell in our body is replaced approximately every two months. So, one can reprogram downbeat (bearish) cells to be more positive and optimistic, hence changing your life for a more constructive and better life.

Hence, it is absolutely imperative for parents, and those responsible for upbringing children, to be accommodative, as they need to provide a decent and productive atmosphere so that the children can benefit. It is scientifically proven that children from age 0-7 will record everything that happens around them in their subconscious mind; and they will behave what they have recorded, affecting themselves and consequently, the society in which they are living. A great majority of our perceptions are hidden below, but directly involved in what we do, since our subconscious mind is extremely attentive from age 0-7 in our thoughts, perceptions, and visual images that we have encountered, as well as beliefs, habits and emotions, what we value, our protective reactions, and everything that we experience around us.

Comparably, our conscious mind takes part in producing thoughts and in choosing which route to take, as the conscious mind proactively decides and controls what to do. Unlike the subconscious mind that has a mind of its own. Therefore, if one wants to alter what one is dealing with, one must change the present perception that he or she is experiencing, and rather believes in.

When our senses receive a signal, they immediately respond and send the message to our brain to process and respond to the situation. It is noteworthy to know that the conscious mind deals with logic and what makes sense. But the desires of the conscious mind have to be in line with the belief system and the values, since it is overpowered by the subconscious mind. The conscious mind makes decisions and forwards orders to the subconscious mind. The subconscious will carry out the directive-oriented position based on what is programmed, not essentially based on what one is requesting.

There are some energy-based dynamics you can reprogram your belief system with, like active meditation, visualization, positive self-talk, affirmations, and adamantly trying to delete the past experiences and flashbacks, not reminding oneself of the past episodes to prevent reoccurrences. Repetition of an affirmation over time alters the neural pathways in your brain to generate new belief, since a fresh network of neurons can be created to manifest a new paradigm shift and manifest a refreshing landscape of thoughts.

It is not nonsense to visualize and focus on mental images in your mind's eye that enable you to make your dreams come true, reach your objectives, and for making your mental images become physical reality. Positive self-talk, meditation, repetition, being receptive, and aligning oneself to actually living your dreams and making your mind a fertile ground for implanting seeds, soaking words and images deep into your sub-conscious mind, will eventually flourish and bear fruit of making your desires a reality. It is all about the incorporeal God that is formless, a superbly magnificent energy, literally so prevalent that oversees everything in existence and knows precisely who we are.

CULTURE OF WARS

"The brave man is he who overcomes not only his enemies but his pleasures"

– Democritus

And I say, if so, then no enemies are manufactured to overcome.

"Good and evil, reward and punishment, are the only motives to a rational creature" – John Locke

As Voltaire says, "It is forbidden to kill; therefore, all murderers are punished unless they kill in large numbers and to the sound of trumpets."

We should take inventory and correct our character flaws in order to resist straying from righteous conduct and become impervious to sinful temptation and wrongdoing.

There is a sacredness of belonging to the human race. We must stop walking sideways along the thick walls of cultural and habitual ignorance that have caused so much tyranny and misdeeds that if persisted upon, will eventually destroy us all.

Many nations are victimized by the culture of war, since culprits must relentlessly manufacture and find sickening reasons to infringe upon a vulnerable nation's affairs and sovereignty to justify wars of aggression. Corporations' piercing power and influence have dominated our thinking pattern for the worse, which has negatively affected the way we live.

Wrongdoings in national and global affairs have mutated like a vicious virus, dominating the way we live, creating havoc that has horrifically affected billions of innocent people. "All war is a symptom of man's failure as a thinking animal," as John Steinbeck so aptly put it.

Ordinary men are not immune to insidious maneuvers furtively executed to make noticeable differences in race, religion, nationality, creed, sexism, creating class war, and in widening income inequality gaps. They have managed to sow seeds of animosity for engendering divisive behaviors to cover up the innate problems and troubling nature of the capitalist economic system.

Relative social stability goes haywire in the midst of troubling times when depression leaves the system in economic paralysis and political gridlock, since there is no way out of its misery and stalemated position except thorough global violence and socio-cultural belligerency. As Mahatma Gandhi noted, "What difference does it make to the dead, the orphans and the homeless, whether the mad destruction is wrought under the name of totalitarianism or in the holy name of liberty or democracy?"

Their conspiracies refute solidarity, encouraging mayhem against fundamentally decisive forces for making a better world, opposing the people, where oligarchical democracy is manifested. Others are illusions about freedom, liberty, and the pursuit of happiness for mankind. This ironically paves the way for a dark ages mentality and activating backward schools of thought that can lead to cultural catastrophe. "Never think that war, no matter how necessary, nor how justified, is not a crime," are the wise words of Ernest Hemingway.

Corporate capitalists claim morality in their legal, social, and business charters. They claim ethics, good faith, and dignity, loyalty and human rights in their establishment protocols. They claim freedom and democracy; they hypocritically seek justice, social welfare, pretending no discrimination or prejudice of any sort, claiming liberty and the pursuit of happiness for everyone. Yet they hypocritically shroud the demons inside to cover up their wicked and inhumane behaviors.

They operate under false pretenses based on lies to further accomplish their objectives for monetary gain, where they willfully distort facts and vicariously execute them via others with revolting intent to cause malice and harm to those who do not conform to the insane and preposterous games they play to provoke troubles.

We must awaken to the culture of fear and manufactured wars that relentlessly solicit the ordinary citizen's vote to engage in neo-colonist conduct and ruthless behaviors for annexing valuable resources from defenseless inhabitants, forcing displacement and illegal migration of the helpless people to nowhere lands. "The world will not be destroyed by those who do evil, but by those who watch them without doing anything," is an apt Albert Einstein quote we need to heed.

They feed on the name of the republic while outsourcing jobs and all the resources available to them, destroying communities. They know no boundaries; multinational corporations act like a magnet towards cheap labor and raw material to exploit and plunder unprotected natural resources. And wherever they are tax exempt, they are free from any legal or financial obligation to compensate for the environmental mess and horrific illness they have cause for so many indigenous and innocent inhabitants.

They have forced the relocation of millions of people because of global warming and rising sea levels, acid rain, fossil fuel and carbon monoxide emission, as well as radioactive byproducts and toxic mine waste. Toxic dust in the polluted air and contaminated water and land which the indigenous live on and must cultivate for their very subsistence cause illness and death. Diminishing ozone layers because of air assault by many global chemical and gas producing companies has caused grave and immediate danger to human health, creating many problems, especially skin cancer.

"Man is born free, but is everywhere in chains" – Jean-Jacques Rousseau.

We are not shielded against the sun's ultraviolet rays, and too many dangerous chemicals and gases have damaged and depleted the ozone to the stratosphere, making it a huge hazard against humanity.

They have shamelessly left no sanctuary or any livelihood for people to unwind and seek immunity from so many hazardous agents, and so much of greenhouse gas emissions and its dire effect without any remorse. Destroying people's health and livelihood through food products immersed with antibiotics, preservatives, MSG, trans fat, glutens, saturated fat, and filled with artificial coloring, preservatives, saturated with chemical and hormonal agents, bleaching flour and sugar, and numerous other food products with a killer agent known as Azodi Carbona mide, sweeteners, and carbonated drinks.

They have taken over the government and conned the public with brazen lies of financial losses, asking the government to bail them out of their economic recession and desperately failed monetary situation with taxpayers' hard-earned money. What these demonic entities sow for profit, people must reap with illness and homelessness.

They unilaterally improvise demonic plans, concocting conspiracies to go to war as corporate media and other corporate lackeys manufacture consent, undermine people's intelligence, and betray inhabitants' trust by deceptive practiced acts, and in bad faith, as the corporate dynasty fabricates and conditions masses of people into irrational exuberance to wage wars of aggression on innocent nations, just because corporate capitalists are rich and have the resources to decimate people, creating bloodbaths, carnage, and forced exodus, and all for hegemonies and territorial schemes but in the name of exporting freedom, democracy, liberty, and human rights through self-made enforceable laws.

And yet, they have hijacked God to shroud the demons inside, to cover up their wicked and inhumane behavior. They operate under false pretenses, based on fibs to further accomplish their objectives for monetary gain, where they willfully distort facts and vicariously execute them with sickening intent to cause malice and harm to whomever is not a conformist to the insane and preposterous game, which they play to provoke and stir troubles ruthlessly and with no clemency at all. For them it is as easy to benefit through creating havoc as it is to catch fish in muddy water. Someone tell me, where is the conscience in that, and where does this patrimonial claim of morality "in God we trust" fit?

This ugly criterion can lead to extremism, which can lead to Hitler-type fascism, since there are already plenty of indicators supporting that. The irony is they govern in the name of the republic, and then, everything public is demeaned and not prestigious, and even bad, including our public schools and public transportation. But everything private is sacred, making them the pillars of society.

Seeing anything public look like an omen against many, with no viable choice, we need to reckon with pluralism and in the meanwhile, we should also give validity to our private life. But let's not become victimized and subservient to the rule of corporate privatization, which is meant to cause ill deeds, taking advantage of isolating people by creepily coaching them through their effective propaganda machines, making them become self-centered and act like remote islands towards each other.

We need to give meaning to human society since by nature, collective activities are the kernel of who we are. Let's not become obsessed with self in a world where no one can survive alone. We should act introspectively and cogitate (think deep), making a choice of a life to co-inspire with each other, as the universe co-inspires with us. We need to realize while progress is the key to human success, it should not take over humankind. We ought to know how cultural agendas and beliefs impact our wellbeing and health, which can in turn influence our mind and thoughts, and therefore affect our physical body for either worse or better. We must treat one another with humane behavior, not acting vicious and indifferent towards others. And stop being disoriented because of mass propaganda and through bombardment of baseless conditioning aimed at keeping us apart while they celebrate our being divided, while they enjoy every minute of their life at people's horrifying expense.

We ought to realize that profound anxiety is the impetus behind our greed. Fear is purposefully played to dominate our life and our degrading social order. They exert fear to dominate and control this inhumane social order. Extreme separation is hurting us all and is an ace in their hand, playing us every which way they want. Humanity has got to understand that the explosion of the concentration of wealth has resulted in our separation, implementing devastating class differentiation, which has caused an upsurge in inequality, raising the potential for a bloody encounter. To avoid violence in its true sense and on a massive scale, we should preemptively strike the culprit of individualism and work towards our collectivism and break through this concrete wall of inequalities, since the resources that are bound for human survival are unconsciously and immorally allocated. It has created a huge financial gap between the haves and the have nots. We need to pay attention and return to our "oneness," witnessed by our biological birth to our very death and to whom and what we return to.

We need to truly understand that we are the byproduct of a cosmic consciousness, giving us the freedom and the liberty to behave as an inseparable part of this awakened force. Not to abuse our freedom and our will, and not to choose evil over goodness. We need to comprehend that we are not self-made, we are not our own property, we are the property of our Creator, and sustained through our beloved God.

It is crucial to understand that human beings are sacred and must not murder anyone or make them perish by the millions via genocide. We must not abuse them. Must not rape them and lie to them, must not infringe on anyone's sovereignty, and must not belittle humanity in any way, because in doing so, you are hence insulting our almighty Creator, abusing God's property and belongings. Our life is a gift; our sustenance through sacred Mother Nature is also a gift. Can anyone in their right mind not think that when people have difficulty breathing the air, cannot drink the water or grow crops to eat because they are contaminated and polluted by multinational corporations, energy and chemical companies, that this is also terrorism? Can anyone in their right mind not think that when people become so cornered and desperate with having nothing to lose, when they see their loved ones perish right in front of their eyes because of hunger and sickness and disease caused by the very species called human corporate, should they not react violently?

This entire human tragedy is caused because only a few powerful 1 percent of the global society wants to keep the status quo, where they hold 70 to 80 percent of the resources, just to have their way, because of greed and because they are totally disconnected from the rest of humanity that live in pain and with agony. They make their decision solely based on profit maximization and what is best for their major stockholders at people's expenses, and have the policing power to enforce it and the media to back them up. That is why many religions insist on "thou shall not kill," "thou shall not rape," "thou shall not lie," "thou shall not steal," and so forth, because when one does, one is messing with God, since no one is self-creator; no one is self-made.

When one knowingly depletes helpless people of their rights and confiscates the very means of their subsistence, that is stealing. And when they die because of so many maladies and hunger, that is murder. And when they are forced to relocate over and over because of turning their livelihood to a horrific situation, that is raiding and looting. And when you pay handsomely to the media to back you up and do the coverup, that is lying. And when you order to imprison and detain and torture innocent people, that is raping people of their rights. This model and economic system that so unethically and inhumanely upholds corporate capitalism exploits and annihilates all that is in its path. It has declared war on God, and God's belongings, humanity and nature. People are God's belongings. They are sacred. The nature that sustains them is sacred. One must not mess with that.

We need to face the reality of the emergence of new thoughts and to identify with the paradigm shift to break through the ills of individualism and push to cultivate a real social and economic renaissance, where collective bargaining and happiness could mean something, and not just be a fad.

Our vision for a good future can be structured at the grassroots level, where happiness is no longer a phantom but a fundamental truth and a sincere expedition into capturing a new life and a better living for all of humanity. But then, to reach true success in our life we need visionaries that are not selfish in their sight to maximize profit and to benefit themselves alone at the expense of others. We must have passion to follow through, and we need an environment supportive of dreamers and for visionaries to have the liberty to act, since for new ideas and creativity to flourish they should be induced and encouraged, not inhibited. We must have an atmosphere that honors freedom of thought, freedom of press, freedom of speech, freedom of assembly, freedom of privacy, freedom of expression, freedom of religion and worship, and freedom of interactions.

It is utterly important to have an atmosphere free of any kind of prejudice and bigotry that can motivate people to participate in daring challenges to overcome their shortcomings and to be the best they can be. As Spinoza said, "Freedom is absolutely necessary for the progress in science and liberal arts."

And I attest that "freedom and democracy is fundamental to the very core of our existence and happiness, it rejuvenates and makes intellectual properties to flourish." We ought to remember those successful visionaries must have had the passion to execute every inch of their plan with the intent to win, and sometimes despite the insurmountable challenges facing them, they have overcome all the hurdles in their life, no matter how difficult the setting. Joseph Campbell said, "Opportunities to find deeper powers within ourselves come when life seems most challenging."

He also said, "It is by going down into the abyss that we recover the treasures of life. Where you stumble, there lies your treasure."

We ought to know when we do not discover our vision, and do not care to locate what we are good for and passionate about, then others will set our vision for us, and I am afraid not to the best of our interest, but theirs, in which we become a vehicle to help them reach their goal. With that said, should our purpose in life and where we stand matter in alleviating others' pain and suffering or not? And if yes, it is vital to truly understand the nature of our existence and why we are here. And why have intelligence if it is not put to good use? We ought to make a difference for the better in the world and persevere to reach our goal despite perhaps facing significant and dramatic challenges in reaching our objectives. We must understand how easy it is to become baffled about God and consciousness in today's materialistically intense society.

This cannot be done unless we explore who we really are as human beings and restore time to meditate on our inner self and perhaps truly connect with God and with nature, and to resist wrongful temptation. We are the heightened state of awareness, trusted with not having to manifest destruction and in not doing wrong. We are an inseparable part of nature, which does not operate hastily but works its way up gradually and with patience. The reason behind our stressful and chaotic life is that we have senselessly prioritized hoarding wealth and quantified living over the quality of life with no limit. We need to take time, as precious as time is, to delve into the very core of our being and to contemplate and savor the goodness of life in its generous offering. We are too absorbed with the culture of entitlement and with the celebrity culture and Hollywood-style action movies, through which we understand the rest of the world. We are into believe that change is to come through government and not via bottom up, but from top to bottom.

We are indoctrinated into nationalism and patriotism just for backing the super-rich up, and just in case their trillions of dollars of outsourcing jobs and resources goes raw, and perhaps they'll have to redeem it via wars and military intervention. Or when they target to extort many nation's natural resources, needing military backup to a point of genocide and making innocent people perish so they can become richer, to tighten the yoke even more around our neck and force us with more austerity.

We are trained into believing everyone is entitled to his or her own. We have evolved into a culture of indifference, where no crime is too big to shock us anymore. We just brush it off as, it is not going to happen to me or to any of my loved ones, and how quickly we forget about the ever present violence. We need to open our neuropaths by repeating compassion through empathy and kindness, to connect to others with love and understanding, letting them know of the serious problem caused by a corporation facing us all.

And finally we must realize when we are not aware, or behave indifferently, we vote to be further enslaved. We need to question more and practice activism to find constructive solutions. We need to uphold morality and righteousness, and continue to dig into the spirit of the whys of the issues from philosophical aspects, as well as the hows of matters from scientific perspectives.

We need to investigate the unjustified allocation of resources. We should give validity to our private life, but not to become victimized by a system of utter individualism where the colossally wealthy can hold onto unimaginable resources to enslave billions of people, as the victims of poverty gradually perish, as they survive on bare minimum with no hope for financial recovery. We know there are other dynamic economic systems that aim at maximizing workers' welfare and enhance people's livelihood.

VISIONARIES AND THE MIRACULOUS UNIVERSE

So many visionaries harnessed nature through zealous leaps, from discovering fire from the times living in caves to an agricultural environment, and inventing tools which peaked in the industrial revolution, reaching the nuclear and electronic age, and to the present age of quantum physics. It seems quantum computation is the next big thing in advancing humanity, transforming our lives from the digital era to the quantum level.

The quantum revolution has already augmented human intelligence through the explanation of the structure of matter, discovering the energy nature of matter, also understanding molecular biology, radiation, lasers, semiconductors, transistors and its derivatives, nuclear reactions, telecoms, nanotechnology, why the sun shines with fusion reaction, and so forth.

It is deservingly just to respect utopians behind scientific discoveries in our universe, but also understand there will always be mysticism in our world; inquiring scientific and scholarly minds are set to demystify them. There are still many intriguing subjects to remain puzzling and outside the scientific realm, and for humans' competency to answer.

Perhaps collective wisdom and philosophy could offer some convincing argument. In his book Computing the Universe, Seth Lloyd describes, "how the simple right atoms bumping into just the right other atoms can effect everything, all interactions between particles in the universe convey not only energy but also information- in other words particles not only collide, they compute."

He carries on to say, "The dance of matter and light had the power to produce our universe and everything in it." Lloyd also acknowledges the universe computes itself and says, "As computation proceeds, reality unfolds."

From this type of cognition, we can culminate that we are the derivatives and the production of energy, consciousness, motion, and matter contacting matter—a huge cosmic dance in its actual sense of comprehension.

In much of what Lloyds believe, also John Wheeler related, thinking about the universe, he explained, "Everything it-every particle, every field of force, even the space and time continuum itself derives its function, its meaning and its very existence entirely from binary choices and bits. What we call reality arises from the posing of yes or no questions."

In other words, Wheeler was suggesting, "The things that make the universe and life, what they 'are' are really information, little specks of polarity. Everything boils down to opposites." Pluses and minuses, male and female, on and off. If what Wheeler sees as the particles of the universe are similar to computer bits of information, and Lloyd states, "The universe is a quantum computer," then they are suggesting that we are living in a simulated reality. If so: Who is the programmer that initiated our cosmic and universe computer simulation?

Can we accept the cosmic architect as the designer replacing God? When did this cosmic computer begin its activity, and how long has it been there? What about when we die; do we just leave our virtual reality and go on to live in another realm outside of our present world and experiences?

Where is the central processing unit in this simulation computer? Is it our brain, or does our brain act as a mediator to link us to the supercomputer mainframe and the cosmic consciousness beyond its limitation? Our simulation of the world and us as its coherent might be begging for an access code that perhaps can help humanity in a far future to upgrade and to upscale programs of life for peace, healing of incurable diseases, finding happiness, and remedying natural disasters. And perhaps rewire the human nervous system and correct other human impasses through conscious binary effect, just as we code the internet connection and word processors.

It is a miracle to historically notice the simultaneousness of a new idea and the technology to deliver it are so coherent that happen when all the ingredients, including the right mathematical formulas and the right experiments, arrive precisely when we need them to connect the pieces of the puzzle to make a new paradigm shift and have a very useful entity for humanity to propel and progress even further and in having a better life.

ENTROPY, AND THE ORIGIN OF UNIVERSE

The dictionary defines the word entropy, which finds its roots in the Greek entropia, as "a turning toward" or "transformation." The word was used to describe the measurement of disorder by the German physicist Rudolph Clausius and appeared in English in 1868. A common example of entropy is that of ice melting in water. The resulting change from formed to free, from ordered to disordered increases the entropy.

Also entropy is known as: a measure of the unavailable energy in a closed thermodynamic system that is also considered to be a measure of the system's disorder which is the property of the system's state and that varies directly with any reversible change in heat in the system, and inversely with the temperature of the system, the degree of disorder or uncertainty in a system.

The degradation of matter and energy in the universe to an ultimate state of inert (inactive, lacking vigor or vitality) uniformity.

The idea of entropy comes from a principle of thermodynamics dealing with energy. It usually refers to the idea that everything in the universe eventually moves from order to disorder, and entropy is the measurement of that change.

1. a thermodynamic quantity representing the unavailability of a system's thermal energy for conversion into mechanical work, often interpreted as the degree of disorder or randomness in the system.
2. lack of order or predictability; gradual decline into disorder.

If energy is high, the randomness and chaos are absolutely present, which indicates a good reason that entropy departs from chance. It must certainly be applicable to life made on planet Earth, so intelligently created, and which is superbly orderly and disciplined, which makes it very far and contrary to being chaotic and disorderly, as it literally is very suitable for human, animal, and plant life, maneuvering in a magnificent low entropy state of being. Wherever we see low entropy in our world, it stipulates hypothetical evidence that intelligence, energy, and design have been put into it, and perhaps what applies to the human world apply to the entire cosmos.

Maybe the universe itself required the input of intelligence, energy, and design from the outside to make it "human-ready." As Stephen Hawking once beautifully put in his book, A Brief History of Time, "What is it that breathes fire into the equations and makes a universe for them to describe? "Be hold that a physicist's equations will never directly make anything; they're maps, not territory. They rationally describe possible structures or entropy states. An equation may provide a description of something that actually is. But an equation doesn't turn "water into sugar cane juice," or nothing into something.

Hence, Mr. Hawking's question still remains. Who or what made the equations of our human-habitable universe that breathes fire into the equation, and evolves into matter, then carbon-based flesh, then minds?

Mr. Paul Davis wrote in his book, God the new Physics, that a mathematical investigation shows that order is exponentially sensitive to rearrangements. That is to say, the probability of a random choice leading to an ordered state declines exponentially with the degree of negative entropy. An exponential relation is characterized by its rapid rate of growth (or decline). For example, a population that grows exponentially doubles its size in a fixed interval of time: 1, 2, 4, 8, 16, 32…

The exponential factor implies that the odds against randomly generating order increase astronomically.

For example, the probability of a liter of air rushing spontaneously to one end of a box is of the order 10 to the power 1o to the power 20 simultaneously, which stands for one followed by 100,000,000,000,000,000,000 zeros. Translated into a cosmological context, the conundrum is this. If the universe is simply an accident, the odds against it containing any appreciable order is ludicrously small." Witnessing creation should be a good enough reason to believe in a supreme being and a divine creator, an absolutely sovereign being who is devoid of any anthropomorphic qualities, beyond space and time. The cosmological argument is an argument for the existence of God that says that God is the First Cause that created the universe (source: Wikipedia).

It's also known as the argument from first cause, the causal argument, or the argument from existence. The argument below is a variant of the cosmological argument, which states: Something outside the universe has always existed.

And I say that nothing cannot create something, at least in a material world, and if quantum physics believes it does, as the physicists believe it can occur in subatomic realms, then that is miracle. There must be a programmer, cosmic energy, conscious-able universe, intelligence, order, purpose, destiny, finite beginning with finite end, responsibility and discipline, space, motion, time, intention, not accidental, with and no chance, no randomness, no probabilities, precursor environmental catalyst, complexity of the structure of living organism, willfulness, dynamism, and not mechanical. These are birds of the same feather, which flock together. Matter is all vibrating oriented energy and conveys all the above although not visible to the naked eye.

Abiogenesis, or the origin of life, is defined as: the natural process through which life originates from non-living matter, but from organic blend, where the change from non-living to living entities was a gradual process of increasing complexity, and not instantaneous. It believes the earliest familiar life-forms on planet Earth were fossilized microorganisms that may have existed as early as four billion years ago, and not long after the Earth's formation about 4.5 billion years ago. Life was harmonized through carbon and water, and construed based on lipids (fatty cell walls), carbohydrates (sugar, cellulose), amino acids (protein metabolism), and nucleic acids (self-replicating DNA, RNA).

Scientists sought their research via paleontology, astrobiology, biochemistry, molecular biology, and scrutinizing fossils digging into geology, etc., trying to determine how pre-life chemical activities initiated life. They believe life arose under conditions that are noticeably different from those on Earth today. The biochemistry of life may have begun shortly after the big bang, 13.8 billion years ago, they say, during a habitable epoch when the age of the universe was only 10 to 17 million years. The panspermia hypothesis suggests that, "microscopic life was distributed to the early Earth by space dust, meteoroids, asteroids and other small Solar System bodies and that life may exist throughout the universe, The panspermia hypothesis proposes that life originated outside the Earth, but does not definitively explain its origin."

The classic 1952 Miller–Urey experiment and similar research demonstrated that, "Most amino acids, the chemical constituents of the proteins used in all living organisms, can be synthesized from inorganic compounds under conditions intended to replicate those of the early Earth. Scientists have proposed various external sources of energy that may have triggered these reactions, including lightning and radiation. Other approaches ('metabolism-first' hypotheses) focus on understanding how catalysis in chemical systems on the early Earth might have provided the precursor molecules necessary for self-replication. Complex organic molecules occur in the Solar System and in interstellar space, and these molecules may have provided starting material for the development of life on Earth."

The troubles kick in when some behave ambiguously and act irresponsibly, throwing in ideological doctoring's that are shallow and depleted of reason. They render insightfulness with grief, because these mal deeds affect many callow minds, as they leave their ill-footprint behind and sometimes with horrific consequences to tragically burden the society in its entirety, as they give mixed signals.

In Charles Darwin's book On the Origin of Species, he wrote: "The exquisite organization of living creatures seems to offer the best possible demonstration of a supernatural designer, yet the evidence of biology and geology provides an adequate explanation for the extraordinary characteristic of biological organism." That is why the proponents of God's existence are pulling their hair, and emphasize the role of a supernatural programmer, programming extraordinary design, not only in biological matter, but in all that exists. He believes in evolution of biological "order" by mutation and natural selection.

Were Mr. Darwin and the like hallucinating when they talked about order? Did they not know "order" is followed by intelligence and consciousness, without which no experience is ever possible? And with responsibility, and a sense of purpose, a role of a live and genius operator that must act magnificently talented and orderly to design such a glorified universe, and absolutely not accidental.

Then we have Mr. Hawking saying oh no, gravity is responsible for our being and the life on planet Earth, and Mr. Marx saying oh no, it is economics which is the spine to our way of life. And Freud's pushing on human sexual behavior, and sees a huge importance in that. Freud even suggests that "God concepts are projection of one's father." And others, like John Paul Sartre, throw in existentialism and seeing (anthropomorphic) the role of human beings attributed as the principle which should rule, along with many other so-called doctorings, lowering his Godhood to believing in fire, manmade statutes, the sun, the moon, the oceans, and nature itself.

Pantheism is very old, even older than Buddhism, which put emphasis on transcendent qualities such as compassion., Most Taoists are pantheists, as are many Chinese, Japanese, and Western Buddhists, deep ecologists, pagans, animists, followers of many native religions, and many Unitarian Universalists.

The central philosophical scriptures of Hinduism are pantheistic. Many atheists and humanists could be pantheist, because of their deep respect for nature and counting it as sacred. Scientific or natural pantheism is a new way of belief for pantheism that deeply reveres the universe and sees nature as sacred, and happily accepts and regards life as the essence of living and body and Earth, but does not believe in any supernatural deities, entities, or supreme beings.

The Shinto religion ("the way of the Kami") is the name of the formal state religion of Japan that was first used in the sixth century CE. Shinto has no founder, no official sacred texts, and no formalized system of doctrine.

Shintoism and Japanese culture, attitudes, and sensitivity are compatible, creating a distinct Japanese consciousness. Belief in kami—sacred or divine beings, although also understood to be spiritual essences—is one of the foundations of Shinto. Shinto understands that the kami not only exist as spiritual beings, but also in nature; they believe kami exists within mountains, trees, rivers, and even geographical regions. In this sense, the kami are not like the all-powerful divine beings found in Western religion, but the abstract creative forces in nature.

Because of the kami (divinity and sacred spirit), the understanding is that the Shinto followers are supposed to live in harmony and peaceful coexistence with both nature and other human beings. This has made it possible for the Shinto religion to exist in harmony with other religious traditions.

Natural deities, supernatural deities, worshiping multiple gods or goddess, monotheism, polytheism, and so many other faiths were addressed in search of God. A deity of good versus evil of equal power by Manichaeism and Zoroastrianism is documented from many years ago. Most Hindus are polytheistic or monotheistic, but relaxed enough to believe in and pray to many gods. Pascal Boyer says, "While there is a wide array of supernatural concepts found around the world, in general supernatural beings tend to behave much like people, the construction of gods, and spirit like person (anthropomorphism), is the oldest characteristic." In the same account, Emile Durkheim was one of the earliest to suggest that "God represent an extension of human social like to include supernatural beings." Psychologist Matt Rossano contends that, "When human beings living in a large group, they may have created Gods as a means of enforcing morality. In small groups morality can be enforced by social forces such as gossip or reputation."

However, it is believed that to enforce morality in a much larger population is harder than in a small group. He also indicates that by including ever watchful gods and spirits, humans discovered an effective strategy for restraining selfishness and in building more cooperative groups. More recently, "Neuro-Theology," a term that was used by Aldous Huxley that studies religious experiences of gods and spirit, digs into the interconnectedness of humans and religion in terms of cognitive neuroscience.

So searching for God is not new; it has carried its track through the entire human history. Some contemplate God as self-reflection and see the Almighty through many other entities, which has rendered humanity with innumerous distorted perceptions of God. The essence of this whole confusion has always been the absence of the beloved through so many distractions, causing sheer abandonment of the truth.

Not noticing that God is the measure of our pain and suffering the further we are from our beloved God, the more fear, loneliness, anxiety, and meaninglessness we encounter. Any cultural novelty should address that, and make people aware of this infinite urge for belonging and to answer our human yearning to know who we are, and where did we come from, why are we here, where are we going to, and so forth. Not through visualization, but via searching souls seeking the divine. And seeking God by visualization alone most definitely makes us mechanical and a reductionist that can never bring about the infinite vastness and the magnificence of the work of God. Referencing Isaac Newton, he said, "Whence arises all that order and beauty we see in the world?" And because we are not our own property, since we did not create ourselves, but realizing that we are a gift, life is a gift bestowed upon us, this alone should change everything. Someone once said, "We are all part of a global lineage of remembrance."

Recognizing our nothingness and our belongingness to the divine, our hearts should be the receptacle of the divine, not saturated with vain and superficial needs. We must truly seek God, not through intellect, but by intuition, wisdom, and faith, where wisdom should mean the search for meaning, where rationality is sought, and where reason should prevail. Joseph Campbell put it this way, "God is a metaphor for that which transcends all levels of intellectual thought. It's as simple as that."

When Prophet Mohammed was asked by an Arab Bedouin, how can I know there is a God? He simply told him: when you see camel dung, you should decipher that a camel was here, and when you see footprints on sands, common sense should tell you a passerby, a human being was here. In seeing the undescribed beauty and the magnificent creation of the sun, the moon, the stars, and the entire life should resonate with you and to acknowledge the derivatives and the undeniable circumstantial evidence of the almighty God.

William Paley wrote in his book Natural Theology that in crossing a heath (a tract of wasteland) suppose I pitched my foot against a stone, and were asked how the stone came to be there: I might possibly answer, that, for anything I knew to the contrary, it had lain there forever; nor would it, perhaps, be very easy to show the absurdity of this answer. But suppose I found a watch upon the ground, and it should be inquired how the watch happened to be there in that place. I should hardly think of the answer I had given before-that, for anything I knew, the watch might always have been there.

"Yet why should not this answer serve for the watch as well as for the stone? The intricate and delicate organization of a watch, with its components dovetailing (to fit skillfully to form a whole, to fit together accurately), is overwhelming evidence for design. Someone who never seen a watch before would conclude that this mechanism was devised by an intelligent person for a purpose."

Mr. Paley went on to say that the universe is similar to a watch in its intricacy and organization, but within a much greater scale. Hence there must be a cosmic designer that has made the world the way it is, and surely for a purpose. It should behold us that the contrivances (concoct, discover, design, excogitate) of the universe does exponentially exceed the contrivances of any art or mechanical device made by man, in terms of its complexity, its purpose, and its subtlety, action, keen hood, and curiosity.

Aquinas said, "An ordered ness of action to an end is observed in all bodies obeying natural laws, even when they lack awareness, which shows they truly tend to a goal, and do not merely hit it by accident." Scientific evidence shows us that the universe hasn't always existed. Here are some of the evidences that support that the universe had begun at a certain point of time.

The Second Law of Thermodynamics says that the amount of spendable energy in an encapsulated and closed system, like in the situation of the universe, is decreasing. In other words, the amount of usable energy will die out, just like the batteries die in any electronic equipment operating with a battery. If our universe, which is a closed system, is in fact running out of energy, then the universe can't be eternal because a finite amount of energy could never have brought the universe through the infinity of time. Hence, it does not make sense to accept an argument that believes in no beginning with no end.

2. The Universe is Expanding

In 1929, Edwin Hubble made a discovery that our universe is expanding. Once scientists realized that the universe was expanding, they then understood the universe would have been smaller in the past. At some point, the entire universe would have been a single point. This point is what many people refer to as the big bang, which is the designated point when our universe began to exist.

3. The Cosmic Background Radiation

Physics.org explains the Cosmic Background Radiation as, "The left-over heat from the fireball of the big bang in which estimates the Universe was born about 13.7 billion years ago." All of science and common sense teaches that life, the world, and the universe is "running down." Thermodynamics teaches that the universe has a fixed amount of energy (taking into account that all mass translates into energy), since the entire system is propelling from a state of higher order to a more disordered state. Eventually, it will reach and enter into a motionless state of complete disorder. We ought to know that all and everything dilapidates; machines rust and wither away, people grow old and die, the birds and the bees, plants and trees, all shrivel and terminate. So do the stars, galaxies and so forth; they burn out, etc.

If matter has always existed, and it always strays off course and divagates to a more disorderly state, then why has the universe not "run down"? It would have already expired, and we would not be here. Our very existence disproves the plausibility of this alternative. The very fact that it is running down demands that it must have had a beginning. The most powerful evidence is the very world that surrounds us. Apostle Paul also spoke of this.

"For since the creation of the world His invisible attributes are clearly seen, being understood by the things that are made, even His eternal power and Godhead, so that they are without excuse" (Romans 1:20).

This creation informs us of God's existence, but it also exhibits his great and eternal power that is part of his divine nature as member of the Godhead. Through what is visible and the seen world, we are able to see something of these otherwise invisible attributes. Even though it cannot be scientifically proven, the evidence is so compelling that if one fails to realize and acknowledge his Creator, he is left without excuse.

While the age of the Earth is assumed by scientists, most do agree that the Cosmic Setting Radiation does point to a finite universe that has a specific age. Therefore, the cosmological argument on God, summarizes that something exists (the universe), which has not always existed. Hence something outside the universe must have always existed, which did create the universe. Nothing cannot create something, at least in our physical world.

Therefore, to avoid cause regression analysis to infinity, where something is to have caused something else, it must at one point have stopped, which did not have a cause, giving into the cause of all causes to prevent regressing to infinity. Something must have always existed in order to cause the universe into existence.

However, the cosmological argument states that "everything that came into existence must have a cause. God didn't come into existence, He always was, is, and will forever be. The cosmological argument refers to the first cause of the universe as someone that has always existed.

If we open-mindedly look at our universe, we can then discern that our God is self-existent, and must be: timeless, non-spatial, and not matter-like; omnipotent, omniscient, and omnipresent, with infinite power and infinitely intelligent, since he has created a flawless universe and the vast cosmos with enormous precision and with awesome ability, turning a state of nothingness into the amazing phenomenon of the time-space universe.

In Stephen Hawking's book The Grand Design, Hawking writes, "Because there is a law of gravity, the universe can and will create itself out of nothing." Both Hawking and Lawrence Krauss suggest that it is theoretically possible for the universe to have come from nothingness, using M-theory, string theory, and quantum mechanics to replace gravity, with God as being the Creator. But evidently there are major shortcomings to M-theory, and there are a number of prominent physicists who point out these mistakes:

1. M-theory requires the law of gravity, and gravity is not "nothing." It's "something. Nothing is no-thing; it's the state of non-existence. One can be certain that gravity isn't nothing, it's something. When physicists talk about nothing, they are talking about a quantum vacuum. But there's a problem. A quantum vacuum is not nothing, since the quantum vacuum has the attributes and the properties of something.

Referencing that "God has made human being in his own image," Mansour al-Hallaj, the Persian philosopher of the eleventh century, said, I saw my Lord with the eye of my heart.

He said, "Who are you?" I said, "I am you."

You are He who fills all place

But place does not know where you are.
In my subsistence is my annihilation;
in my annihilation, I remain you.

It is now scientifically substantiated that the world we see and experience is actually made of molecules, and molecules are comprised of atoms, and atoms are made of subatomic particles like protons and electrons that according to scholarly minded physicists, are 99.99999 percent empty space and electrical spin.

Physicists tell us atoms are made of particles, and particles are waves, and waves are possibilities, where these possibilities exist in nothing. By today's findings, the tiniest of them all are quarks, which in turn are part of a superstring field that comports frequencies and vibrating strings, which make the actual particles relating to the nature of their vibration. Bottom line is, the astrophysicists tell us when they search beyond molecules with the most sophisticated telescopes into the microscopic realm and subatomic cloud, they are unable to find anything. Hence, many of them conclude we come from nothing.

Forgetting that nothingness is the source of all that has existed and is impregnated with all there will ever be, humanity should expect the infinite possibilities from nothingness. We ought to study the microscopic realm and the unseen world of the subatomic world through our third eye, and with mindfulness, and to welcome these amazing matrixes and discern them fully in our contemporary age.

Neil Bohr, the Nobel Prize-winning father of quantum mechanics, said, "Everything we call real is made of things that cannot be regarded as real. In quantum mechanics hasn't profoundly shocked you yet, you don't understand it well enough." We are active in a world of physical objects, but this is how our brain accords and translates captured sensory data and information. From the tiniest and at the largest scale of nature and the way we interact with our world, this physical reality is not in existence.

Mr. Bohr believed the constituents of matter have absolutely no physical structure. He continues to address the idea of reality, which he believes is a cosmic concoction of non-localized energy and empty space. He carries on to say, "It becomes clear that our thoughts and the signals they register in the brain also have these same properties at their smallest level. Our thoughts are also an activity of the universe, and all activities take place within the same quantum realm prior to manifesting in physical reality."

Referencing objectivity and subjectivity, scientists keep them apart, to only reflect on external and the material world as they sever and isolate subjectivity in assessing their findings from the external world to objectify their results. They have no clue why subjective experiences exist at all, and why there is intelligence, and why sentiment evolves. We should awaken to the fact that consciousness and reality are not separate, as many scientists want us to believe. Many prominent physicists accept that there is no way to explain how something as material as chemical and physical processes can give rise to something as immaterial as experience.

The sudden realization happens when the essence of the remarkable world is conscious and not matter. It so happens that when our mindfulness is elevated and our consciousness is raised, we look at the world differently. It is because of cosmic energy (consciousness) that connects and makes our cognition ability and experiences possible. Deepak Chopra summarizes consciousness:

"As subjectivity/awareness, the ability to experience or feel having a sense of self-hood, and the executive control of the mind, and in Vedanta, consciousness is the potential for experience, consciousness is beings or existence, and it is prior to subject/object split, consciousness is the ground of existence, Sat-Chit-Ananda."

Deepak Chopra carries on to say, "Science depends on the experiences of the external world which is the perceptual reality, but not the fundamental reality." Perceptual realities are the description of the mode of observation; in other words, different species see the world differently. Reality is the species-specific description of the mode and the culture of observation.

Indicating science, Deepak says, "As systematic enterprise that builds on and organizes knowledge in the form of testable explanation and prediction about the universe, science is based on loop of observation theory experimentation and validation, science is based on facts, science relies on empirical measurement, it quantifies, unusually in terms of unit of mass, energy, velocity, and position, science is the objective truth."

Professor of theoretical physics Amit Gozwami indicates some principles on quantum mechanics. He expresses his finding's first as wave-function. Saying a quantum object can simultaneously be at many places, like an electron, which can be seen at different places at the same time. It can be sized in space as a wave, known as the wave property. Secondly is the discontinuity, a quantum object disappears at one point and appears elsewhere without having ever being notice to depart and travel the intermediate space, it is known as quantum jump, it basically teleports. Then, is what professor Amit calls Action-At- Distance, when a quantum object is seen, at the same time predisposes its interdependent twin object, regardless of the distance. Anything that happens to the electron, he says, the exact same or the opposite will occur to the proton. It is believed that Einstein named this "spooky" action at a distance. Then is the observer effect.

Which says a quantum object cannot be detected in ordinary space-time until we can notice it as a particle. It adheres to the fact that the quantum object can infinitely subsist as a non-local wave until is being directly noticed. Consciousness literally breaks apart the wave-function of a particle as soon as is observed. And insinuates that: if not consciously observed, it would physically stay un-seen in an opposition of potentiality. Hence observation not only produces the consequences but also shifts what needs to be measured. This rather bizarre posit (axiom, presumption, hypothesis) of quantum theory, which has long intrigued physicists and renowned philosophers alike, says that by the very act of watching, the observer affects the observed reality. This was validated in what is recorded as the double-slit experiment, as the presence of a conscious observer altered the action of an electron from a wave state to a particle state, which is familiarized as the observer effect, and entirely shakes what we presume to be the fact about the physical world. The findings of this experiment were published in the peer-reviewed journal Nature, in which the scientists summarized saying, "The introduction of a which-path (welcher Weg) detector for determining the actual path taken by the particle inevitably involved coupling the particle to a measuring environment, which in turn results in DE phasing (suppression of interference)." What is literally saying interprets that: the measurement system used to notice the activity of the particle affected the action of that particle.

> "[T]he atoms or elementary particles themselves are not real; they form a world of potentialities or possibilities rather than one of things or facts."
>
> — Werner Heisenberg

> "Not only does God play dice but... he sometimes throws them where they cannot be seen."
>
> — Stephen Hawking

The double-slit experiment repeated

As scientist Dr. Dean Radin said in a paper replicating the double-slit experiment, "We compel the electron to assume a definite position. We ourselves produce the results of the measurement." Now, a common response to this is, "It's not us who is measuring the electron, it's the machine that is doing the observation." A machine is simply an extension of our consciousness. This is like saying, "It's not me who is observing the boat way across the lake, it is the binoculars." The machine does not itself observe anything any more than a computer that interprets sound waves can "listen" to a song.

This has led some scientists to speculate that without consciousness, the universe would exist indeterminately as a sea of quantum potentiality. In other words, physical reality cannot first exist without subjectivity. Without consciousness, there is no physical matter. This is known as the Participatory Anthropic Principle, and was first proposed by physicist Dr. John Wheeler.

Essentially, any possible universe that we can imagine that it does not have conscious observers in it can be ruled out immediately. Consciousness is therefore the ground of being, and must have existed prior to the physical universe. Consciousness literally creates the physical world.

These findings provide huge implications regarding how we can understand our interconnectedness with the external world. "We create our reality" is used to refer to the fact that our thoughts create the perspective we have of the world, but we now have a more concrete and literal understanding of this phrase. We actually give rise to the physical universe with our subjectivity.

"I regard consciousness as fundamental. I regard matter as derivative from consciousness. We cannot get behind consciousness. Everything that we talk about, everything that we regard as existing, postulates consciousness." – Max Planck, Nobel Prize winning originator of quantum theory, as quoted in The Observer (25 January 1931). The bottom line in the world of quantum physics is that physical objects can lodge and occupy several different states simultaneously, which is related to abnormal situations of parallel worlds. Particles subatomically and at microscopic level show up in many places at the same time, denoting them by scientists as "superposition," where a single electron can be found in many places playing many possibilities, where a single particle uses all the possible progression or a line of development resembling a trajectory to travel from point A to B, and so forth, and not limited to one single progression or trajectory.

Scientists now believe quantum computation is necessary to perform and compute the collaboration that occurs among parallel universes at microscopic scales, since it needs to search through the enormous landscape of possibilities, to explore many directions, perhaps within millions of parallel universes at the same time. Scientists believe physical systems can maneuver with all the possibilities available to them at the same time, where those possibilities can converse and interact together, miracles are in the making beyond our imagination and wildest dreams.

They also tell us that we do not see objects as they are, we see them as we are. And the way our brain is set up and our DNA is structured, not a single person is going to ever show up like any one of us in millions of years before we existed, or in millions of years to come after we are gone.

The scientist and astrophysicist claim 70 percent of our universe is made of dark energy, and also claim that millions of galaxies are drifting apart travelling at more than the speed of light as they drop into the unknown. And 25 percent is made of dark matter, which means it is not visible and does not reflect light, give off, or suck up light, therefore known by the scientific community as not atomic. The scientists address their findings as 99.9 percent of the universe is made of hydrogen and helium that has not shaped into stars, and also tell us only 0.1 percent of 1 percent is visible because the rest of it is not atomic. And what they conclude is we are depending on this 0.1 percent of the 1 percent that is atomic, and perhaps we are made of that. And if the gravitational forces of galaxies in dark energy collapse, we would not be here.

Perhaps it is good enough reason for astrophysicist Mr. Hawking to conclude that an inanimate force of gravity is the cause of everything and has replaced God in his mind. I wonder if we could have ever formulated any practical scientific theory if science was to decide on o.1 percent of 1 percent from a total of the 100 percent unknown in question, which was assumed and undertaken to be experience on. Mr. Hawking is limited to planet Earth from an apparently infinite number of planets, trillions of galaxies, and billions of universes, which should make his findings very limited and not credible at all.

Let's check into related and peripheral issues, where they are a preponderance and play an enormous role in our life. We'll delve into the subject of spirit and consciousness and also look into matter, which science feeds on and believes in the doctrine of materialism referencing having no mind, no spirit. Scientists accept nature as mechanically oriented, having no awakening concept or any consciousness. They see and analyze our world as machine-like; conveying sets of fixed rules so it will be easier for scientists to adequately assess findings, and hence, for scientists to draw their conclusions while avoiding too many variables and elusive changes without interference. They forget this wonderful structure and beautifully designed world, richly textured, is just an illusion, and all of it takes place in our brain. Scientists view events as empirically as they actually experience them, and they quantify their findings, since they factor in human perception utilizing the human nervous system and consciousness. Since they cannot measure or mathematically quantify consciousness, they are also not able to directly observe conscious energy, so they throw the baby out with the bathwater and claim perhaps none exists.

On the other hand, the world of business is also preoccupied and contemplates on wealth creation, and capitalist ideology encompasses a broad cultural spectrum which leads to the world of materialism as investors adamantly pursue consumer-oriented environments. It seems customers are mesmerized with possessing a life of luxury at any cost and behaving skeptically towards non-material thoughts, but are obsessed with wealth-creating ideas over any spiritual endeavors. Too many people are driven to believe and are encouraged by material philosophy over spiritualism.

CYBERSPACE

As imperative as technology is for modernized living and in making further progress, we should not lose sight of what makes us human.

Unfettered freedom, impulsive behaviors, disinhibiting activities in the cyberworld ought to be alarming.

A cyber-psyche can bring trouble, where an extreme cyber realm can invite apocalypse (disaster), where loss of identity is surprisingly relevant, as if those exorbitantly (unduly, excessively) engaged have no soul.

Questions such as who are we, and who are we becoming in the cyber world, would not be out of line, and actually should be inspiring for alerting industrialized nations to avoid a chaotic atmosphere where turning into mechanical humans can become quite harmful.

In cyberspace, anonymity is fostered, making us vulnerable to exploitation, cheating, insensitivity, deception, irresponsibility, social brutality, and inflammatory and impulsive behaviors.

The culture of cyberspace can well become an underground for criminal activities and illicitly ubiquitous maneuvers, where evaluating mates and appraising cyber companions is visceral. Not actually knowing who we are dealing with, since one lacks daily face-to-face experience and instinct in evaluating and appraising mates can safeguard cyber predators to victimize others, and often with impunity.

The issue is of concern, since online conduct has become socially acceptable, where harmful behaviors are changing fundamental human relationships, where an array of misconduct is not funny or silly anymore but compulsive, threatening, hyper-stimulating, addictive, and potentially dangerous.

It seems the law and forensic perspective can be of little help, what with lack of regulation, privacy, accountability, and naïveté (inexperience, callowness), proclivity, disguising, and other insidious behaviors where the end justifies the means for the malefactors (criminals, culprits) for feeding their wrongful and addictive behaviors, while often harming the innocents, where so many can be emotionally impaired for life.

Not to forget that cyberwarfare is already of tremendous concern in the use or targeting in a battlespace linking computers and online networks and control systems, where operational cyberattacks, espionage, sabotage, hacking, and other menacing cyber offensives can most definitely disrupt our daily living for the worse.

INTROVERTS VS. EXTROVERTS

Extrovert personalities are much more common in freedom-oriented societies, since Western culture is basically synonymous with democracy and human rights, leaving not much space for one to easily become finger-pointed or blamed for behaving outside the traditions, They can say what they want without persecution, contrary to dictatorial countries, where introvert behaviors are as common, as even defending one's right is prohibited, as freedom of speech, freedom of press, freedom of assembly, and even freedom of religion is prohibited. In feudal agrarian cultures, dictatorial behavior is frequently exercised. They are the products of fear and illiteracy, where open-mindedness is punished, where lack of education does barely question if perhaps the entire cultural setup is wrong, where one does not have to become brainwashed to either kill or be killed for one's beliefs.

> "I would never die for my beliefs because I might be wrong"
>
> — Bertrand Russell

It is a pick your poison scenario, since dictatorial cultures are geared to low socio-cultural stimulation, without a robust economy, which often produces introverts, where they normally shy away from others, especially the opposite gender. And since the overall society is tilted towards a lower social arousal, and not diversified in economic stimuli, inhibiting excitement in socio-economic productivity; and since unisex activities are not the norm, as males and females cannot freely intermingle without legally being engaged or married, as sexism is definitely alive, where women are biased against in finding jobs and discouraged from pursuing higher education, and so on.

On the other hand, some extroverts can exaggerate in behaving fearless, enacting mal-mannerism, where sometimes reverence is lost, or when no value boundaries are set in dealing with others, as if rationale should not be of an essence, exhibiting an aggressively intrepid (dauntless, bold) attitude. And because Western socio-cultural and socio-economic criterions produce independence, since comparatively the employment rate in socio-agrarian nations, known as developing countries, is much lower than industrial-oriented societies with a much higher rate of employment, this potentiates the younger generations to influence the rules, rebel, and even change the cultural settings.

Extreme chivalrousness, shying away, irrationally hiding personal agendas, not sharing one's problems for seeking help are usually common when introverts are forced to live within the family rules, also facing social dilemmas, and confronting economic hurdles. There are often single breadwinners responsible for their family's well-being, as many developing countries lack providing enough jobs to adequately fulfill employment for so many that are competent to work, but cannot find vocation. The cultural settings often demand respect, especially in a strict disciplinary atmosphere. And since maneuvering within traditional dilemmas can often be misunderstood, leaving gaps in people's participatory and communicative discourse, as they often could not freely say what they mean or do what they say, mixed signals are quite common in dealing with sex, love, and of course, sexual orientation.

The truth is that we heal when we connect. We can adjust better and make progress in an open-minded society. It is human nature wanting to belong. Being honest about how we feel can heal us; it can expedite to remedy the problems. We are more resilient, and often more courageous when in groups. Collaboration is the key to success, especially within the global scale; good foreign policy and cooperation can identify with prolonging existence in this rather fragile worldly social and economic atmosphere. A constructive extrovertist's attitude can be a blessing, when people can freely speak their mind and professionally communicate in decisive matters to bring peace and happiness to all, because everyone should matter.

In a closed circuit environment, people do fear social judgements, which forces so many to mind and worry about what other people think of them. That is not encouraged in open societies. This is not to say there are no introverts in advanced societies, of course they are; but within lower rates, since free cultures relatively do not foment being excessively worried about other people's opinions or care what others think of them.

Overall, introverts prefer quiet settings; they shy away from the crowd, which can be difficult to deal with in school or in any other group activity, place, and social gathering where classmates, teachers, and grownups can make remarks about those quiet children and silent participants.

Generally speaking, we get more introverted as we grow older. Many elders have less interest in making friends; perhaps not needing to be praised, domineering, and not carrying a Napoleon syndrome attitude. People become more reclusive as they get older. It may be low testosterone, inducing less energy, and since much of our needs diminish in finding mates, finding jobs, finding new friends, sometimes not even eager enough to locate family members, peers, colleagues, and old lovers, there is just less incentive for conquering the world.

In advanced and industrial nations, technology, information, media, and market dynamics are catalysts for motivating people into upper mobility and in changing their lives for the better. This even influences the introvert, especially the youth, to become part of the excitement, to engage in a free market society where the inhabitants forgo cultural and social taboos, which leaves fewer obstacles to improve self. Whereas comparatively feudally agricultural oriented nations convey plenty of forbidden issues, or the so-called "out-of-bounds matters" as they play as brick walls, literally prohibiting individual and social progress. It becomes exponentially difficult when imperial governments hire terrorist states to ambush their own nation into poverty and silence, where crying out loud, complaining, and any criticism is punished, forcing so many into acting introverts and minding your own business mannerisms.

In many underachieving nations, tribal mentality still rules, where they lack social, political, and economic dynamics to authenticate true democracy and human rights. It is unlikely for minority groups to dominate the socio-political and socioeconomic agendas, as they are disfranchised, and as most bear prejudice, racial hurdles prevent them from reaching upper-mobility status.

It is also so sad that nepotism (the practice among those with power and influence of favoring relatives or friends, especially by giving them jobs, and endorsing individuals that have been recommended by other powerful colleagues) is very much alive in many third world countries, and even the United States under the Trump administration. They get preferential treatment, the old boy network, and looking after one's own. Acting biased and partially towards others is often exercised by the elites and the influential authorities. No transparency is ever allowed, keeping the citizens in the dark; no one dares to question the authorities and/or criticize the culprits in charge. Being outspoken can be dangerous, where the introvert behaviors and in keeping quiet is a blessing that might help one to stay alive.

Either way, extrovert traits are valued over introvert customs and behaviors where socio-cultural and socioeconomic dynamics can play a magnificent role in awakening billions and in goading introverts that we have already arrived into the twenty-first century, which requires a very competitive atmosphere where quality characters are demanded for success. It is imperative to know that solitude and a meditative mind should help in brainstorming to manifest creativity, open-mindedness, and passion for reaching for the stars, which sure can help one to become marketable and engage in communicating with other inquisitive minds, not become a remote island. And since many successful businesses look for extrovertly intelligent persons with good attitudes to maximize profit, employers seek extroverts with good quality for better productivity.

THE AMAZING HUMAN BRAIN

Can you imagine that everything in existence is perfunctory (lacking in interest or enthusiasm, just mechanical), operating as machines? If so, why not label and call it the planet of robots, where there are no goal-oriented organisms, only a mechanical world of machines. That is how our brain seems to be.

Let's assume we are robots, and nothing shorter than assimilated computers. If so, it would be unwise to imagine a digital world without software, lacking an absolutely powerful script writer, a competent programmer, in which trillions of species convey DNA and are so meticulously designed, an absolute miracle, since every single species, including humans, is assigned with an identity that is uniquely different than others, and for practical purposes. Precise blueprints of who, and what we are, so exquisitely planned that should put any inquisitive mind in awe.

We need to be reminded that a gene is part of DNA, which carries an individual's genetic information relating to one's characteristics. As informative as DNA is, it is callous not to see the urgency of a magnificent designer in manifesting entities as complicated as DNA and genes, demanding a breathtakingly animated being, and in understanding that matter and energy cannot produce data, lacking an intelligent designer. DNA is a map for the amplification of the living organism.

Some assume a pool of chemicals can perhaps form a living cell, or perhaps a primordial bacterium of some kind is responsible for DNA. Not fathoming that even the simplest life form requires a highly complex message with some 500,000 DNA characters. DNA is written with a combination of four chemicals: adenine, thymine, cytosine, and guanine, which scientists abbreviate as A, T, C, and G. Those are the letters of the DNA alphabet that encode all information necessary for life. In the simplest microorganisms, it takes 500,000 letters to produce a living organism.

Researchers, biologists, neurologists, and those active in genetics and related fields, medicine and anthropologists, believe there are five hundred thousand A's, or C's, or T's, or G's in a human being. It takes three billion (3,000,000,000) of those letters to manifest a copy of you, and there is one of those three-billion-letter messages inside every cell in everyone's body. Wouldn't it be insane to posit the cause to an inanimate, unintelligent matter, where such a magnificent task as DNA could take place by chance, and to occur in the realm of probabilities?

Many scientists take the human brain as having no conscious. They believe that our thoughts, memories, our vision, imaginations, our dreams, ideologies, values, interest, compromise, compliance, dignity, emotion, insensitivity, cruelty, and feelings of fear, shame, sadness, despondency, grief and sorrow, pain and suffering, willingness, courage, accountability, happiness, ecstasy, joy and longing for love, depression, transfiguration (metamorphosis, spiritual change, exalting, glorifying), deity, our sense of purpose, our intuition, pride, wit, talent, reasoning power, intelligence, ingenious, ingenuity, generosity, wisdom, aspiration, hopes and desires, inspiration, dialogue, patience, behaving hastily, diplomacy, satisfaction, courage, gratitude, gratefulness, affability, our love and empathy, apathy, ill feelings and brutality, hatred, tension, animosity, scorn, feeling of disdain, positive attitude, optimism, pessimism, rejection, loneliness, sexual temptation, reluctance, acting desperate, ire (rage anger), worry, revenge, offense, defense, homicidal, suicidal, feeling of regret, preserved, feeling of guilt, betrayal, mistakes, humiliation, resentment and despair, ineffable (taboo-like, indescribable), competitiveness, sacrifice, loyalty, devotion, sympathy, caring, longing for justice, fairness, rivalry and cooperation, ambition, withdrawal and shying away, introvert, extrovert, playfulness, domineering attitude, laid-back and laziness, persistence, perseverance, jealousy, eagerness, our sense of solitary, reclusiveness, feeling of resentment, meanness, blame, optimism, bliss, trust, pride, ego, selfishness, vision, righteousness, passion, obsession, captivation, compassion, transcendence, responsibility, meditativeness, focusing, confidence, intuitiveness, engaging, creativity, our sense of comprehension and resonance, despondency, revelation, reverence, serenity, affinity, gratitude, understanding, our sense of wonder, peace and tranquility, puzzled, abstract (general, not specific), exclusiveness, acceptance, forgiveness, anxiety and stress, clarity, rationality, our beliefs, craving, aggressiveness, satisfaction, trustworthiness, defiance, temptation and desires, our sense of neutrality, our sense of affiliation, belonging, faith, and so forth, are only supposed to be the byproducts of a mechanical brain that is fueled through electro-chemical charges, and is because of some chemical reaction.

The question is, how would our brain know what sort of hormone or electrical impulse should generate to manifest a particular thought, or designated feeling? And how does a human brain activate billions of neurons, where trillions of synapses spark to make us think and function the way we do; often so brilliantly, which should make one believe in magic, intuition, revelation, telepathy, and the like? It makes one overwhelmed by the rush of verve (mental strength), leaving little doubt that our human mind is of cosmic energy, where the presence of God is felt.

Do we really know the mechanics and the process in which hormonal secretion happens, and why? And how would our brain know and distinguish the joy hormones from the sad hormones? And why not exude exhilarating feel-good hormones when we are in pain? If done erroneously, mixed signals should be expected with a confused central processing unit. And why not emit sad hormones when we are really happy and vigorous?

Our brain reacts to the outside stimuli through electrochemical activities. It produces the precise amount of joy hormone in a peaceful and serene atmosphere, as well as generating the exact scale of agonizing and distressful hormone when in hostile and frustrating situations.

The question is, how would our brain know what kind of hormone to release for specific situations, and what quantity of variety of hormones available should exactly be produced to fit different scenarios and not go haywire, where excreting out of balance hormones can mean irreparable damage?

If our senses are responsible for us behaving as humans, senses are not of matter, and if it is our brain, the brain is also energy-oriented, with great ability of relating to formlessly ubiquitous cosmic energy, literally mindful, and magnificently aware, which reverberates (echoes) to the outside world.

The nervous system is impacted by our senses; what mechanism actually takes place for our brain to activate messages to the rest of our body for complying to the outside world?

What really triggers a lump of fatty tissue with trillions of microscopic nerves, blood vessels, capillaries, neurons, and synopsis, where they connect with no flaws, to create consciousness, manufacture thoughts, build experiences, derive messages, keep memories ... and why? And why convey intent and intelligence?

Quantum physics has enlightened us in subatomic realms, where the world of string theory, invisible quarks, and vibrating waves actively maneuver, as their operational frequencies are as intricate and way beyond our human senses to reckon with.

Our thoughts, feelings, and emotions, the human nervous system, and the entire planetary life, sensations, intelligence, and mindfulness, are played at different frequencies that are quite different from the frequencies played in the invisible world of subatomic particles. The wave parameters in the unseen realm sing a much different song, limiting us to make evidence of the cause, but to see the effects.

What we invent and magically create are the byproducts of a thought and ingenious ideas, often brilliantly imaginative like building shuttles, conquering other planets, playing Mozart, curing the deadliest of diseases, or when one perishes or is glorified in the name of love. We are not apart from the very imperative forces of our universe, and although they are invisible, they play an extremely essential role in nature.

The five forces of nature as they sustain our universe are:

Gravity, which pulls and pushes on energy and momentum, also based on Einstein, who generalized Newton's idea saying gravity pulls on mass, as the gravitational field holds planets, stars, and entire planetary system and galaxies together.

Electromagnetism, which includes both electric and magnetic forces, pull and push on particles that convey electric charge, and keep atoms together. Electromagnetism is linked with electric and magnetic fields, and also with the particle of light, known as the photon.

The Strong Atomic (Nuclear) Force, a force that pulls and pushes on quarks, anti-quarks, and gluons, also holds protons and neutrons together;

a remnant version of this force keeps atomic nuclei together. The strong atomic force is associated with the fields and particles known as gluons.

The Weak Nuclear Force (a force that affects most particles but is too weak to hold them together; its main effect is to cause many types of particles to dilapidate (decay) to other particles, and to let production and observation of neutrinos. The weak nuclear force is related to the fields and particles called "W" and "Z."

The Higgs Force, an extremely weak force, not currently observed, but expected to be present, the Higgs force is affiliated with the Higgs field and particle.

The above five forces of nature play decisive roles to maintain, balance, and prolong life. Our mind, spirt, or soul, call it as you wish, can respond to the awakened forces of the universe. That is exactly why we can identify with the unseen energy oriented in cyberspace, internet, cell phones, GPS, and medical diagnostic equipment, not to exclude diagnostic imaging machines (i.e. ultrasound, MRI, PET, and CT scanners), and x-ray machines, infusion pumps, medical lasers and LASIK surgical machines, etc.

It seems that everything happens in our brain. Not only is the human brain the most complex part of the human body, but it is known to be the most intricate entity in the universe. Our brain is the center of consciousness; it controls the entire voluntary and involuntary movement and other bodily functions. The brain dialogues with each part of our body via the nervous system, in which it carries electrochemical signals to execute orders received from the central processing unit.

An adult human brain is about three pounds. This jelly-like matter interrelates our mind to cosmic consciousness. The universe is fueled by this ever present cosmic life which our mind is an inseparable part of, and without life, couldn't be possible.

Our senses are impacted by the real world, interpreted by the brain into making sense. It is acknowledged that our conscious experience of events is actually delayed, giving the brain milliseconds to sort and synchronize the information, match it, package it, and deliver it.

Neuroscientists also credit that when our brain receives data with cross references of sight, sound, touch, hearing, and smell, they move together to make different tasks possible for each varied sensory information received by our brain.

It takes a delay gap to process and deliver it for us, and then reflect. It is also scientifically known that even if we are deprived of the outside world, our brain depicts its own reality related to its internal model, since there is already a model existing in our brain.

Our brain is the closest thing to gamut (range, spectrum) of electromagnetic radiation, x-rays, ultrasound, MRI, gamma rays, radio waves, air compression waves, and electrochemical signals, which also makes all sensory perception possible relevant to our dreams, feelings, memories, intelligence, our desires, emotions, and retro diction events (information or ideas to infer past events or states of affair), and so forth.

Our brain is pertinent to what we perceive, as our mindfulness literally relates to experiences of the moments in our life. Have you not noticed how time flies when in love, how time passes so quickly and elated when we are engulfed with joy and pleasure?

And amazingly enough, when fear is induced, or a bad accident of some kind occurs, it feels like eternity, like time is moving in slow motion. We now understand that from cradle to grave, human beings are networks in progress. We are not fixed entities, since our neurons continuously alter, showing the human brain's plasticity because of creating new and fresh neurons, especially for studiously inquisitive minds.

Diversifying and mental challenges, gaining knowledge and experience, and for exercising our mind through posterior hippocampus potentiates the brain for getting physically bigger.

The longer and the more mind challenges and learning new thing with years of practice, the more we should expect for our brain to enlarge in certain areas. It is also believed our brain secretly controls all that we do, even that which is hidden and not revealed to us.

It is interesting to notice many newborn animals are ready to encounter the challenges they face when they are born, since they are already instinctually programmed before being born. Humans take the longest time span among other species to competently manage their environment and the world around them. They can be conditioned to fit, and become compatible with their surroundings.

We can grow, learn, and progress through experience, and we can adapt accordingly. The hidden agendas to our human brain are in the connection of millions of new neurons as they flourish as we take new learnings and become skilled in accomplishing new tasks. The secret is not in the number of cells, because they seem to be the same in their number in young and old people.

Our early learning, even before two to three years of age, is very crucial, as it will play a critical role for the rest of our life. Not engaging our brain in mental activities and in experiencing fresh ideas can dramatically shift our memory perception for the worse, and make us lose our cognitive ability. The human brain can be compromised if left with no access to mental strength, leading to lack of vigor and recollection problems.

When faced with a critical situation, amygdales located in the temporal part of our brain activate and play a huge role in our response to emotion and fear. Amygdala is almond-shaped and is situated within the temporal lobe of brain. it is engaged in emotions and motivation specific to our survival. Amygdala processes feelings of fear, pleasure, and joy, and is also responsible for memory storage in different parts of the brain. It is also understood that determination is based on how big an emotional response an event invokes.

Amygdala is automatically connected with fear and anxiety and hormonal excretion. When we become startled and fearful of an unexpected and a bitter sound, the amygdala heightens our perception of the sound, which causes us to react with a fight-or-flight response. And this response activates the sympathetic branch of the peripheral nervous system, which causes accelerated heart rate, dilated pupils, increase in blood flow to muscles, increase in metabolism rate, and sometimes showing the victim with a pale face, since blood accumulates in our limbic system from other parts of our body for better maneuverability in fight-or-flight response.

Amygdala is also involved with memory, hormonal secretion, emotional responses, arousal, and automatic response to fear. It is located deep within the temporal lobes, median to hypothalamus, and right next to hippocampus. The amygdala gets sensory news from the thalamus and from the cerebral cortex.

The thalamus is also a limbic system structure, and it links areas of the cerebral cortex that are involved in sensory perception and movement with other parts of the brain and spinal cord that also have a role in sensation (conveying nerve impulses from sense organs to the nerve centers) and movement. The cerebral cortex processes sensory information captured from vision, hearing, touch, and other senses, and is engaged in decision-making, problem-solving, and planning.

It is through our sense of vision, hearing, touch, smell, and taste that we connect and respond to the environmental changes around us and with each other. Various environmental activities impact our senses, which are then captured by our nervous system to be assigned to many different parts of our brain accordingly, making specific parts of our brain respond to a variety of incoming messages, which we are then instructed to fulfill the tiniest or a major function.

Trillions of brain cells and capillaries, one hundred billion neurons and trillions of synopsis, quadrillions of interactions and more are constantly at work to make what and who we are. No one can claim to have seen the mechanics of how our senses record and reflect upon environmental activities, which are then sent to different parts of our brain via our nervous system.

It is wondrous how messages are laser-precise and directed to specific parts of our brain, then the brain orders our body to react in accord with the incoming messages. It should not be surprising to call them senses, since we cannot materialize any of them, if not of spirit, then, why call them senses? Our senses, the nervous system, and our mind are energy-oriented and derivatives of the cosmic energy field.

Messages retrieved and commands sent from the brain to our nervous system are not received by insensitive tissues, deadened nerve cells, and a network of irresponsive arteries, capillaries, bones, and muscles, etc. And yes, our brain commands messages back to the nervous system for us to execute them, but then again which us, who is the operator, who is behind I, or behind any of us? Is it the one hiding behind our brain, the subconscious mind, or the one perhaps hiding behind the physical body, within our spirit and into our soul, or the operator is probably the soul, ruling over us, but where?

Whom are we actually addressing these massages to? Who is really running the show? Is it our brain that is self-governed that is responsible for all of what is happening?

Surgeons work on physical bodies (patients) to operate on, utilizing sharp knives and scalpels, and physicists, chemists, biologists, and so on, need laboratories for experiencing on actual matters. It habituates them to developing a one-track mindedness, which makes them so anxious looking for results that necessitate actual findings. They forgo the reality of mind over matter, acting negligent of the higher realms. They wave to denote the ever present soul and the ubiquitous spirit.

Most scientists persist on having viable results, not for the convenience of their undertakings, but because of the plausible and confirmed results they are looking for. Most scientists are reluctant about the unseen world that lurks behind all and everything we do. They make the material world prominent without paying attention to the elephant in the room, the spirit of things, which makes it misleading.

The average human brain contains approximately100 billion neurons (nerve cells) that are the core component of our nervous system, and our brain enables transmitting information by electrochemical signaling. Our brain sends a great deal of electrical impulses to other neurons, which makes our perception of reality possible.

With millions of neuroglia (or glial cells) to support and protect the neurons, each neuron may be connected to up to 10,000 other neurons, passing signals to each other, constituting a network of as many as 1,000 trillion synaptic connections, since every spark executes a thought for processing. That is believed to be about an average of four to five thousand thoughts taking place within each hour; you do the math. Similarly, by some measure, scientists equate our brain to a computer that renders a 1 trillion bit per second processor.

Bear in mind, the estimates on the human brain's memory capacity vary wildly from 1 to 1,000 terabytes (for comparing our brain terabits with the 19 million volumes in the US Library of Congress, which only represents about 10 terabytes of data). Each terabyte is 1,024 gigabytes, or 1,099,511,627,776 bytes, one trillion bytes.

The information process within the brain occurs during the processes of memory <u>encoding</u> and <u>retrieval</u>. It happens when the brain utilizes a combination of chemicals and electricity. It is a very complicated process that involves a variety of interconnected steps, intricately designed.

Every neuron keeps a voltage gradient (grade, slope, inclination) across its membrane (plasma, nucleus) due to metabolically driven differences in ions of sodium, potassium, chloride, and calcium within the cell, each of which has a different charge. If the voltage changes significantly, then an electrochemical pulse called an action potential, or nerve impulse, is generated. This electrical activity can be measured and displayed as a wave form called brain wave, or brain rhythm.

A typical neuron generates a soma (the bulging, stretched into a more rounded shape cell body that contains the cell nucleus), dendrites (long, feathery filaments connected to the cell body in a complex branching "dendritic tree"), and a single axon (a special, extra-long, branched cellular filament, which may be thousands of times the length of the soma).

Unlike other body cells, most neurons in the human brain are only able to divide to make new cells (a process known as neurogenesis) during fetal processes and for a few months after birth. Brain cells may grow in size until the age of about eighteen years old, but they are essentially designed to last for a lifetime.

Surprisingly enough, the only area of the brain where neurogenesis (the birth, the origin of neurons) has been shown to continue throughout life is the hippocampus, an area vital to memory encoding and storage. Deepak Chopra said, "Our minds influence the key activity of the brain, which then influences everything; perception, cognition, thoughts and feelings, personal relationships; they're all a projection of you." Our sensory and neuron networks are bound to exclusive frequency, and experience our world within the possibilities of those vibrations. And when information is received by our brain, then our brain alters and interprets those incoming signals according to its potential and active cells available for percentage usage, which makes our perception of reality possible.

The Gospel of Thomas talks about how beliefs are so powerful, when referring to Jesus saying how the union of thought and emotion can literally alter our reality. "When you make the two one, thought and emotion," he begins, "you will become the son of man, and when you say mountain move away, it will move away."

This so-called empirical realty is based on mode of observation, which varies in many species of animals, since their perception of reality is very different from one another, including us. For example, snakes see through infrared, and dogs have great sense of smell, and honey bees see through ultraviolet, whales and dolphin operate with ultrasound and through echo location, so does the bat. How a chameleon sees the world and operates on several vision axes is much different than us; insects having many eyes see the world entirely different.

Dr. Andrew Jackson, from Trinity College, Dublin, who led the study, said, "A lot of researchers have looked at this in different animals by measuring their perception of flickering light.

"Some can perceive quite a fast flicker and others much slower, so that a flickering light looks like a blur.

"Interestingly, there's a large difference between big and small species. Animals smaller than us see the world in slow-motion. It seems to be almost a fact of life.

"Our focus was on vertebrates, but if you look at flies, they can perceive light flickering up to four times faster than we can.

"You can imagine a fly literally seeing everything in slow motion.

"The effect may also account for the way time seems to speed up as we get older," Dr. Jackson said.

This is why animals notice natural hazards a bit sooner than humans. When we see the sky as blue, it is not what other species see as blue. The significant issue is that dissimilar species with different nervous system operate at different frequency rates and since they resonate with the outside world unequally, they do as they are wired.

Hence, how millions of species functions depends on the specific description, with the mode of observation and culture in which they maneuver. This signifies that perceptual reality is not actual and fundamental reality; it is through our brain and nervous system that our world is shaped, a world that scientists tell us is odorless, tasteless, sightless, and so on.

When scientists claim realism and objectivity, they do not consider the subjectivity of consciousness, since they cannot prove its existence. Some scientists imply take "the observer" as hallucination, and if so, and the observer is an illusion, then the observed should also be an illusion, since logic tells us illusion creates illusion, and cannot make reality form delusion. Either the observer is an illusion, which does not comply with our very nature, or it is outside space and time as we know it.

How can we imagine, how can we formulate theories, how can we constitute design in our consciousness, how can we manifest beauty, aesthetics, art, poetry, love, and grasp the meaning of any non-matter entity at all? Where are observations made, if not in our very conscious?

Our brain processes wondrous amounts of information. It captivates colors for the eye to see, the temperature around us, the amount of pressure we feel, the sound, even the dryness of our mouth. It holds and resonates with our emotions, thoughts and feelings, our memories. It simultaneously keeps track of our bodily functions, including breathing, eye and eyelid movements, hunger, blood circulation, and so forth.

Our brain processes a million messages a second, while it weighs in all of these data, and filters and discards the unimportant ones. This screening operation lets you concentrate efficiently in the world. It carries intelligence; it reasons, it dreams, generates feelings, and meditates on taking action as it interacts with its environment and with other people. Imagine many parts of the entire brain, each with a very complex and crucial task, playing in a mechanically oriented atmosphere with no dynamics, and without a competent programmer or an omnipotent planner.

I wonder how this amazing organ behaves so marvelously as a control center by receiving, translating, and directing sensory information throughout the entire human body. Our central nervous system includes the brain and spinal cord. There are three major branches that comprise our human brain. They are the forebrain, the midbrain, and the hindbrain (the lower part of the brainstem, the posterior of the three primary divisions of the developing vertebrate brain). Each and every division of our brain does exactly what it is known for and specified to do. But then again, how does the same material brain recognize the particular task assigned to each and every part of it with an awesome awareness and discipline?

The intricacy and the anatomy of human brain and its subcategories are imperative. The forebrain is responsible for a variety of routines, not to exclude receiving and processing sensory information, thinking, perceiving, generating and understanding language, and controlling motor activities.

There are two major parts of forebrain, which are known as the diencephalon and the telencephalon. The diencephalon includes the thalamus and hypothalamus, which are both responsible for such deeds as motor control, relaying sensory information to other parts, and controlling autonomic functions. The telencephalon holds the largest part of the brain, the cerebrum. Most of the actual information processing in the brain takes place in the cerebral cortex.

The midbrain and the hindbrain collectively comprise the structure of brainstem. The midbrain is the portion of the brainstem that links the posterior, also recognized as hindbrain and the forebrain. This region of the brain is active in visual and auditory responses, as well as motor function.

The hindbrain extends from the spinal cord and is composed of the metencephalon and myelencephalon. The myelencephalon, or "afterbrain," is the most posterior region of the embryonic hindbrain, from which the medulla oblongata develops.

The metencephalon contains structures such as the pons and cerebellum. These regions assist in maintaining balance and equilibrium, movement coordination, and the conduction of sensory information. The my.elen.ceph.alon is the posterior part of the developing vertebrate hindbrain or the corresponding part of the adult brain composed of the medulla oblongata, which is responsible for controlling such autonomic functions as breathing, heart rate, and digestion.

Other vital parts of the brain contain various structures that have a multitude of functions. Below is a list of major structures of the brain and some of their functions.

Basal Ganglia: Involved in cognition and voluntary movement. Diseases related to damages of this area are Parkinson's and Huntington's.

Brainstem: Relays information between the peripheral nerves and spinal cord to the upper parts of the brain. Consists of the midbrain, medulla oblongata, and the pons.

Broca's Area: Speech production, understanding language.

Central Sulcus (Fissure of Rolando): Deep groove that separates the parietal and frontal lobes.

Cerebellum: Controls movement coordination. Maintains balance and equilibrium.

Cerebral Cortex: Outer portion (1.5mm to 5mm) of the cerebrum. Receives and processes sensory information.

Divided into cerebral cortex lobes.

Cerebral Cortex Lobes:

Frontal Lobes: involved with decision-making, problem solving, and planning.

Occipital Lobes: involved with vision and color recognition.

Parietal Lobes: receives and processes sensory information.

Temporal Lobes: involved with emotional responses, memory, and speech.

Cerebrum: Largest portion of the brain. Consists of folded bulges called gyri that create deep furrows.

Corpus Callosum: Thick band of fibers that connect the left and right brain hemispheres.

Cranial Nerves: Twelve pairs of nerves that originate in the brain, exit the skull, and lead to the head, neck, and torso.

Fissure of Sylvius (Lateral Sulcus): Deep groove that separates the parietal and temporal lobes.

Limbic System Structures:

Amygdala: involved in emotional responses, hormonal secretions, and memory.

Cingulate Gyrus: a fold in the brain involved with sensory input concerning emotions and the regulation of aggressive behavior.

Fornix: an arching, fibrous band of nerve fibers that connect the hippocampus to the hypothalamus.

Hippocampus: forwards memories out to the designated part of the cerebral hemisphere to be stored for long-term and retrieves them when necessary.

Hypothalamus: directs a multitude of important functions, such as body temperature, hunger, and homeostasis.

Olfactory Cortex: Receives sensory information from the olfactory bulb and is involved in the identification of odors.

Thalamus: Mass of gray matter cells that arranges sensory signals to and from the spinal cord and the cerebrum.

Medulla Oblongata: Lower part of the brainstem that assists in controlling autonomic functions.

Meninges: Membranes that deal with and protect the brain and spinal cord.

Olfactory Bulb: Bulb-shaped end of the olfactory lobe, activates the sense of smell.

Pineal Gland: Endocrine gland involved in biological rhythms. Secretes the hormone melatonin.

Pituitary Gland: Endocrine gland involved in homeostasis, regulates other endocrine glands.

Pons: Arranges sensory information between the cerebrum and cerebellum.

Reticular Formation: Nerve fibers located inside the brainstem that regulate awareness and sleep.

Substantia nigra: Helps to control voluntary movement and regulates mood.

Tectum: The dorsal region of the mesencephalon (midbrain).

Teg.men.tum: The ventral region of the mesencephalon (midbrain).

Ventricular System: links system of internal brain cavities filled with cerebrospinal fluid.

Aqueduct of Sylvius: canal that is situated between the third ventricle and the fourth ventricle.

Choroid: generates cerebrospinal fluid.

Fourth Ventricle: canal that passes between the pons, medulla oblongata, and the cerebellum.

Lateral Ventricle: largest of the ventricles and situated in both brain hemispheres.

Third Ventricle: makes a pathway for cerebrospinal fluid to flow through.

Wernicke's area: This area of the brain assists with spoken language and how it is understood.

To summarize some of the activities of human brain, a marvel of a creation where genius and miracles are discovered.

Our human brain is the central organ of the nervous system, located in a thick, bony skull that relatively protects it from damage that might occur. It is similar to and has the same general build as the brains of other mammals, but with a much more highly developed cerebral cortex than any other animal. This has led to the evolutionary success of widespread supremacy of the human species across the planet.

Larger beasts, such as whales, sharks, crocodiles, and elephants, have larger brains, but when sized and measured using the cephalization ratio, which compensates for human body size, the quotient for our brain is almost twice as large as that of some dolphins, and three times as large as that of a chimpanzee.

Much of the increase in size comes from the cerebral cortex, especially the frontal lobes, which are associated with the thinking brain, executive functions, such as having a choice, with having will, taking risk, self-control, planning, reasoning, and in general, abstract thought. The portion of the cerebral cortex related to vision and the visual cortex is also greater than other animals, and enlarged in humans.

One hundred captivating facts about the human brain gathered by scientists and medical society in their scholarly rendered research. The human brain has bewildered and puzzled masses of people throughout history. Some scholars, scientists, and medical authorities have spent their whole lives trying to figure out how the brain works.

It should not be of any surprise why curious minds enjoy learning facts about this astonishing organ in the human body. Below, you will find 100 facts about the brain, including how it maneuvers, how it expatiates (to explain by setting forth in careful and often elaborate detail), what it controls, how it affects sleep, dreams, emotions, and the power of our memory and the way we think. Furthermore, let's debunk some of the brain misconception myths that people accept as gospel truth.

Physical make up and attributes of the human brain.

Weight. The weight of the human brain is about three pounds.

Cerebrum. The cerebrum is the largest part of the brain and makes up 85 percent of the brain's weight.

Skin. Your skin weighs twice as much as your brain.

Gray matter. The brain's gray matter is made up of neurons, which gather and transmit signals.

White matter. The white matter is made up of dendrites and axons, which create the network by which neurons send their signals.

Gray and white. Your brain is 60 percent white matter and 40 percent gray matter.

Water. The brain is made up of about 75 percent water.

Neurons. Your brain consists of about 100 billion neurons.

Synapses. There are anywhere from 1,000 to 10,000 synapses for each neuron.

No pain. There are no pain receptors in the brain, so the brain can feel no pain.

Largest brain. While an elephant's brain is physically larger than a human brain, the human brain is 2 percent of total body weight compared to 0.15 percent of an elephant's brain, meaning humans have the largest brain to body size.

Blood vessels. There are 100,000 miles of blood vessels in the brain.

Fat. The human brain is the fattest organ in the body and may consists of at least 60 percent fat.

The Developing Brain. Starting from within the womb, fetal brain development begins the amazing journey that leads to a well-developed brain at birth that continues to grow for 18 more years.

Neurons. Neurons develop at the rate of 250,000 neurons per minute during early pregnancy.

Size at birth. At birth, your brain was almost the same size as an adult brain and contained most of the brain cells for your whole life.

Newborn's growth. A newborn baby's brain grows about three times its size in the first year.

Stopped growing. Your brain stopped growing at age 18.

Cerebral cortex. The cerebral cortex grows thicker as you learn to use it.

Stimulation. A stimulating environment for a child can make the difference between a 25 percent greater ability to learn and 25 percent less in an environment with little stimulation.

New neurons. Humans continue to make new neurons throughout life in response to mental activity.

Read aloud. Reading aloud and talking often to a young child promotes brain development.

Emotions. The capacity for such emotions as joy, happiness, fear, and shyness are already developed at birth. The specific type of nurturing a child receives shapes how these emotions are developed.

First sense. The first sense to develop while in utero is the sense of touch. The lips and cheeks can experience touch at about 8 weeks and the rest of the body around 12 weeks.

Bilingual brains. Children who learn two languages before the age of five alter the brain structure, and as adults have a much denser gray matter.

Child abuse and the brain. Studies have shown that child abuse can inhibit development of the brain and can permanently affect brain development.

Brain Function. From the invisible workings of the brain to more visible responses, such as yawns or intelligence, expose how the brain works with these facts.

Oxygen. Your brain uses 20 percent of the total oxygen in your body.

Blood. As with oxygen, your brain uses 20 percent of the blood circulating in your body.

Unconsciousness. If your brain loses blood for 8 to 10 seconds, you will lose consciousness.

Speed. Information can be processed as slowly as 0.5 meters/sec or as fast as 120 meters/sec (about 268 miles/hr.).

Wattage. While awake, your brain generates between 10 and 23 watts of power–or enough energy to power a light bulb.

Yawns. It is thought that a yawn works to send more oxygen to the brain, therefore working to cool it down and wake it up.

Neo cortex. The neo cortex makes up about 76 percent of the human brain and is responsible for language and consciousness. The human neo cortex is much larger than in animals.

10 percent. The old adage of humans only using 10 percent of their brain is not true. Every part of the brain has a known function.

Brain death. The brain can live for 4 to 6 minutes without oxygen, and then it begins to die. No oxygen for 5 to 10 minutes will result in permanent brain damage.

Highest temperature. The next time you get a fever, keep in mind that the highest human body temperature ever recorded was 115.7 degrees–and the man survived.

Stress. Excessive stress has shown to alter brain cells, brain structure, and brain function.

Love hormones and autism. Oxytocin, one of the hormones responsible for triggering feelings of love in the brain, has shown some benefits in helping control repetitive behaviors in those with autism.

Food and intelligence. A study of one million students in New York showed that students who ate lunches that did not include artificial flavors, preservatives, and dyes did 14 percent better on IQ tests than students who ate lunches with these additives.

Seafood. In the March 2003 edition of Discover magazine, a report describes how people in a 7-year study who ate seafood at least one time every week had a 30 percent lower occurrence of dementia.

Psychology of the Brain. From tickling to tasting to decision-making, find out how the brain affects what you experience.

Tickles. You can't tickle yourself because your brain distinguishes between unexpected external touch and your own touch.

Imaginary playmates. A study from Australia showed that children with imaginary playmates between the ages of 3 and 9 tended to be first-born children.

Reading faces. Without any words, you may be able to determine if someone is in a good mood, is feeling sad, or is angry, just by reading the face. A small area in the brain called the amygdala is responsible for your ability to read someone else's face for clues to how they are feeling.

Ringing in the ears. For years, medical professionals believed that tinnitus was due to a function within the mechanics of the ear, but newer evidence shows that it is actually a function of the brain.

Pain and gender. Scientists have discovered that men and women's brains react differently to pain, which explains why they may perceive or discuss pain differently.

Supertasters. There is a class of people known as supertasters who not only have more taste buds on the tongue, but whose brain is more sensitive to the tastes of foods and drinks. In fact, they can detect some flavors that others cannot.

Cold. Some people are much more sensitive to cold and actually feel pain associated with cold. Research has shown that the reason is due to certain channels that send cold information to the brain.

Decision-making. Women tend to take longer to make a decision, but are more likely to stick with the decision, compared to men, who are more likely to change their mind after making a decision.

Exercise. Some studies indicate that while some people are naturally more active, others are naturally more inactive, which may explain why getting out and exercising is more difficult for some.

Boredom. Boredom is brought on by a lack of change of stimulation, is largely a function of perception, and is connected to the innate curiosity found in humans.

Physical illness. The connection between body and mind is a strong one. One estimate is that between 50-70 percent of visits to the doctor for physical ailments are attributed to psychological factors.

Sadness and shopping. Researchers have discovered that those experiencing the blues are more willing to spend more money in an attempt to alleviate their sadness.

Memory. Learn how scent, jet lag, and estrogen affect memory, plus plenty of other information, with these facts.

Jet lag. Frequent jet lag can impair your memory, probably due to the stress hormones released.

New connections. Every time you recall a memory or have a new thought, you are creating a new connection in your brain.

Create associations. Memory is formed by associations, so if you want help remembering things, create associations for yourself.

Scent and memory. Memories triggered by scent have a stronger emotional connection, therefore appear more intense than other memory triggers.

Anomia. Anomia is the technical word for tip-of-the-tongue syndrome when you can almost remember a word, but it just won't quite come to you.

Sleep. While you sleep at night may be the best time for your brain to consolidate all your memories from the day.

No sleep. It goes to follow...lack of sleep may actually hurt to create new memories.

World Champion. A world champion memorizer, Ben Pridmore memorized 96 historical events in 5 minutes and memorized a single, shuffled deck of cards in 26.28 seconds.

Estrogen and memory. Estrogen (found in both men and women) has been shown to promote better memory functions.

Insulin. Insulin works to regulate blood sugar in the body, but recently, scientists have discovered that its presence in the brain also helps promote memory.

Dreams and Sleep. The amazing world of dreams and what happens during sleep is a mystery rooted in the brain.

Everyone dreams. Just because you don't remember your dreams doesn't mean you don't dream. Everyone dreams!

Nightly average. Most people dream about 1-2 hours a night and have an average of 4-7 dreams each night.

Brain waves. Studies show that brain waves are more active while dreaming than when you are awake.

Lost dreams. Five minutes after a dream, half of the dream is forgotten. Ten minutes after a dream, over 90 percent is forgotten. Write down your dreams immediately if you want to remember them.

Blind people dream. Dreams are more than just visual images, and blind people do dream. Whether or not they dream in pictures depends on if they were born blind or lost their vision later.

Color or B&W. Some people (about 12 percent) dream only in black and white while others dream in color.

Virtually paralyzed. While you sleep, your body produces a hormone that may prevent you from acting out your dreams, leaving you virtually paralyzed.

Snoring. If you are snoring, you are not dreaming.

During a dream. If you are awakened during a dream, you are much more likely to remember the dream than if you slept until a full night's sleep.

Symbolism. As those who invest in dream dictionaries can attest, dreams almost never represent what they actually are. The unconscious mind strives to make connections with concepts you will understand, so dreams are largely symbolic representations.

Adenosine. Caffeine works to block naturally occurring adenosine in the body, creating alertness. Scientists have recently discovered this connection and learned that doing the opposite–boosting adenosine–can actually help promote more natural sleep patterns and help eliminate insomnia.

Dream showings. Japanese researchers have successfully developed a technology that can put thoughts on a screen and may soon be able to screen people's dreams.

Airplanes and headaches. A study showed a correlation between flying and headaches, and states that around 6 percent of people who fly get headaches brought on by the flight itself.

Juggling. Juggling has shown to change the brain in as little as seven days. The study indicates that learning new things helps the brain to change very quickly.

Disney and sleep. A study published in the journal Sleep Medicine describes how Disney creators used real sleep disorders in many of their animated pets.

Blinking. Each time we blink, our brain kicks in and keeps things illuminated so the whole world doesn't go dark each time we blink (about 20,000 times a day).

Laughing. Laughing at a joke is no simple task, as it requires activity in five different areas of the brain.

Yawns are contagious. Ever notice that you yawned after someone around you did? Scientists believe this may be a response to an ancient social behavior for communication that humans still have.

Brain Bank. Harvard maintains a Brain Bank where over 7,000 human brains are stored for research purposes.

Outer space. The lack of gravity in outer space affects the brain in several ways. Scientists are studying how and why, but you may want to hold off on your next trip to the moon.

Music. Music lessons have shown to considerably boost brain organization and ability in both children and adults.

Thoughts. The average number of thoughts that humans are believed to experience each day is 70,000.

Ambidexterity. Those who are left-handed or ambidextrous have a corpus collosum (the part of the brain that bridges the two halves) that is about 11 percent larger than those who are right-handed.

Brain tissue has a consistency that is very similar to tofu.

Our brain can generate twenty-five watts of power at any given time. It could power a light bulb.

During pregnancy, a woman's brain will shrink. It will take up to six months to regain its size.

When we are born, our brain is about the size it is now. That is one reason why babies have such large heads relative to their body.

Our brain is more active when we are sleeping.

Information can go in between parts of our brain at a speed of two hundred sixty miles per hour.

We have over one hundred thousand miles of axons in our brain. They could wrap around the Earth four times. Axon is a long and single nerve-cell process that conducts impulse away from the cell body.

Our brain does not have pain receptors. It cannot feel anything. That is why brain surgeon can perform brain surgery on a conscious patient.

One can survive only having one side of one's brain.

There are more than one hundred thousand chemical reactions happening in our brain every second.

Our brain will continue to develop until we are in our late forties.

Every day we have about seventy thousand thoughts.

Experts estimate that over a lifetime, the modern human brain retains up to quadrillion pieces of information. We have more brain cells when we are two years old than we will have at any other point in our life.

Our brain accounts for 2 percent of our mass, but uses 25 percent of our oxygen and energy. The human brain is the greatest wonder of creation. This little organ weighs only 1,500 grams but contains billions of nerve cells. Each nerve cell is joined to others by hundreds of little offshoots, and the exchange of information between them is quicker than the telephone exchange of a busy capital city.

The number of telephone links in one brain exceeds the number of stars in a galaxy. It would be more than 1,000,000,000,000! No computer or telephone exchange is in a position to store and swap so much information in such a small space as that occupied by the human brain. Most people talk casually about their little grey cells without ever taking hold of what happens inside them.

While you are reading these words, your brain is carrying out a vast number of highly complex functions. You are turning the pages with the most delicate movement of your muscles. The muscles in your eyes are adjusting so that you can see with equally sharp clarity in changing light conditions. Your retina is picking out the letters on the paper and reducing them to tiny points, which the optic nerve sends on in the form of an impulse code to the visual center, where the words are reassembled into a new picture.

If our brain should be mechanically defined, why would anyone need to be mindful of his or her environment? They ought to automatically take place. Further, should we not take psychogenesis and other psychiatrically related fields, or analytical psychology as a mockery and futile, since they delve into the origin and development of mental functions, traits, and states that investigate patients from cognitive health, sound-mindedness, abilities and perspectives? Psychiatrists, psychologists, neurologists, and so forth, evaluate individuals mentally and assess abnormalities of the brain in identifying specific mental illness in search of a cure. Is the world of unseen, the word of telepathy, dreams, imagination, and so on, just illusions?

Quantum consciousness rather than quantum physics is what gives birth to all that we know, and the unknown. What we perceive as nebulous (not clear) consciousness is what manages the void, where the womb of nothingness has delivered all that we know and is potentiated with miracles to be discovered. Our brain is linked to cosmic energy, through which our mind and thought processes function.

We are the byproducts of an awakened, thought-oriented entity where no senseless, unintelligent matter can ever be produced. You might ask, if so, then everyone should uniformly carry the same level of intelligence and consciousness, and perhaps think the same, since it is fed from the same source via our brain. "I do not feel obliged to believe that the same God who has endowed us with senses, reason, and intelligent has intended us to forgo their use" (Galileo Galilei).

With learning new things, acquiring information and knowledge, brain plasticity becomes possible, which makes more neurons and intensifies the connection with other neurons as it fires up more synopsis, leading to higher IQ and intelligence, arriving at a higher cognitive ability, and often dynamic thinking, just like a cell phone or a radio transmitter, a TV or a satellite dish that is a tool and a means which enable us communicate, but then the actual signal is provided from elsewhere. An intelligent person with an alert mind is similar to advanced cell phones that should make a difference in sound resonance, diversity in overall functions, and clarity of hearing and conversation. To have an intelligent brain is like having an advance Apple iPhone, which can make better connection acting as a smart intermediary.

Graham Hancock said, "I don't believe that consciousness is generated by the brain. I believe that the brain is more of a receiver of consciousness."

CONSCIOUSNESS

How would you define consciousness? What precisely is consciousness? One can become aware of something because of one's consciousness. Consciousness is the essence of existence that allows you to have an experience. Without consciousness, we cannot participate in anything personally at all. As birth is an experience, life, near death, and everything that is ever known to man is an experience, which if we lack consciousness, no experience is ever possible.

Crawling, walking, running, and exercising, are experiences. Falling in love, making love, liking, getting hungry, and becoming thirsty are all experiences. Learning a new language, hearing, listening, and talking to someone is an experience. Singing and having an accident are all experiences. Cleaning your room, yawning, napping, listening to music, fighting, making peace, making friends, giving birth, becoming sick, catching cold, worrying, feeling melancholy, dreaming, fear, depression, happiness, sadness, and so on, are all experiences.

The bottom line is, our lives are the sum total of our experiences. With the absence of memory and consciousness, no living and no experience is ever possible, since consciousness is the very foundation and the actual basis for having to experience anything. Consciousness and experience are a two-sided coin. Thus, without consciousness, experience cannot exist. We would have no intelligence, no mind, no memory, no thoughts, no emotions, no dreams and imagination, and no sensory perception of any kind.

Consciousness is absolutely crucial and extremely provisional for our existence, which, as intangible as it is, without it, we cannot truly live even in millionth of second. Yet there are those naïve souls that still emphasize the superiority of matter, and ignore the utter validity of energy-driven consciousness over matter-based agendas. Consciousness is cosmic; it is the source that does not change but miraculously feeds infinite variance phenomenon.

What electricity is to millions of lamps with various shapes and sizes, consciousness is to our diverse experiences that are enormously mutable. Consciousness is never interrupted; there is never a gap in consciousness. It is always there. Even when sleeping we can remember our dreams after we wake up, which signifies no gap in consciousness. Perhaps a bit of experimental memory lapse, but no interruption in consciousness, prevalence, continuity, and without change. The same is true with expanded consciousness. Consciousness is an infinite source. It is beyond what enlargement means to human beings.

It is our mind that can advance, and perhaps become more intelligent, wiser, because of the expansion in experience. Neurons, nerve cells, or brain cells are the fundamental component of the nervous system in general and the brain in particular. A neuron is an electrically charged cell that develops and offloads information by electrochemical signaling.

Neurons are not like other cells. They neither die off to be replaced by new ones, nor divide, and they can't normally be replaced after being lost, although there are a few exceptions. It is noteworthy to know that because our brain is malleable, our mind can be expanded and further grow intelligently. The average human brain has about 100 billion neurons (or nerve cells) and many more neuroglia (or glial cells) that serve to protect and support the neurons.

Behind every great mind lays a super energy-driven brain with dynamic features, just like a highly advanced satellite and up-to-date Apple cell phones that are utilized as they brilliantly communicate as the brain identifies and grasps cosmic energy and renders thoughts that are also energy driven to make sense of our world.

If our brain was anything less than an energy-based entity, it could not recognize and identify with an energy driven cosmic, the higher memory capacity, the higher terabytes where more neurons firing means higher intelligence with raised IQ. It is imperative to know that consciousness is not limited to any boundaries. It is not confined. It is boundless in its nature, and contrary to space, it has no outer edge. The vibrating frequencies of our mind to comprehend are limited, which are not the limits of consciousness.

Further, no scientist has ever located consciousness anywhere within the brain, which has incited them to believe consciousness as an epiphenomenon (spin-off, by-product) of existence. Logic dictates that what is boundless is everywhere; it is not contained within any perimeter to be found in a specific place.

It is natural to think that we have an apart consciousness because of individual experiences. We are under the impression that consciousness is located in our brain, or someplace within our nervous system which the body carries everywhere we go. Believing that consciousness is generated by the human brain is delusional, and as egotistical and anthropocentric (human-centered) as it can be. This paradigm shift is to know that consciousness is not within us; we are within the consciousness.

The point should gravitate towards knowing that everything thing is utterly energy-driven, constructively managed and disciplined to produce goodness. And because we are also an undeniable part of nature with a conscience, we need to identify with virtues and positive energy to constructively generate moral excellence. Other than that, our efforts will be repudiated and eventually haunt us for worse; since doing right is structured within the entire universe and not excluding human beings. The essence of living is to do right, and believe that without good conscience, no good experience can ever be possible. We are not exempt from the infinitely creative and immensely resourceful nature, and we need to properly converge and run along the same lines.

Many scientists see nature as aimless, where evolution is objectified with no purpose. This should mean no beginning or an end, making it a hypocritical (charade, farce) thought, and far from reason. They simply choose not to see the reality of matter, the reality of motion and time which are intertwined, and one cannot exist without the other. Evolution means a gradual moving forward, and any evolutionary motion must convey purpose. What I mean is: wherever there is matter, exists motion, and where there is motion, exists time, and where there are motion and time, there must be purpose.

There are many controversial subjects dealing with the context of God and science. Inquiring minds want to delve into knowing if matter and science are the root cause of all there is, or is it God that is sovereign and in control. And there are millions, if not billions, of pious and curious characters that postulate (hypothesis, suppose, assume, posit) and ruminate (to think deeply, to ponder) trying to reach positive gain in discerning the reality of life deemed to our Creator, or perhaps atheists interested in knowing if matter and science are the anchor to everything.

And those who fanatically believe in grotesque (unheard-of, bizarre) concepts referencing life and existence without inference, they are depleted of any puissant (powerful) and convincing arguments. Either way, there is no doubt that science or technology has transferred humanity from the clenches of ignorance and has protected us from dark ages and inquisition-like atmosphere to modern times.

Our safety and security has tremendously been improved and positively shifted. We have progressed gradually but surely to an advanced era where miracle-like discoveries are employed and give humanity encouragement and impetus to conquer what seems to be the impossible, and to hope for the best which is yet to come in contemporary times.

Science and technology have made it literally practical to access brilliant ways of communication via the internet, Twitter, Facebook, Skype, blogging, cell phones, fax, satellites, and many other advanced intermediaries and digital entities. They have immensely affected and played a catalyst in positively shaping our life, and have made it possible to know the world in dynamic ways, where decisive changes take place and resonate where most applicable. Technology has made our life easier and more productive and promising.

There is no doubt that science has mitigated trepidation (fear, dreadfulness) and human superstition from the unknown. And also through which the mastery to our planet is appreciated and still propelling. With that said, we should not give all the credit to such tasks as science, no matter how advanced we are in our scientific endeavors or with having cutting edge technology in producing creative products available to us. "The more I study science the more I believe in God" (Albert Einstein).

And yet, science cannot tell us why we should be good. Science cannot tell us who are we, and where we came from, and why we are here, or where are we headed. Is existence real? Why did life come about? What is the meaning of life? Is self-awareness and knowing of the world around us real? Or does everything just happen in our brain and our reality is just an illusion?

And what is consciousness? Where does our consciousness and awareness come from? And is there life after death? How and why do we experience things, and why intelligence? Furthermore, why can't the most scholarly and scientific-minded of all times even collectively simulate a human brain having the same characteristic and attributes? Scientists awaken us to the uncharted territories and possibilities, like if we did not have to die, perhaps live up to an average age of three to four hundred years, or to experience parallel universes, and so forth.

To manifest a much more innovative brain, which has already led us from the hunter and gatherer environment to present position, where conquering other planets is the norm, neuroscientists tell us no region of the brain works in separation from other parts of brain, as they all work in concert and in interconnectivity with each other.

They state that our senses of seeing, sound, smell, taste, touch turn into electrical signals and then are directed to our brain, and our brain makes meaning out of those incoming electro signals. They continue to express at the beginning the signals are unintelligent, but our brain figures out a way to decode encrypted signals, making sense of them.

Mr. David Engleman, a contemporary neuroscientist, disclosed an exciting view, saying, "A new chapter in our life might be at the horizon where our brain flexibility can perhaps change our physical body. And that advanced robotic could very much influence our neurotic brain. Where technology can enhance our body through human fragility to human indestructibility."

Mr. David Engelman also elaborated on how the scientist can use liquid nitrogen to preserve people's brains, giving them a chance at life again after they die. This is a monumental leap of faith, where jaw-dropping endeavors can boldly claim beyond belief criterion like storing one's unique pathways and links to store memories. Every brain that stores a lifetime of wisdom information and experience is preserved, an option that scientists are trying to make sense of.

In a nutshell, what they are saying is, our mighty brain has the potential to make sense of the complicated stuff, where transparency of millions of signals sent to it become immediately clear and understood, which in return are made applicable to command our body to execute them in an orderly manner.

This gives rise to the idea that we can perhaps try to program the brain through biorobotic engineering and computer-like simulation, where extraordinary tasks can be sent to our brain via electrochemical signals, which at first might seem vague and unintelligent to our brain, but it will soon decipher and decode any related message received, enabling us to conquer the next phase of human revolutionary endeavors. If so, it can land us in unimaginable places that presently seem and sound just like fiction, not reality.

There is a saying that if you cannot take the horse to the water, then take the water to the horse. Scientists are trying to externally influence the brain through biorobotics to access the other 90 percent of human brain that is not activated, which might supposedly be manifested in a distanced time. And since it is commonly believed that we are currently using only 7 to 10 percent of our brain, then obviously there should be 90 percent availability left to become exploited and explored into uncharted territories, completely unknown to man, expediting to opening up the brain's potentiality for the comfort and progress of humanity—I hope.

Mr. Engelman narrated, "If we can make a digital view of the brain, then we can run software on brain creating simulation on what the brain can do. This will be a colossal step in exploring some of the incredible potentiality of human brain in uncharted areas.

Pavel Osten and Troy Margrie, on mapping brain with a light microscope, wrote:

The beginning of the 21st century has seen a renaissance in light microscopy and anatomical tract tracing that together are rapidly advancing our understanding of the form and function of neuronal circuits. The introduction of instruments for automated imaging of whole mouse brains, new cell type–specific and trans-synaptic tracers, and computational methods for handling the whole-brain data sets has opened the door to neuroanatomical studies at an unprecedented scale.

We present an overview of the present state and future opportunities in charting long-range and local connectivity in the entire mouse brain and in linking brain circuits to function. Neuro scientist are trying to map out the entire brain circuitry and wiring that is to underpin all and the total work of the brain, with its memory, information and experiences, by magnifying each part of the human brain one hundred times or more. Scientists say a super organism is created when each segment of the brain works in concert as a complex colony.

Like the ants and the bees do, since an ant or a bee cannot serve its purpose if left alone, unless are able to work collectively and within the entire net-work, and with the whole system, and since a single bee or a single ant is lost, going in a circle, while a colony of ants or bees works just fine in reaching their objective. It is now certain that consciousness has to do with integrated circuitry and activity of the entire brain, and not to single out singular cell behavior.

The challenges that Mr. Engelman pointed out were: can we become a non-biological being where we can be digitally uploaded to the unthinkable, like living in a restructure of the past, or to practically make sense of parallel universes, or even stop death and dying, or simulating anything we wish to occur? Perhaps analogous to the fictional genie in the bottle, which if freed from the limited environment of the capped bottle, then even the entire world is not a limit.

Where the interconnectivity of our mind, our physical body, and the become, no simulation leveraged by bio robotics, or other automation reassembly can ever create human conscious, emotion and feeling in its authenticated form as we can experience as actual human beings. So you're made of detritus (pieces left from exploded stars); get over it. Or better yet, celebrate it. After all, what nobler thought can one cherish than that the universe lives within us all? Rene Descartes said it more plausibly when he stated, "How can we even know what we are experiencing is the reality."

CONSCIOUSNESS AND THE EMPTINESS

A mind can perhaps live in a computer machine, where mechanically it makes it possible to do gargantuan tasks, making the artificial intelligence possible beyond our dreams, where it can solve enigmatical issues and dynamically resolve beyond-belief problems, but not to ever be trusted in manifesting a truly innate human fulfilment. Our sense of consciousness and spirit is an extraordinary concept that cannot be simulated no matter how far we go in exploring our brain, since our brain is matter and a medium that links our energy-oriented mind to the cosmos.

With all of that said, the question again that will rise to surface is: who is this shadowy observer inside each and every one of us that thinks, feels, sees, hears, tastes, smells, is curious, has emotion and will with memory, can choose; imagine, desire, and hope, has intuition and is creative, has conscious with a subliminal entity working below the threshold of one's consciousness—but cannot be found with even the most sophisticated and scientifically advanced instruments.

And no matter how deeply and thoroughly we search into the tiniest of cells, neurons, or any other biological network, we cannot find anyone there. The question that remains is, are we not real? Are we all hallucinating or imagining things? Can illusion experience a real world, or is our world also an illusion? Or are we perhaps under some kind of spell that is meant to condemn us in not understanding more than what we are supposed to? If not, who is this ghostly observer within us that self-inspects without being detected and is not identified?

Tezin Gyatso, His Holiness the fourteenth Dalai Lama, explains,

We all have a valid, proper sense of self, or "I," but then we additionally have a misconception of that "I" as inherently existing. Under the sway of this delusion, we view the self as existing under its own power, established by way of its own nature, able to set itself up.

However, if there were such a separate I—self-established and existing in its own right—it should become clearer and clearer under the light of competent analysis as to whether it exists as either mind or body, or the collection of mind and body, or different from mind and body. In fact, the closer you look, the more it is not found. This turns out to be the case for everything, for all phenomena.

The fact that you cannot find them means that those phenomena do not exist under their own power; they are not self-established."

His holiness carries to say on the subject of emptiness and existence,

A consciousness that conceives of inherent existence does not have a valid foundation. A wise consciousness, grounded in reality, understands that living beings and other phenomena—minds, bodies, buildings, and so forth—do not inherently exist. This is the wisdom of emptiness.

Understanding reality exactly opposite to the misconception of inherent existence, wisdom gradually overcomes ignorance.

Remove the ignorance that misconceives phenomena to inherently exist and you prevent the generation of afflictive emotions like lust and hatred. Thus, in turn, suffering can also be removed. In addition, the wisdom of emptiness must be accompanied by a motivation of deep concern for others (and by the compassionate deeds it inspires) before it can remove the obstructions to omniscience, which are the predispositions for the false appearance of phenomena—even to sense consciousness—as if they inherently exist.

Therefore, full spiritual practice calls for cultivating wisdom in conjunction with great compassion and the intention to become enlightened, in which others are valued more than yourself. And further on the subjects of no self, emptiness, and if objects exist, His Holiness says,

Selflessness,

Both Buddhists and non-Buddhists practice meditation to achieve pleasure and get rid of pain, and in both Buddhist and non-Buddhist systems the self is a central object of scrutiny. Certain non-Buddhists who accept rebirth accept the transitory nature of mind and body, but they believe in a self that is permanent, changeless and unitary. Although Buddhist schools accept rebirth, they hold that there is no such solid self. For Buddhists, the main topic of the training in wisdom is emptiness, or selflessness, which means the absence of a permanent, unitary and independent self or, more subtly, the absence of inherent existence either in living beings or in other phenomena.

The Two Truths

To understand selflessness, you need to understand that everything that exists is contained in two groups called the two truths: conventional and ultimate. The phenomena that we see and observe around us can go from good to bad, or bad to good, depending on various causes and conditions. Many phenomena cannot be said to be inherently good or bad; they are better or worse, tall or short, beautiful or ugly, only by comparison, not by way of their own nature. Their value is relative.

From this you can see that there is a discrepancy between the way things appear and how they actually are. For instance, something may—in terms of how it appears—look good, but, due to its inner nature being different, it can turn bad once it is affected by conditions. Food that looks so good in a restaurant may not sit so well in your stomach. This is a clear sign of a discrepancy between appearance and reality.

These phenomena themselves are called conventional truths: they are known by consciousness that goes no further than appearances. But the same objects have an inner mode of being, called an ultimate truth that allows for the changes brought about by conditions. A wise consciousness, not satisfied with mere appearances, analyzes to find whether objects inherently exist as they seem to do but discovers their absence of inherent existence. It finds an emptiness of inherent existence beyond appearances.

Empty of What? by His Holiness Tezin Gyatso

Emptiness, or selflessness, can only be understood if we first identify that of which phenomena are empty. Without understanding what is negated, you cannot understand its absence, emptiness.

You might think that emptiness means nothingness, but it does not. Merely from reading it is difficult to identify and understand the object of negation, what Buddhist texts speak of as true establishment or inherent existence. But over a period of time, when you add your own investigations to the reading, the faultiness of our usual way of seeing things will become clearer and clearer.

Buddha said many times that because all phenomena are dependently arisen, they are relative—their existence depends on other causes and conditions and depends on their own parts. A wooden table, for instance, does not exist independently; rather, it depends on a great many causes such as a tree, the carpenter who makes it, and so forth; it also depends upon its own parts. If a wooden table or any phenomenon really were not dependent—if it were established in its own right—then when you analyze it, its existence in its own right should become more obvious, but it does not.

This Buddhist reasoning is supported by science. Physicists today keep discovering finer and finer components of matter, yet they still cannot understand its ultimate nature. Understanding emptiness is even deeper. The more you look into how an ignorant consciousness conceives phenomena to exist, the more you find that phenomena do not exist that way. However, the more you look into what a wise consciousness understands, the more you gain affirmation in the absence of inherent existence.

Do Objects Exist?

We have established that when any phenomenon is sought through analysis, it cannot be found. So you may be wondering whether these phenomena exist at all. However, we know from direct experience that people and things cause pleasure and pain, and they can help and harm. Therefore, phenomena certainly do exist; the question is how? They do not exist in their own right, but only have an existence dependent upon many factors, including a consciousness that conceptualizes them. Once they exist but do not exist on their own, they necessarily exist in dependence upon conceptualization.

However, when phenomena appear to us, they do not at all appear as if they exist this way. Rather, they seem to be established in their own right, from the object's side, without depending upon a conceptualizing consciousness.

When training to develop wisdom, you are seeking through analysis to find the inherent existence of whatever object you are considering—yourself, another person, your body, your mind, or anything else. You are analyzing not the mere appearance but the inherent nature of the object. Thus it is not that you come to understand that the object does not exist; rather, you find that its inherent existence is unfounded. Analysis does not contradict the mere existence of the object. Phenomena do indeed exist, but not in the way we think they do. What is left after analysis is a dependently existent phenomenon. When, for example, you examine your own body, its inherent existence is negated, but what is left is a body dependent on four limbs, a trunk, and a head.

If Phenomena Are Empty, Can They Function?

Whenever we think about objects, do we mistakenly believe that they exist in their own right? No. We can conceive of phenomena in three different ways. Let us consider a tree. There is no denying that it appears to inherently exist, but: We could conceive of the tree as existing inherently, in its own right.

We could conceive of the tree as lacking inherent existence. We could conceive of the tree without thinking that it inherently exists or not. Why is science mute about many things of great concern, like the big bang, and why there was transformation of inanimate matter to animated matter? And why changes from plants to beasts, and eventually to the human animal. And as science states: The big bang explosion took place in a millennium of a second. If so, such an explosion must have made absolute destruction, rather than making a very intricate and orderly life such as ours possible.

And where in the world have you ever heard, or seen, that an unintelligent, lifeless substance, a spiritless matter of any kind, can give birth to such bright, skillful, and vivacious life like ours? With thousands of other sensible questions pending, science cannot come close to answering.

It should make one puzzled when a leading scientist like Mr. Steven Hawking addresses such important issues as time and believes the big bang and time originated simultaneously, and somehow the big bang gave birth to time, forgetting that leading physicists and scholarly minded scientists also adamantly believe that where there is matter, there is motion, where there is motion, there is space, and wherever there is space, there is time. And is it not fair to say evolution must have encompassed everything, including the big bang?

And because evolution occurs gradually within things, moving them to alter from simplest to more complex beings, then, if so, shouldn't we assess and conclude that time must have existed before the big bang, since the big bang also must be relevant to the gradual accumulation of matter, in which it must have reached its limit and apex before the big explosion?

You might say, even evolution started at the same time as the big bang. But then, to probe and follow reason with a sensible mind, shouldn't we agree on the accumulation and the gradual buildup of matter, like lava, which eventually became unimaginably hot that should have caused the big bang? I am sure no reliable scientist would attest to the big bang happening out of nowhere with the "abracadabra" incantation.

Either way, we need to know matter must have existed before the big bang, innately with motion and naturally driven with time. What does it take to convince humanity that there is an absolute power with unimaginable influence and order ruling everything there is and all of which there will ever be? And unless we believe in this literal ultimate power other than ours, in which human conduct and a moral compass should be directed to and evaluated with, we will be perplexed and ought to run into mental and spiritual confusion and into the unknown, where trouble is to perceive us.

Therefore, we should not behave maledicted (to speak evil), and not be spurred into behaving malevolently, but explore benediction (blessing, benevolence) and seek authenticity in our character when referencing the almighty Creator; and to convey honesty and goodness in our heart towards mankind with no prejudice or ill will.

Knowing that even the best of man's behavior is relative, no matter how righteous, we are bound to make mistakes, as we cannot be perfect by nature.

Hence, the omniscient and omnipresent God is the absolute power, which makes it possible for our relative and sometimes convoluted (twisted) mind to seek clear-sightedness, and through which we should be alerted with our behaviors. Believe in the world of the unseen, as you should reckon that it is the world that makes the world we experience possible. Behold in "what goes around, comes around." The problem starts when people cannot connect their wrongdoings with later punishment they receive in life. You might claim there are those who do wrong with no ill consequences. But that cannot be any further from the truth, since no one is in anybody's heart to truly know what pain and suffering they are wretchedly entangled with.

In reference to the world of the unseen, I should mention the world of planets, entire stellar system, galaxies, the universe, the world of the atom, photon, protons, neutrons, electrons, quarks, lepton, and the world of Higgs, and Higgs bosons, Higgs field, the world of wave links and frequencies, the world of the entire energy field. The world of quantum, the world of string theory and other subatomic particles, the world of electromagnetic forces, strong and weak atomic forces, the forces of gravity, the world on parallel but unseen universes, and so on.

I am sure there are many other unseen forces to be discovered in the near future by talented and curious-minded people. This should tell us it is definitely not all about what we are able to discern with our limited senses, but should very much be about the invisible world we cannot see. Deepak Chopra said, "Observation is made in conscious (awareness), theories are conceived in consciousness (awareness), science cannot explain consciousness, but consciousness can conceive and construct the scientific method, science itself is the off-spring and the product of consciousness."

It is important to see the role of consciousness in an UNseen world that makes our reality possible and expresses the visible world through our senses so that we can experience real living. Persian poet Jalal Adin Rumi, in the book I Have Passed Beyond all Thoughts by Craig Person, is quoted as saying,

Normally our minds are continuously stirred by perceptions, thoughts, and feelings, much as the ocean is constantly swept into waves by winds and currents.

This mental activity obscures the mind's true nature. But like an ocean the mind can settle down. It can become calm, quiet, and silent, while remaining awake. When it does, one experiences the mind's essential reality—unbounded pure consciousness. This inner field lies beyond thought and feeling, even beyond space and time.

Essentially, it takes open-mindedness and awareness to relate to delicate and complex matters, where events maneuver in the microscopic realm and beyond our senses to adapt to these magnificent happenings. Consciousness is a matrix that acts on a different level, but evidently is the operator of the unseen world and what it holds as intrinsic value and the essence of every phenomenon that the external and the extrinsic world experiences, including humans and what they relate to.

There is consciousness in everything, but different entities express consciousness differently. Of course, animals cannot relate to consciousness and direct it as we do, since consciousness is implanted in humans much deeper than in animals and plants, and is much more subjective to the human mind and spirit.

The world we recognize is generated in our mind through consciousness utilizing our brain. Cosmic conscious holds infinite potential that engulfs material phenomenon, which makes the world of matter secondary in cosmic existence. When we see the color green it is consciousness working through our senses and simultaneously with our nervous system to make the color green relevant to our eyes and visionary system.

We can see the color green as light reflect off the retina, which is defined by the dictionary as "the sensory membrane that lines the eye, is composed of several layers including one containing the rods and cones, and functions as the immediate instrument of vision by receiving the image formed by the lens and converting it into chemical and nervous signal which reach the brain by way of optic nerve." Evidently, a bundle of nerves goes to the back of our brain, known as the occipital lobe. The occipital lobe is the back part of the brain that is involved with vision, to make us see the color green.

Most of us see the color red the same, the color green the same, the color blue and white the same, and so forth, despite our retina or group of nerves involved and our brain not being exactly similar. It is the cosmic conscious imprinting on our brain to make these realities the same. Now imagine if we would all see colors and other objects differently; it would be a world so chaotic and impractical beyond anyone's imagination. If so, how would anyone be able to identify a thief, a murderer, a rapist, or anything at all, since witnesses would all give a much different description of the culprit, one seeing black, one seeing white, and the other seeing burgundy, or perhaps short, tall, fat, or skinny? This is also true with any other object.

And by the way, have you ever paid attention to the trillions and trillions of deletions done on your computers, cell phones, and other digital gadgets and electronic equipment? This is perhaps done every minute by billions of users, and have you asked yourself, where do these cleanups and expunging's go?

In 1927, many prominent physicists, including Albert Einstein, Bohr, Marie Curie, Schrodinger, Marconi, Werner Heisenberg, and others, gathered in Brussels, Belgium, to discuss consciousness and atomic war.

Albert Einstein was approached by the others, and was told that the mind of the researchers was affecting the conclusions of their experimental work, where it seems that the observer and the observed are in the same loop. The presence of the observer eventually destroys the information; disabling the researcher to substantiate any reliability in results while testing for consciousness.

Einstein could not believe that, since he thought this would violate all the scientific knowledge on mathematical models and behaviors. Later on he acknowledged and referenced this, saying, "Anyone who became seriously involved in the pursuit of science becomes convinced that there is a spirit making evidence in the laws of our universe much greater and undeniably superior than that of man." Max Plank, the father of quantum physics, also said, "All matters originated and existed only by the virtues of a force which we must assume behind this force there is an intelligent and conscious mind, this mind is the matrix of all matters … Science cannot explain consciousness, because the presence of the observer interfered with the result of every experience he is doing, since the observer happens to be part of the same loop; he would cause the collapse of the wave function, making a chaotic effect on the situation."

He defined the wave function in the mathematical structure as, "The waviness of the probabilities of events at quantum level." They all believed that the language of quantum communication is how the universe communicates through wave links with frequencies beyond what we can practically and visibly participate in, and via subatomic particles. They concluded that spirit is not a force like an electromagnetic force, or the strong and weak atomic forces, or the force of gravity. They believed spirit is consciousness.

They agreed collectively that consciousness was too potent, and if it ever got a chance to be fully administered and exercised, it could surely one day enter staller civilization and perhaps communicate with parallel universes. It is believed that our bio-consciousness has the ability to transfer information and communicate with the spirit of the universe. And since our collective consciousness can significantly influence our life for the better, if ever given a chance, we ought to act keenly to what science believes in. Scientists tell us that atoms are particles, and particles are waves, and waves are possibilities, where these possibilities exist in nothingness. Henceforth, nothingness should mean everything, including cosmic energy and awakened consciousness. In another words, nothingness is the potential for experiencing awareness and becoming conscious of the consciousness, which is the nervous system of our existence. Heisenberg said, "What we observe is not nature itself, but nature exposed to our method of questioning."

I believe it is the absolute and the omnipotent Creator that rules this whole being through the energy of consciousness. The good news is that humans are adamant they'll even further explore into the world of microcosms known as the "submicroscopic world." Prominent physicists and scientists tell us there are trillions of planets and galaxies, and billions and billions of universes beyond our imagination that should only comprise and count for .01 percent of what there is. The rest is dark energy and dark matter. They also say the universe is still expanding, since Hobble Edwin showed the distance galaxies are all moving away.

It should at least give us the clues, not to be cocky about the things we can understand, since there are an infinite number of things we still cannot fathom. Believe in the unseen almighty God, which could be the best self-defense ever known to man. And since we could not be far from being sadistic and mentally sick to truly claim believing in God and the heaven above, but still be wicket and cause evil. If one sincerely believes in God and can identify with our Creator of the heavens and the Earth, but still cause harm to others, then he or she should immediately seek treatment.

We need to understand that without holding high moral ground and prioritizing virtues in seeking compassionate thoughts and empathy, we will not reach tranquility in our life, and will be denied from having fidelity and trust with others. The gist of the matter should be about the energy that is prevalent in everyone and everything, not apart from the sanctified energy of the cosmos, which should not be abused. Every time we purposely and knowingly do wrong we are abusing the living sacred energy within, which is granted and empowered within us by the absolute power, the omniscient, and the omnipresent God. We are abusing our Creator.

Humanity is at a point where any demonic character can push a nuclear button and cause pandemonium and panic when rushing to judgment and being hasty with our decision to retaliate. They can desecrate life and leave our ashes behind. Many nations are now so advanced with their digital arsenals and diversified weaponry but they are not conscionable enough to scrutinize the consequences of their inhumane action.

Such frail behavior could release annihilation to whom it may concern and ensue the wrath of God on us, killing and destroying millions of innocent people without a morsel of regret on the culprit's part. But naïve and negligent enough not to comprehend when indicted because of one's wrongdoings by inescapable and justified laws of the universe and the heaven above, you are guilty as charged, and being easily acquitted won't be the case. In conclusion, I'd like to quote several prominent scientists and physicists referencing consciousness, our life and the universe.

Information is everything

In the final decades of his life, the question that intrigued Wheeler most was: "Are life and mind irrelevant to the structure of the universe, or are they central to it?" He suggested that the nature of reality was revealed by the bizarre laws of quantum mechanics. According to the quantum theory, before the observation is made, a subatomic particle exists in several states, called a superposition (or, as Wheeler called it, a "smoky dragon"). Once the particle is observed, it instantaneously collapses into a single position.

Wheeler suggested that reality is created by observers and that "no phenomenon is a real phenomenon until it is an observed phenomenon."

He coined the term "Participatory Anthropic Principle" (PAP) from the Greek anthropos, or human. He went further to suggest that "we are participants in bringing into being not only the near and here, but the far away and long ago" (Ref. Radio Interview with Martin Red fern).

This claim was considered rather outlandish until his thought experiment, known as the delayed-choice experiment, was tested in a laboratory in 1984. This experiment was a variation on the famous double-slit experiment, in which the dual nature of light was exposed (depending on how the experiment was measured and observed, the light behaved like a particle, a photon, or like a wave).

Unlike the original double-slit experiment, in Wheeler's version, the method of detection was changed AFTER a photon had passed the double slit. The experiment showed that the path of the photon was not fixed until the physicists made their measurements. The results of this experiment, as well as another conducted in 2007, proved what Wheeler had always suspected—observers' consciousness is required to bring the universe into existence. This means that a pre-life Earth would have existed in an undetermined state, and a pre-life universe could only exist retroactively.

A universe FINE-TUNED for life

These conclusions led many scientists to speculate that the universe is fine-tuned for life. This is how Wheeler's Princeton colleague, Robert Dicke, explained the existence of our universe:

"If you want an observer around, and if you want life, you need heavy elements. To make heavy elements out of hydrogen, you need thermonuclear combustion. To have thermonuclear combustion, you need a time of cooking in a star of several billion years. In order to stretch out several billion years in its time dimension, the universe, according to general relativity, must be several years across in its space dimensions. So why is the universe as big as it is? Because we are here!" (Cosmic Search Vol. 1 No. 4)

Stephen Hawking has also noted: "The laws of science, as we know them at present, seem to have been very finely adjusted to make possible the development of life." Fred Hoyle, in his book Intelligent Universe, compares "the chance of obtaining even a single functioning protein by a chance combination of amino acids to a star system full of blind men solving Rubik's Cube simultaneously."

Physicist Andrei Linde of Stanford University adds: "The universe and the observer exist as a pair. I cannot imagine a consistent theory of the universe that ignores consciousness" (Biocentrism: How Life and Consciousness are the Keys to Understanding the Universe)

Wheeler, always an optimist, believed that one day we would have a clear understanding of the origin of the universe. He had "a sense of faith that it can be done." "Faith," he wrote, "is the number one element. It isn't something that spreads itself uniformly. Faith is concentrated in few people at particular times and places. If you can involve young people in an atmosphere of hope and faith, then I think they'll figure out how to get the answer."

Conclusion

Wheeler died of pneumonia on April 13, 2008, at age 96. His whole life he searched for answers to philosophical questions about the origin of matter, the nature of information, and the universe. "We are no longer satisfied with insights into particles, or fields of force, or geometry, or even space and time," he wrote in 1981. "Today we demand of physics some understanding of existence itself" (The Voice of Genius: Conversations with Nobel Scientists and Other Luminaries)

Let's hope that young scientists will continue to be encouraged by these words and will push the boundaries of human imagination beyond its limits, and maybe even find the elusive final theory – a Theory of Everything.

Keep up your contiguity (nearness) with science, philosophy, and educate yourself, and be of benefit to eager minds to a point of sacrifice. Enlightenment needs to become an epidemic.

Words will push the boundaries of human imagination beyond its limits, and maybe even find the elusive final theory – a Theory of Everything.

BREEDING MERCENARIES' CULTURE / DARK MONEY

"All that is necessary for the triumph – of evil is that good men do nothing" mistakenly attributed to Edmund Burke.

Mercenaries are the most treacherous individuals known worldwide. They instigate demonic acts and work for mean-spirited people with a Mafia mentality. They know no boundaries in murdering people or assassinating the opposition, as they normally are experts in sabotage, espionage, and infiltration, disguise and deception. They kill and maim, and do the unthinkable without a conscience, just for the love of receiving a paycheck. Presently we have mercenaries in Africa, unemployed men throughout the Middle East, terrorists who are actually mercenaries as they ruthlessly slaughter innocents in the name of Allah (God) to obtain money for their own survival and the West's corporate armies hired for money.

The anonymity of so many evil-minded culprits behind hiring these assassins makes them immune to prosecution. They would become futile in their devilish conduct if they couldn't motivate others to do the work for them. They seduce and fund the hungry, accommodate the broken, the hopeless, the needy, and entice the hate fools and the greedy to accomplish their beastly and inhumane tasks. Mercenaries are the invisible hands of barbarism, and they do come in many shapes and forms. Other kinds of mercenaries are the lackeys of corporations. They come in the form of media, as they first bellow the bullhorn of propaganda, misleading the public, and softening the road for Godfathers of crime and their mischievous conduct in the name of profit. They accumulate more wealth fueled with spilled blood wherever they deem necessary. A new era of corporate exploiters and financial elites have so far managed to play as the neo-colonist to bribe and enslave high state officials, even presidents and prime ministers, to change the fate of less powerful nations for the worse with the stroke of a pen, often overpowering the majority vote of the citizens. Where people's democratically elected president is either assassinated or a coup-d'état is formed against them and they're removed from the office of presidency, dark money plays a huge role in their inhumane schemes.

They are anonymously powerful people behaving in anonymous ways to circumscribe the very laws that ensure our democracy, illegally shifting dark money (secret money) in campaign contributions to install who they want in public office. They are in cahoots with public officials who have sold people out. The concentrated financial influence of special interest in our politics is the elephant in the room of politics, when spending gargantuan amounts of money has blinded the public to not notice the problem our nation faces. The survival of American democracy is on the line if we choose not to act, since dark money lurks at the heart of our political crises.

History is loaded with conspiracies by government officials who colluded with powerful and the very influential people to change what people favored for the benefit of the few. Roman politicians paid mobs to riot on their behalf. It is extremely essential to understand the role of dark money in politics and its perennial (everlasting) menace to our democracy. Dark money is cash whose source is not known, and which is spent to alter political outcomes to favor the financial elites.

Dark money can be noticed as the underlying corruption from which our crises eventually arrive: the collapse of public trust in politics, the rise of demagogic anti-politics, losing faith in the system, assaults on the living world, public health and civic society. They clearly manifest that democracy is senseless without transparency. The tobacco industry, gun industry, fossil fuel, biotechnology, junk food companies, the pharmaceutical industry, petroleum industry, and so on, have influenced our democratic elections by contributing very large sums of money aimed at placing their favorite congressmen, senators, and even presidents into office. They manufacture false identities, bogus scientific controversies, and fake news, as the ultra-rich manipulate the media outlets and manage to buy the political systems with the help of their affiliated mercenaries and devoted goons.

"Total liberty for wolves is death to the lambs." — Isaiah Berlin

— Jane Mayer, Dark Money: The Hidden History of the Billionaires Behind the Rise of the Radical Right

Many believe that because of having the will to choose, and since we are able to think and make conscious decisions, then we should be immune to perils of bizarre conditioning and not so susceptible to being influenced and perforated by its ongoing lies and tricks that brainwashing conveys. But I am afraid that is not the case, as we are very vulnerable to the malicious conduct of brainwashing, and pay a heavy price for it, without even noticing its forcible inculcation: to instill or impress an idea on someone, so inculcation is the process of instilling or impressing ideas, beliefs.

The perpetrators' premeditated plans are subtly manufactured, as they carry no reliable information. They wittingly deliver fake news in bad faith as they hit consumers with humbugs to establish their morbid objectives. Corroborative (supporting, confirming) evidence is not quite easy to obtain, which is very sad and inhumane, and should remind us of tampering with mail, which is considered a federal offense.

They have convinced the populace to participate in their pernicious behavior and into augmenting their position. Media are immune to dissidence and meaningful complaints against them, by orchestrating people to get accustomed to junk information through hideous tactics, where false propaganda has become ill-intended and unfortunately the norm. Mass propaganda manipulates people's emotions and preys on citizens through demagoguery, which historically is proven to be more effective than reason, since it does efficiently move people towards the intended target and into accomplishing the culprit's wicked task, icing its forcible inculcation of belief (brainwashing) with lies and deception.

Joseph Pulitzer said, "A cynical, mercenary, demagogic press will in time produce a people as base as itself. They act profoundly undemocratic without the consent of people, as they implement covert missions with significant wrongdoings." And Henry A. Wallace said, "A fascist is one whose lust for money or power is combined with such an intensity of intolerance toward those of other races, parties, classes, religions, cultures, regions or nations as to make him ruthless in his use of deceit or violence to attain his ends."

We are faced with the worst kind of mercenaries: the religious mercenaries. For them, God is an excuse to reach their filthy objectives. Most are fake at heart and malignant in nature, since they behave hypocritically and aim at raping and murdering in the name of Allah (God). This should alert freedom-loving people to stay away from being dragged into the war of religion, because that is what they are after, the war of ideology, where doctrines of many denominations are to supposedly clash and eventually slaughter millions of innocents under the allegiance to and duty for one's faith.

These malefactors and the messengers of hate are ignorant enough not to realize humanity has reached the age of awakening, and will not be mouse-trapped into a medieval cultural of thinking and enslaved by their dirty schemes, since wise and conscionable people of the world are enlightened enough to side with democracy, liberty, and human rights and they will stand united to protect lives and the pursuit of happiness.

Without knowing who is who, so many live hypocritically. With boisterous living they exhibit a good front and behave meticulously in public, as they hide their growth negligence of God. They behave cryptically, and are estranged with morality and extinct from virtues. They forfeit the truth and arrogantly tell people what to think, and dictate to them how to behave in the name of God and goodness while they literally derail from what they profess and secretly incite ruinous and bizarre conduct. We need to look at the bigger picture, aimed at acting compassionately towards the entire humanity and not only for the faith-based group that we happen to belong to. We must insist on crumbling the walls of religious prejudice and racial hatred, and truly believe in one nation under God.

We are deliberately kept apart, living a sectarian lifestyle blinded with pride and self-centeredness. The potential for provocative and ill behaviors are constantly present so the preacher of resentments and disunity can live on manufactured vanity (narcissism), breeding a culture of ignorance and with people's financial support. Dalai Lama said, "There is no need for temples, no need for complicated philosophies. My brain and my heart are my temples; my philosophy is kindness." And Yehuda Berg wonderfully said it thus: "I do believe that the original sources of all religions should be taught, because with that we will find our similarities, not just our differences."

I believe that if Mohammed, Buddha, Jesus, and Moses all got together, they would be best of friends because the spiritual basis of all religions is something that builds unity. But that is not what the demons of our times ever consider and hope for. They don't want a better world, to make peace and unify under one God where sociocultural and socioeconomics would not and could not keep us so far apart. These mercenaries of evil disseminate fear and choke off the opposition, no matter how significant and justified the opposition are in their demand for a better life.

People should be aware of tyranny by the invisible hands of misfortune silently driven, presiding at the most vulnerable and heart-wrenching places. Media pipes in with rage and anger towards the target to win citizens' vote for the state and the corporations to break into all-out war with the less powerful nations, to devour people's natural resources, to confiscate their wealth, and all in the name of bringing freedom and democracy to them.

This bizarre and inhuman conduct is possible because indignant corporates are in cahoots with their cronies and puppets, as they confabulate (talk informally) in secret to mandate vicious plans against the innocents, as culprits' diabolical ideas affect millions for the worse—and apparently with no shame. The state and corporations implement sanctions, crippling trade embargos and militarism to decimate the designated prey, forcing displacement and homelessness and the exodus of natives from their homeland and into concentration camps. All aimed at annexing their resources for profiteering, making a deliberate mockery of democracy, character, virtues, and human rights.

this reminds us of colonialism phase two, strategized with devastating sanctions, modern weaponry, and complex tactical combat, where collateral damages include murdering innocent and godly people of faith. You might not believe in God, which you hypocritically claim and perhaps grasp in the privacy of your mind as not real, but fasten your seat belt, as you are to face a ride so tragic, with the curses of mishaps descending on you beyond anyone's imagination. The Almighty never misses his just and laser-precision punishing the perpetrator in the most unexpected places and times.

We ought to comprehend that "no leaf is to ever fall without the Almighty noticing it." One can perhaps be invincible and manage to hide one's hands from doing wrong, but rest assured, godly retribution in the name of Heaven and Earth is closer to you than the aorta of your neck. Common sense should foresee mitigated punishment from the Almighty if one is callow and sterile of intelligence and handicapped with no wisdom. But God help you when you knowingly cause such deliberate atrocities beyond belief.

Many tycoons and business biggies obnoxiously see themselves as the creators of affluence and consider other hardworking people—the real wealth-makers—as moochers. They do not realize that societies run by policing and capital punishment are those where fascism is constantly at work to chastise desperate people against their will and just demands for employment, food, and shelter. They keep people at their mercy, since they have expropriated all the resources and choose not to fix the root causes of the social and economic problems.

Corporate takeover by the elites has turned capitalist institutions into despotic regimes and plutocracies, where fair play and decent competition is denied and public welfare, humanism, and people's wellbeing is vilified. And because the inequality gap has sadly widened beyond belief, forgetting it is "we the people," as stated in the Constitution, that hold all the political power, not "we the corporations and the oligopolies." People delegate some of that power to the government of their choice to do their job in the name of God and the masses.

They have lost integrity in not keeping people's interest at heart. This should be the case before all hell breaks loose, and in the midst of panic and fear, some type of weird government will take over and endanger the essence of freedom and democracy that is the most sacrosanct entity known to man.

It is urgent that we wake up to access the core human values and become enlightened, where saving lives over profit is practiced. And to know when people's morale is lifted with the hope for a better future, it will motivate many to cooperate and attain vital agendas that everyone can identify with to accomplish them successfully and to reach their relative objectives. Entering into collective bargaining with decent conscience and in good faith, whether in our foreign policies or domestically, can benefit us all, and hence, everyone willing and able to work should not be denied such, thus becoming a productive member of society.

It is long overdue to call for redistribution of wealth and the need to lessen economic gaps so everyone can be sheltered with basic subsistence. Exercising genuine care for the needy should help to keep out hatred from our heart and perhaps shun belligerent encounters and crime-related tragedies where peace, safety, and tranquility of mind is restored. Holding onto 90 percent of resources by the few, while billions are fed dirt, and with no place to rest their head, is not freedom.

Freedom is only sacred when one's liberty does not infringe on others' sovereignty. Holding onto 90 percent of the resources by the few is declaring an economic war of aggression on humanity that is forfeiting people's right of existence and literally taking their freedom away. I believe this is even worse than conventional wars, since it causes gradual but sure destruction of a nation. Pope Francis said, "Human rights are not only violated by terrorism, repression or assassination, but also by unfair economic structures that creates huge inequalities." Pope Francis justly believes money should serve and not rule; so should any decent human being.

MIRACULOUSLY INTRIGUING PHENOMENA

Many wonders of the Milky Way universe and beyond are so enthralling, it strikes any inquisitive mind with awe. And yes, the ever present cosmic energy, or if you like, "quantum consciousness," as eternal as it seems to be, is influenced by our God, the infinite source of wisdom, with supernatural ability, flawlessly overseeing all there is and all that might ever exist. Bear in mind that mass energy as imperatively life-bearing it is not eternal. Scientists tell us it wears out, empowering reason to believe our mighty God is only eternal.

For instance, the Sun is 93,000,000 miles away from Earth, yet sunlight is our main source of energy. The sun is so fervent (flaming), the scorching heat at the core of our sun is 27,000,000 million degrees Fahrenheit. It gives more output energy in one second than mankind has generated since human existence.

The speed of light is 186,000 miles per second. If we travel at the speed of light going around the Earth, we can circle the Earth seven times per second. And remarkably enough, it will take 28 billion years or more to circle the universe at the speed of light. As the Bible tells us, God stretches out the heavens. It appears that the entire universe is stretching, as more than 100 billion galaxies, planets, nebula (groups of stars that are very far away), constellations, galaxies, cloud of gas or dust in space can sometimes be seen at night. And the stars in our universe are moving away from each other. Einstein shed light on some of the mysteries of our world with the well-known equation of E = mc2, where(E) is energy, (m) is mass or matter, and (c) is the speed of light. It is possible to turn mass into full-blown energy; if you expunge (annihilate) mass, it will produce energy, light, power, and sound, since there is incomprehensibly vast energy in all matter.

Bear in mind that even light and energy carry weight if scalable. Hence, one can convert mass into whole energy. It is fascinating to know that if the mass of an average-size tree could be changed into energy and possibly conserved, the power produced would be 45,000,000,000,000 KWH. Bear in mind that the USA yields 4,000,000,000,000 KWH of power annually. So if a single tree was converted into energy, and of course harnessed, the single tree would supply all of the USA with 10 years of electrical power.

The vast energy in a single grain of salt can electrically charge an entire household for several months. We are endowed with a universe potentiated with infinite energy. Some illuminating thoughts on the ingenuity of the design behind DNA, which contains a marvelous blueprint for all living things, where the intensity of information in a pinhead of DNA is nothing short of a miracle indeed. The amount of information conveyed in a pinhead volume of DNA will pile up books 500 times higher than from here on Earth to the moon.

DNA is very powerful information storage, written in codes as a linguistic system that can only come from an intelligent source. This denotes the impossibility of any matter-oriented entities giving rise to myriads of fascinating data, as matter is not insightfully driven to give imperative information. Scientists clearly know that DNA language can only be written in code by an intelligent source. DNA is three-dimensional molecules that are self-replicating and competent to make identical copies quickly and efficiently.

DNA are molecules that are self-correcting. There are special enzymes that can detect and correct replication errors on a minute-to-minute and second-to-second basis. The laws of information science say that information never originates by itself, it must come from an intelligent source. The information conveyed by DNA are transcendently enlightening, which should debunk any nomadic idea that an unintelligent matter devoid of any sense can create life.

Further insight on DNA molecules should convince anyone about the absurdity of the universe appearing by random chance. The DNA code informs; it programs a cell's behavior. All precepts, all advice, all instructions and plans come with volition and with having aims. Those who write teaching manuals do so with purpose. It should be enlightening to know that in every cell of our bodies there exists a very detailed instruction code, much like an infinitesimal (miniature) computer program. As you may be aware, a computer program is constructed of ones and zeros, like this: 110010101011000. The way they are arranged instructs the computer program what to do. The DNA code in each of our cells is very alike. It's made up of four chemicals that scholarly minded scientists abridge (shorten, abbreviate) as A, T, G, and C. These are suitably sequenced in the human cell like this: CGTGTGACTCGCTCCTGAT, and so on. There are three billion of these letters in every human cell!

As you can program your phone to alert you for specific reasons, DNA instructs the cell. DNA is a three-billion-lettered program telling the cell to comply in a certain way. It is a complete instruction manual. One needs to ask: how does this information program end up in each human cell? These are not just chemicals or formulas without intent, they are chemicals that instruct, coded in a very detailed way specifically how the person's body ought to develop.

Natural, biological, and physical reasons are absolutely lacking as an explanation when programmed information is involved. One simply wouldn't find instruction, exact information like this, without someone purposefully contriving (building) it.

Within each cell there is an area called the nucleus, which contains the all-important chromosomes. Chromosomes are microscopically small, rod-shaped structures that carry the genes. Within the chromosomes is an even smaller structure called DNA. This is the most important chemical substance in the human body—or in any other living thing. Increasing scientific revelation of DNA molecules has caused enormous problems for materialism.

DNA is a super-molecule that stores encrypted innate(hereditary) data. It coheres of two long tethers (cord) of chemical building blocks twined and put together. In humans, the strands of DNA are about two yards long, yet less than a trillionth of an inch in thickness.

In function, DNA is similar to a computer program on a floppy disk. It stores and relocates encoded information and tutelage. It is said that the DNA of a human being keeps enough facts and figures code to fill 1,000 books, each with 500 pages of tiny printed type. The DNA code generates a product much more complex than that of any computer. Surprisingly, this giant set of education fits comfortably within a single cell and routinely directs the formation of entire adult humans, initiating with just a single fertilized egg. Even the DNA of a bacterium is superbly complicated, which conveys at least three million units, all arranged in an extremely precise meaningful procession. The molecules that engulf DNA constitute an amazingly fabulous mechanism beyond belief - a truly microscopic prodigy (a miracle, marvel.)

The data is so tightly stored that the amount of DNA requisite (needful) to cipher (encode) the entire people living on planet earth would possibly fit into a space no bigger than an aspirin tablet!

Many scientists are persuaded that cells having such a complicated code and with such complex chemistry could never have come into existence by pure chance and with undirected chemistry. No matter how chemicals are vitiated (amalgamate, mix, blend), they do not engender DNA coils—or any intelligent code—at all. Only DNA propagate (multiply, spawn) DNA. Biology is the most powerful technology ever created. DNA is software, protein is hardware, cells are factories. Arvind Gupta

A couple of prominent scientists computed the aberrant (deviant, abnormal, odds) of life made by natural projection. They evaluated that there is less than 1 chance in 10 to the 40,000 power that life could have come from by disorderly trials. That's 10 to the 40,000 power, which is a 1 with 40,000 zeros after it! Why is natural selection not a random process? Evolution is not a random process. The innate variation on which natural selection acts may happen randomly, but natural selection by itself is not anarchic what so ever. The survival and procreation success of an individual is straightly connected to the ways its inherited traits behave in the context of its local environment.

Essentially Fodor & Piattelli-Palmarini are saying that "Darwin denies God as an agent but then gives Mother Nature all the qualities of God. That is, in a scientific book you might read on page 2 that God does not exist but then on page 5 you will see Mother Nature "choosing", "selecting", "deciding", "having wisdom", etc... It is simply a bait and switch,"

Life couldn't have had a random start. The problem is that there are about two thousand enzymes, and to fortuitously acquiring them all in a disorderly manner and disciplinary trial is solely one part in 10 to the 40,000power, an infinitely small possibility that could not be met even if the entire universe comported (tally, agreed, consist) of organic soup. If only one is not biased either by social acceptance or by a scientific training into the belief that life originated on the Earth. This simple math should convince any savvy individual, and utterly annihilates the idea of having no intelligent designer out of any judicious and decent court ruling.

Further, so many evolutionists act like they are irrelevant with the meaning of the word "selection." They keep saying "natural selection", which Selection according to any dictionary means (to pick, to choose, to select), if so, who is selecting, choosing by whom? Any sensible picking acquires intelligence, and intelligence demands savvy mind.

How can one gain some conception of the size of such a huge number? According to most Evolutionists, the universe is less than 30 billion years old—and there are fewer than 10 to the 18th power seconds in 30 billion years. So, even if nature could somehow have produced trillions of genetic code combinations every second for 30 billion years, the probabilities against producing the simplest one-celled animal by trial and error would still be inconceivably immense. In other words, probabilities greatly favor those that believe an intelligent designer was responsible for originating even the simplest DNA molecules.

Chemist Dr. Grebe notes, "That organic evolution could account for the complex forms of life in the past and the present has long since been abandoned by men who grasp the importance of the DNA genetic code."

Researcher and mathematician I. L Cohen adds, "At that moment, when the DNA/RNA system became understood, the debate between Evolutionists and Creationists should have come to a screeching halt. the implications of the DNA/RNA were obvious and clear. Mathematically speaking, based on probability concepts, there is no possibility that Evolution vs. the mechanism that created the approximately 6,000,000 species of plants and animals we recognize today."

Evolutionist Michael Denton stated, "The complexity of the simplest known type of cell is so great that it is impossible to accept that such an object could have been thrown together suddenly by some kind of freakish, vastly improbable, event. Such an occurrence would be indistinguishable from a miracle."

Famed researcher Sir Fred Hoyle is in agreement with Creationists on this point. He has reportedly said that supposing the first cell originated by chance is like believing a tornado sweeping through a junk yard might assemble a Boeing 747 from the materials therein.

It is important to note that the information written on DNA molecules is not produced by any known natural interaction of matter. Matter and molecules have no innate intelligence allowing self-organization into codes. There are no known physical laws that give molecules a natural tendency to arrange themselves into such coded structures. Like a computer disk, DNA has no intelligence. The complex, purposeful codes of this "master program" could have only originated outside itself. In the case of a computer program, the original codes were put there by an intelligent being, a programmer. Likewise, for DNA, it seems clear that intelligence must have come first, before the existence of DNA. Statistically, the odds are enormously in favor of that theory. DNA bears the marks of intelligent manufacture.

Dr. Wilder-Smith is an honored scientist who is certainly well-informed on modern biology and biochemistry. What is his considered opinion as to the source of the DNA codes found in each wondrous plant and animal? "An attempt to explain the formation of the genetic code from the chemical components of DNA. is comparable to the assumption that the text of a book originates from the paper molecules on which the sentences appear, and not from any external source of information. As a scientist, I am convinced that the pure chemistry of a cell is not enough to explain the workings of a cell, although the workings are chemical.

"The chemical workings of the cell are controlled by information which does not reside in the atoms and molecules of that cell. There is an author which transcends the material and the matter of which these strands are made. The author first of all conceived the information necessary to make a cell, then wrote it down, and then fixed it in a mechanism of reading it and realizing it in practice—so that the cell builds itself from the information."

One only need to look carefully at any living creature to gain some concept of their enormous complexity. If you have a pet, consider the complexities that must be involved—enabling that "package of matter" to move about, play, remember, show signs of affection, eat, and reproduce. If that is not enough to boggle your mind, imagine being given the task of constructing a similar living pet from carbon, calcium, hydrogen, oxygen, etc.—the animal's basic constituent parts.

If you have ever held a beloved pet in your hands, completely limp and dead, you may have some comprehension of the helplessness of even the most intelligent and sophisticated scientist when it comes to the overwhelming problem of trying to create life.

In contrast, the natural world does not have the advantages people bring to the problem. In nature, there are only matter, energy, time, chance, and the physical laws—no guiding force, no purpose, and no goal.

Yet, even with all of modern man's accumulated knowledge, advanced tools, and experience, we are still absolutely overwhelmed at the complexities. This is despite the fact that we are certainly not starting from absolute zero in this problem, for there are millions of actual living examples of life to scrutinize.

We all begin with a single cell, then grow to more than 100 trillion cells, as each cell is an incredibly complicated nano-chemical machinery, with thousands of variations, and beyond anyone's imagination how each cell works. Cells come with a manufacturer's manual, referencing instructions of how each single part needs to operate.

Absolutism and relativism

Absolutism can mean different things in various situations. Prescribing value judgment would be difficult to comply with, for example, ethical decisions based on objective rules. It constitutes that some things are always right and some other things are always wrong. They are the same for all time, places, cultures, and people. A common example of Absolutism is Kantian Ethics, which is difficult to institute due to circumstances that arise in different situations.

People will do what they think is the right thing to do, since they are often influenced by their environment and because how people are brought up can sharply affect them in what they believe. One cannot expect universal civility of mind and manner, where morality could decisively count, since so many places are simply exhausted from having constructive means and the rudimentary ingredients to barely enlighten them with the most basic requirements for education and insightfulness.

To even make a relatively just society economically prosperous, with learning opportunity and training, proper education, good role models, wisdom, compassion, and awakened consciousness, it is required that consumers distinguish the intricacies between right and wrong, and to realize, as Plato puts it: "Goodness is its own virtue."

There are so many variables that can affect one's decision, starting with self-interest, greed, inferiority complex, desire, economic deprivation, lack of empathy, not having the right education and training, being deprived of analytical and reasoning skills, dignity and worth of the person, proper role models, peer pressure, wrongful environmental effects, and so on, which make one prone to irrational thinking and a static mindset. For instance, is it wrong or right to abort a living baby inside one's mother womb, where the mother desperately seeks abortion and pleads for her freedom to do so? This and many other dilemmas facing us often cannot be justly resolved.

For Kant, morality is only possible if free will exists. If deprived of being free, we would not be able to select which action to take. In which case, we could not be held responsible, since we are forced to do as we are told (in a positive or negative way) for our actions (we would be like programmed robots). But then again, we can be victimized by our own freedom of decision-making and by our own free will, if not having enough mind power and intelligence to manifest the right resolution. And morality can sometimes contradict rationality. This contradiction indicates that an act (or maxim) is immoral, no matter how desperate one's condition.

Like it is immoral to steal a loaf of bread when one's loved ones are almost perishing because of being hungry and homeless. Often it is not right to treat people the same due to circumstances that arise due to different situations. Put simply, not everyone can live by the same rule, because of wrong socioeconomic and sometimes immature sociocultural and callous sociopolitical agendas that have unjustifiable influence over all mentality in accepting extreme inequality in the allocation of resources. That is fundamentally wrong, since it can only happen where fear rules.

We all know that a hungry mob is an angry mob. No matter how anyone should persist on morality and the correct rule of conduct, deprived masses of people will mostly not budge. Some say it is the era of consciousness and we can constitute progressively oriented maxims to implement morality and perhaps reference flawless ethical rules and absolute dogmas. We are human beings and we are bound to make mistakes; no human mind is an exception to the rule.

Moral truths are subjective feelings about human conduct, which can never obtain the status of fact, as they are the result of ways of life and ideas that differ from culture to culture or person to person, depending on people's position and circumstances. We cannot make absolute moral rules where its dynamics could not be questioned. Man's commandments can be questioned; only God's references to morality and ethics need to be relied on and taken as absolute.

The bottom line is, we as human beings need to have references throughout our lives; call them rules, or laws and regulations, call them what you like. The point is, we must have reference points to make our interactivities practical and to make sense of what we are engaged in, and abide by the correct standard, since without make sense, mottos we would be lost. We can become reckless and perhaps chaotically exposed. For instance, when weighing something, you ought to have pound or kilogram as your reference point.

When measuring long distance, you need to reference mile or kilometer; when measuring height, you must reference foot, inches, meter, or centimeter, etc. When you measure volume, you need to reference gallon or liter; monetary units, dollars, pounds. Numbers, signs, colors, and thousands of other things can manifest references to help us manage our lives.

References give meaning to our lives. They bring order, enabling us to manage things. But it does not mean they cannot be changed and perhaps replaced. Referencing morality is not as easy, because human beings are complex beings, and difficult to deal with. Godly ways and ethical conduct cannot be as relaxed as we sometimes want them to be. Contrary to what Kantians believe, that one should be free to choose what one designates as being "ethical," this can bring disorder, since people and society's morals cannot homogeneously be agreed upon.

And for practical reasons, divine laws and "absolute maxim" cannot be compromised (e.g., thou shall not murder, thou shall not rape, thou shall not steal, thou shall not lie, no pedophilia, do not discriminate, and so on). These must be exercised to give meaning to the expression "live and let live," where empathy can avoid cruelty, and orderly conduct would prevent mayhem.

In comparison, relativism believes that nothing is intrinsically right or wrong. It can be influenced due to cultural and societal differences, since not every group, nation, or country should be run with the same stick. Relativism can alter due to historical events and modernization. What was perhaps true fifty or one hundred years ago might not hold water at the present time. Some traditions can even be counterintuitive and extremely backward, affecting everyone if still practiced.

"God is the absolute truth, there exists an absolute truth." Suppose we assert the negation of the statement, that is: there is no such thing as absolute truth. By making that assertion, we claim that the sentence: "There exists no absolute truth" is absolutely true. The statement is self-contradictory, so its negation, "There exists an absolute truth," is true.

But God, absolute divinity, must not be confused with mortals having utter power. No mortal, because of its nature in self-interest and greed, must be allowed to have absolute power. No mortal should be trusted with absolute morality, since human beings are definitely bound to make mistakes and cannot be an absolute role model. We all make mistakes and can sin in one way or another, but our wrongdoings are relative in their nature. Some are heavy players in behaving horrifically and inhumanely in doing felony crimes, and some perhaps engaged in petty crime. That is why we must have a just judiciary system to enforce due process of the law to accordingly render punishment. And there are those that are not noticed or caught when acting immorally, or perhaps made an unintentional mistake.

I believe when Kant talks about "Categorical Imperative" as a basis of morality by criticizing the golden rule is a bit of a stretch. Kant expects everyone to play as a universal role model; that is certainly a utopian idea, where fear of punishment makes a relative living possible. And since progressive behaviors are undeniably ingratiated with high consciousness through elaborate wisdom that we lack, not too many can abide by the rule of choosing what is "right" over what is "pleasing." That is what morality is, to choose right over wrong.

It is difficult, not to say that is impossible, for an individual's act per the short-term pleasure of the senses to be ignored, which can deliberately or unknowingly harm others and the environment. In the process, individuals are indirectly inflicting harm on themselves. What is good for self should be good for the universe; or what is good for the universe should be good for the individual as well.

This should remind one of the materialism and capitalism that might be pleasing to individuals in the short-term, but they are eventually harming the overall humanity by over-production and over-consumption. Choosing moderation in accumulation of wealth, and spirituality over materialism, is good for the individual as well as the universe.

Catholics believe that after death we wait in purgatory, a limbo state, before our fate is decided on for ending up either in the inferno or sent to Heaven. And I say millions are already experiencing hell; ask anyone with old age, who is weak, often sick, has no income, or is a single parent, widow, or homeless. Capitalists cannot in any way identify with social programming, where the needy could have realistic welfare, assistance for the elderly, disabled, and the working class after they are laid off or kicked out of the work force without benefits.

Rich elites are smoke-screened with conveniences and are confident with resolute influence and financial might. This has since overpowered their ethical behavior for the worse. They have caused irreparable damage to humanity and what they stand for by selfish ideas and how they so arrogantly refuse to attend to the suffering of the world around them. There is an expression that says: "Power tends to corrupt, and absolute power corrupts absolutely."

The rich elites are neither rational enough to insightfully commit to correcting the painful socioeconomics, the unjustifiable socio-politics, nor responsible enough to pay any attention to the global warming and the environmental disasters that are literally escalating as they accumulate so much wealth at the price of spilled blood. "Live simply that others may simply live" (Mahatma Gandhi).

A good reminder is that too much of anything can become lopsided, where moderation is ignored and too much power is in too few hands.

This can exponentially hurt people for the worse; it's just human nature. No one should be allowed to have absolute might. It can eradicate the God within us. God's absence can bring out the demons to leave their footprint with destruction and demise, giving true meaning to the word hell, and in witnessing how the sanctity of God and the sovereignty of nature is dull-mindedly infringed upon.

They act nocturnally (diurnal, mainly active at night) and are surreptitious in their conduct, betraying the consumer's trust. This should put shame on the expression on our entire monetary system that says "in God we trust." As William Shakespeare put it, "What a terrible era in which idiots govern the blind."

POSITIVISM DOCTORING

Positivism says that all real knowledge permits proof, and that all authentic knowledge assumes that the only worthy knowledge is scientific. Thinkers such as Henri de Saint-Simon (1760–1825), Pierre-Simon Laplace (1749–1827) and Augusts Comte (1798–1857) believed that the scientific method, the circular dependence of theory and observation, must replace metaphysics in the history of thought. Émile Durkheim (1858–1917) reformulated sociological positivism as a foundation of social research.

Wilhelm Dilthey (1833–1911), in comparison, fought stringently against the thought that only explanations derived from science are valid. He reprised the argument, already found in Vico, that scientific explanations do not reach the inner nature of phenomena and it is humanistic knowledge that gives us insight into thoughts, feelings, and desires. Dilthey was in part influenced by the historicism of Leopold von Ranke (1795–1886).

Countering positivism

At the turn of the twentieth century, the first wave of German sociologists, including Max Weber and Georg Simmel, rejected that doctrine, thus founding the anti-positivist tradition in sociology. Later, anti-positivists and critical theorists have associated positivism with "scientism"; science as ideology.

Later in his career (1969), German theoretical physicist Werner Heisenberg, Nobel laureate for pioneering work in quantum mechanics, distanced himself from positivism by saying: "The positivists have a simple solution: the world must be divided into that which we can say clearly and the rest, which we had better pass over in silence. But can anyone conceive of a more pointless philosophy, seeing that what we can say clearly amounts to next to nothing? If we omitted, all that is unclear we would probably be left with completely uninteresting and trivial tautologies."

"Everything we call real is made of things that cannot be regarded as real" (Niels Bohr).

Everything that we see is ruled by what we do not see.

With the rate humanity is progressing, knowing about string theory and similar breakthrough theories, where scientists are digging into other dimensions, such as "eleven dimensions," befits their findings that can perhaps soon substantiate success. Miracle-like experiences as such wouldn't be a thing of the past, as with newer discoveries we can exponentially grow to one day see and kneel to God, giving us the heavenly chance to swirl into deep cosmos with pure joy and extreme delight, whence, with no doubt, we can feel and taste the infinitely glorious forces of the universe and be able to activate them at will.

To those that persist in thinking, I must see God to believe in God, the adequate question should start with self-cultivation, to know self-first. No disrespect, but not everyone can honestly digest the complexities of metaphysical subjects. When one says, "I love God," one must first know correct self-awareness, which is the key. Ralph Ellison, the invisible man, said: "When I discover who I am, I'll be free." Then perhaps one is to take on knowing God. And when one insists on denying God unless one can see God, he is stretching it not a bit, but a whole lot. "Wise men speak because they have something to say; fools because they have to say something" (Plato).

Forget that the most impressive and beautiful things cannot be seen, and not even tangible, they must be felt with the heart. Looking beyond our reach into a higher realm, looking for a physical God that is not inhibited within space and time, will certainly prove futile. We can only see the effects of our mind and our thoughts. We can only notice the reflection of our intelligence, IQ, talent, beauty, imagination, and thousands of other things that most definitely play gigantic roles in our lives that are not tangible and cannot be seen, but we certainly can notice the effects.

Just as our nervous system and senses are applicable to the visible world, it is the infinite potential of our brain we should strive for to one day have access to ultimate reasoning power. That should clearly resonate with the intricacies of the unseen world.

Can we ever see or feel our bones lengthen as they grow to make us taller? On average, sixteen to eighteen million magnificent thunderstorms occur each year, releasing adequate amounts of hydrogen and nitrogen to fertilize crops. This phenomenon is not seen by the naked eye, but it exists nonetheless. The vital energy activated in every animated being is not seen, and yet without it, no life is possible. There are millions if not billions of other undetected agendas that can practically make us or break us. They are not visualized or detected by the naked eye, but they exist.

We cannot see our memories that without life, becomes practically impossible; ask any Alzheimer's patient. Our pain and suffering, our anger and resentment, our happiness, our hopes and desires, our intentions, cannot be seen, only felt. We can only feel hunger and thirst; we can only feel when we are in love. We can see the utterance (expression) on people's faces, detect certain parts of brain change in response to stimuli, but their emotions are utterly intangible. We cannot see consciousness, despite numerous scientists trying their utmost effort to locate consciousness anywhere in the brain, but utterly with no success.

Atoms are the tiniest building blocks of matter and every other thing in an observatory universe such as ours, but they cannot be seen with the naked eye. Do you see thousands of pressure points pulsing throughout your body? No. But one can feel them. Do you see when your senses report to your brain and impact your nervous system, making it aware of certain tasks, which then your body respectively responds to accordingly?

Air, the oxygen we breathe, which ironically is what keeps us alive, cannot be seen, but felt.

Ultraviolet light is a type of electromagnetic wave that makes sunburn. They say bumblebees can see ultraviolet light, but humans cannot see it. The Hubble space telescope utilizes ultraviolet light to detect stars and galaxies in space.

We can see gravity's effects, but we cannot see it, as we cannot see light and heavy atomic forces, but the effect can absolutely be devastating.

No electromagnetic force can be seen, but the effect of electromagnetics is very much alive.

Infrared, which emits heat, radiates infrared waves, for instance our body infrared, which is a sort of electromagnetic wave. We can see the brain and brain's chemical activities but our mind, memories, and thoughts are utterly intangible.

Quantum particles exist in the subatomic realm, which scientists tell us they pop in and out of for a split second, and can only be realized through electrostatic forces.

We can imagine the whole universe is out there, which can be seen partially by telescope. But we cannot know where it actually ends. It is mind-bending to think about our universe. But imagining the limit of the entire cosmos, if any, is not practical, at least in the present era.

Radioactivity is one sort of electromagnetic wave. Some are approximately one foot long to several miles in length. Electromagnetic frequencies transmit data and are utilized for radio, satellites, computers, and things of that nature.

Dark matter does not vent light or energy, yet it can be seen by mathematically calculating the motion of planets. Scientists tell us that about 80 percent of matter in the universe is made up of dark matter.

Anti-matter owns qualities that are antithetical (reverse, opposite) to regular matter. When matter and anti-matter collide, they both become destroyed. Scientists tell us they exist through the world's particle accelerators and other scientific methods.

Numbers are not seen, but in almost every imperative undertaking, we need to rely on numbers to manifest correct assessments. Our private finances and business affairs, and science-related endeavors, or any other vital undertaking, will practically go haywire without mathematics. Just because we cannot see what rules us, even on our earthy planet, does not mean they do not exist. I cannot reiterate (say again) it more that the world we do not see manages the world that we see.

Just as our nervous system and senses are applicable to the visible world, it is the infinite potential of our brain we should strive for to one day have access to ultimate reasoning power that should clearly resonate with the intricacies of the unseen world.

Can one see what literally keeps one alive? Can you see your jugular beating? Can you see your carotid arteries pulsating? Not unless you feel it with your fingers. Can you see your food digesting? Can you see the oxygen you breathe? Can you see your thoughts and memories? Can you see the urge to mate and to multiply? Can you see your cravings and desires?

Can you see thousands if not millions of acting hormones and enzymes where every thought and movement and every biochemical, biomechanical, biophysical activity has to happen for one to function properly and not in disarray? Can you see your mind, and can you see God? No. You feel most of them, and without them, we expire.

The vital energy activated in every animated being is not seen, and yet without it, no life is possible.

Our faith is not seen, but it is an inseparable part of our daily lives and a decisive factor in all that we undertake. For instance, we put our trust in the pilot's hand that airlifts the jumbo jet we are in, or the taxi driver who transports us home. Every time we drive and are behind the wheel we have faith and expect to reach our destiny, but our expectation is not seen or materialized. We take a leap of faith when we expect our parachute to open in midair as we jump out of a plane and then guide us to where we should land. A pregnant mother expects in good faith no complications during delivery, and impatiently expects to hold her healthy baby right after it is born. And when soldiers are placed on the front line of nasty wars and in devastating combat situations, they expect to return to their loved ones.

We expect to wake up every morning as we lay in bed and sleep at night. Millions of other faith-based beliefs and the over-arching concept of "in God we trust" are the impetuses and the moving forces we cannot deny or do without; such forces are not seen, and yet are the essence and irrefutable attributes to our lives.

Mr. Michio Kaku, professor of theoretical physics and the co-founder of string field theory, states:

The latest version of string theory is called "M theory" (M for membrane), so we now realize that strings can coexist with membranes. So the subatomic particles we see in nature, the quarks, the electrons, are nothing but musical notes on a tiny vibrating string. What is physics: physics is nothing but the laws of harmony that you can write on vibrating strings. What is chemistry? Chemistry is nothing but the melodies that you can play on interacting vibrating strings. What is the universe? The universe is a symphony of vibrating strings. And then what is the mind of God that Albert Einstein eloquently wrote about in the last thirty years of his life? We now for the first time in the history have a candidate for the mind of God. It is cosmic music resonating in eleven-dimensional hyperspace.

It is appropriate now to indicate a couple of mind-boggling situations where eventful design creation should perplex and amaze any savvy-oriented mind.

Reductionist vs Holism Positivism

I must see God to believe in God.

"Astronomers now find they have painted themselves into a corner because they have proven, by their own methods, that the world began abruptly in an act of creation to which you can trace the seeds of every star, every planet, every living thing in this cosmos and on the earth. And they have found that all this happened as a product of forces they cannot hope to discover.... That there are what I or anyone would call supernatural forces at work is now, I think, a scientifically proven fact." (Astronomer, physicist and founder of NASA's Goddard Institute of Space Studies Robert Jastrow).

Confucius said, "Real knowledge is to know the extent of one's ignorance." There is much truth in what Confucius said, which can probably help many not to behave conceitedly, at least as it evolves around our actions, and in what we take as truth, for one: we have lopsided belief in self so much, and I might add unreasonably emphatic in self-adequacy, that we have forgotten about who actually is in command.

THE BOTTOM LINE ON THE ORIGIN OF LIFE

During all recorded human history, there has never been a proven case of a living thing being generated from anything other than another living thing.

As yet, evolutionism has not made a scientifically credible explanation for the origin of such tremendous complexities as DNA, the human brain, and many other elements of the cosmos.

It is highly callous for materialists to say that all living things evolved into existence from nothing and without any conscientious instruction and with no scrupulous blueprint. Science has yet to discover how even one protein molecule could have truly come into existence by dull natural processes rather than dynamically guided energy-driven evolution.

There is not a scientific fact that life did (or ever could) have evolved into existence from non-living matter. Further, there is not even a slight evidence that spontaneous generation is possible.

Only DNA is known to produce DNA. No chemical interaction of molecules has even come close to producing this ultra-complex code that is so essential to all known life.

Posted July 22, 2012 Alan McDougall, the 1/1040, 000 probability actually refers to the chance of obtaining the required set of enzymes for the simplest living cell. How was this probability derived? We know that amino acids are the building blocks of enzymes, so what part of probability that you give is the chance of obtaining the required amino acids for those enzymes?

The researchers probably calculated the odds for a limited set of molecules to combine to the desired configurations. What they fail to take into account is that there are an exponential number of molecules performing exponential random combinations over billions of years. Some of which will combine to the desired configuration. Combine those together, and the odds shorten to the extent that it obviously becomes a certainty, judging by the fact that DNA, enzymes, et al. (together with further example of that sort) are extant (currently or actually existing).

On Sunday, July 22, 2012 at 2:42 PM, Joatmon said:

I would say that the odds against life evolving by chance is very large. This is evidenced by the fact that so far we haven't found any except here on earth.

I would say we haven't looked, and that we don't have many places to look. The only planets in the Sun's habitable zone are Venus, Earth, and Mars. There's a lot more to habitability than merely being in a star's habitable zone. Venus has too thick an atmosphere. Mars, too thin. Neither Venus nor Mars has an active plate tectonics (climatology, meteorology, geophysics, oceanography, seismology, geo chemistry) system. Mars might have been habitable long ago, and Mars does show some signs of having borne life long ago. It shows some signs that it still bears life right now. We do see life on the one planet that is habitable, and that life originated very shortly after conditions became hospitable for life. Judging from a sample size of one, maybe two (which is all we've got), it appears that primitive life is very likely to arise if conditions are right. That said, judging from a small sample size is always an iffy proposition. We need more data.

The theory of evolution discloses that life started, and evolution progresses by random chance. Yes, fortuitous (accident) hugely maneuvers in evolution, but this debate utterly disregards the principal role of natural selection which is contrary to chancy behaviors, and disorderly conducts.

Chance, in the form of mutations, brings about genetic volatility (variance), which is the basic material that natural selection has to work with to create what is necessary. Then, natural selection extricates (disentangle) definite variations. Those variations that render higher reproductive success to their holders (and chance makes sure that such beneficial mutations will be inescapable) are kept, and less successful variations are eliminated. When the atmosphere changes, or when organisms move to a different environment, different vacillations are chosen, eventually succession to different species. Harmful modifications normally expire out quickly, so they don't obtrude (impose, barge in) with the process of beneficial mutations amassing.

Nor is abiogenesis (the origin of the first life) merit to chance. Atoms and molecules arrange themselves not merely randomly, but due to their chemical properties. Complex molecules form spontaneously, and these complicated molecules can influence each other to make even more complex molecules. Once a molecule molds that is essentially self-replicating, natural selection will direct the formation of ever more efficacious (most effective) replicators. The initial self-replicating object didn't need to be as complicated as a new cell or even a strip of DNA. Some self-replicating molecules are actually not really all that complex.

A calculation of the probabilities of abiogenesis (the idea of impromptu origination of living organism straight from lifeless matter) is good-for-nothing, unless it accounts for the colossal range of starting materials that the first replicator perhaps has formed from, the chancy innumerable various forms that the first replicator might have held, and the fact that much of the construction of the replicating molecule would have been non-random to start with.

One ought to also realize that the theory of evolution doesn't rely on how the incipient (inaugural, first) life began.

In short, life does not evolve by chance alone, nor does the theory of evolution have anything to do with how life began. That's a completely different theory.

The universe functions by steady laws of nature. Why does it?

In the midst of global social, political, and economic mayhem, as the chaotic world threatens us all, there are so many dire gridlocks and uncertainties torturing humanity without mercy it makes man guilty as charged, not God.

But look at what we can depend on day after day: all the forces of the universe, not to exclude gravity, remain consistent. Imperative resources are produced to sustain and to keep us going. A hot cup of cocoa left on a kitchen counter will get cold. The earth rotates in the same 24 hours, and the speed of light doesn't alter—on Earth or in galaxies far from us. How is it that laws of nature never change? Why is the universe so orderly, and conducts so faithfully, refreshed after a deep and tranquil sleep for a day of hard work? And when a healthy baby is delivered after nature's time span of nine months has matured from one's mother womb, and so on.

"The most prominent philosophers and the greatest scientists have been impacted by how strange this is. There is no formal principle of reasoning necessity for a universe that obeys rules, let alone one that abide by the rules of mathematics. This consternation (amazement) springs from the acknowledgement that the universe doesn't have to act this way. It is easy to envisage (fancy, imagine) a universe in which conditions change unpredictably, and criterions modify from instant to instant, or even a universe in which things burst in, and pop out of existence."

Richard Feynman, a Nobel Prize winner for quantum electrodynamics, said, "Why nature is mathematical is a mystery...The fact that there are rules at all is a kind of miracle."

Why can't we feel Earth's spin, and other miracle-like phenomena?

We do not feel Earth's spin as it rotates ceaselessly because we're all moving with it, at the same constant speed. Earth rotates on its axis once in every 24-hour day. At Earth's equator, the speed of Earth's spin is about 1,000 miles per hour (1,600 kilometers per hour). The day and night come and go and carry us all along around and around in a lofty (formidable, grand) circle under the stars every second of the day, yet we don't feel Earth spinning. Why not? It's because utterly everything, including Earth's oceans and atmosphere, are spinning along with the Earth at the same constant speed. We'd feel the spin if unexpectedly the Earth stopped moving, which then would be a feeling similar to riding in a fast car and the driver suddenly slamming on the brakes! Why can't we feel Earth's spin?

Think about riding in a car or flying in a plane. When you're smoothly riding, you can feel as if you're not moving. An airbus jumbo jet or a Boeing jumbo jet flies at about 600 miles per hour (about 950-1,000 km per hour), or about half as fast as the Earth spins at its equator (lines of latitude and longitude.) But, while you're riding on that jet, close your eyes; it would seem to you as if you do not move at all. And when the flight attendant comes by and pours drinking water, or any of the beverages available (tea, coffee, hard liquor, or soft drink of any kind) into your cup, what you are drinking doesn't fly to the back of the plane.

That's because your drink, the cup you are drinking with, and you, are all moving at the same rate as the speed of the plane. Now meditate about what would occur if the car or plane wasn't moving at a constant rate, but instead speeding up and slowing down. But because they couldn't feel Earth move, they decoded this observation to give meaning that Earth was motionless and "the heavens" moved above us. It was the Greek scientist Aristarchus who initially proposed a heliocentric (Sun-centered) model of the universe hundreds of years BCE. The world's great thinkers upheld the idea of geocentric (Earth-centered) of the macrocosm for so many centuries.

It wasn't until the sixteenth century that the heliocentric model of the solar system, taking a particular body as central, began to be understood. While having some errors, Copernicus' model finally convinced the world that Earth spun on its axis beneath the stars and also moved in orbiting the sun. Bottom line: the reason we don't feel Earth spinning on its axis? It's because Earth rotates steadily and moves at a fixed rate in orbit around the Sun, carrying us all as passengers along with it. If that is not a miracle, I do not know what is.

The elaborateness of planet Earth indicates a purposeful designer who not only made our universe, but also sustains it as we speak. God's endless design can infinitely be manifested.

The Earth is perfectly sized. The Earth's size and corresponding gravity keeps a thin stratum (layer) of mostly nitrogen and oxygen gases stretching approximately 50 miles above the earth's surface. If Earth were smaller, an atmosphere would be impossible, like the planet Mercury. If Earth were bigger, its ambience (climate, atmosphere) would keep free hydrogen, like Jupiter. Earth is the only known planet furnished with an environment of the proper mixture of gases to nourish plants and animals, including human life.

Our planet Earth is situated the right distance from the Sun. Reckon the temperature swings we face, about -30 degrees to +120 degrees. If the Earth were any further distant from the Sun, we would all freeze to death. Any nearer and we would incinerate. Even a fractional volatility (vacillation) in the Earth's location to the Sun would make life on Earth just not possible. But the planet Earth maneuvers perfectly within desirable distance from the Sun while it spins around the Sun at a speed of virtually (almost) 67,000 mph. It is also rotating on its own axis, letting the entire surface of the Earth be properly cooled and warmed each day.

The moon is the perfect size, and within the exact distance from the Earth for its gravitational pull. The moon makes imperative ocean tides and movement so ocean waters do not stagnate, and yet our incredibly huge oceans are inhibited from spilling over across the global continents.

Water, as colorless, odorless, and without taste as it is, keeps every living thing alive. Plants, animals, and human beings consist mostly of water (about two-thirds of the human body is water). The distinguishing traits of water are specifically made for life.

Water can reach a boiling point and can be frozen; water allows us to live in an atmosphere of vacillating temperature changes and keeps our bodies a steady 98.6 degrees.

Water is a universal solvent. The liquidity of water means that different chemicals, minerals, and nutrients can be carried all over our bodies and permeate the smallest blood vessels.

Water is chemically neutral by nature, meaning it does not affect the makeup of the substance it carries. Water enables food digestion and helps nutrients, vitamins, and minerals to be absorbed and used by the body for creating energy.

Amazingly enough, water has a unique surface tension (tightness). Water in plants can flow upward against gravity, carrying life-giving water and nutrients to the uppermost of the tallest trees. Water freezes from the top down and floats, so that fish can carry on living in the winter. Oceans contain 96 percent to 97 percent of the Earth's water. There is a system designed on our planet Earth which purifies and cleans salt from water, and then dispenses it throughout the entire globe. The evanescence (evaporation) takes the ocean waters, leaving the salt, and forms clouds, which are then carried by the wind to distribute water over the land for vegetation, animals, and humans. It is a system of cleansing and supply that maintains life on this planet, a great recycling system.

The human brain concurrently (at the same time) projects an astonishing amount of information. Our brain discerns all the colors, the things we see, the temperature we feel around us, the pressure we feel against the floor, the sounds, the dryness of your mouth, even the texture of anything we feel. The brain holds and processes our sentiments and emotions, thoughts, the power of reasoning, and memories. Our brain simultaneously keeps track of the ongoing functions of our body, like breathing patterns, heat, eyelid movement, thirst, hunger, and the movement of the muscles in the entire body. It retrieves messages and renders order to other parts of our body.

The human brain develops more than a million messages a second. It weighs what is crucial of all this data, filtering out the unimportant items. This screening work permits one to focus and function effectively in our life. The brain acts differently than other organs. There is an intelligence to it; the ability to be logical, to generate feelings, to dream and devise, to take action, and connect to the environment and people.

The eye can perceive among seven to eight million colors. It has automatic focusing and manages an amazing 1.5 million messages at the same time.

Evolution insists on mutations and changes from and within existing organisms. Yet evolution alone does not fully clarify the source of the eye or the brain—and how in heaven's name did the start of living organisms happen from nonliving matter? The universe had a start—what caused it?

Scientists are now confident that our universe originated with an extremely colossal explosion of energy and light, which we know as the big bang. Everything that exists: the beginning of the universe, the start of space, and even the initial start of time itself, is due to the big bang effect.

Astrophysicist Robert Jastrow, a self-described agnostic, stated, "The seed of everything that has happened in the Universe was planted in that first instant; every star, every planet and every living creature in the Universe came into being as a result of events that were set in motion in the moment of the cosmic explosion. The Universe flashed into being, and we cannot find out what caused that to happen."

Steven Weinberg, a Nobel laureate in Physics (the recipient of honor or recognition for achievement in an art or science) said at the moment of this explosion, "the universe was about a hundred thousand million degrees Centigrade...and the universe was filled with light."

The most prominent scientists say that the universe has not always existed. It had a start. what caused that? They have no explanation for the sudden explosion of light and matter. THE BOTTOM LINE on the origin of life, unless one is to tie up evolution, which in some cases makes scientific sense, to the umbilical cord of the almighty God. It will become nothing less than a farce to believe the criteria the nonbelievers offer on how life incepted from nowhere, in random chance, and without a superbly intelligent source.

To further cultivate the agnostic's claim for an absentee of design and lack of a designer, any stable mind should ask: can any architect, draftsman, planner, builder, mechanic; chemical, electrical, electronic, computer, industrial, or construction engineer; or any other professional analyst ever substantiate a meaningful and mindful design without a reliable blueprint and masterfully composed schematic?

Imagine a world where anything and everything can be built, managed, sustained, and preserved without anyone lifting a finger. All activities of the world we live in would have no one to effectively think, and would be barren of anyone from spending time, not able to devote funds, skill, and energy to make them.

Imagine your dinner with a variety of food is served to you out of nowhere, and without a cook. Imagine the place you live, poof, appeared overnight, out of nowhere, without building materials, denied of helping hands, and without a crafty schemer, plotter, mason, or a builder. The thought of such a ludicrous (inept, absurd) claim is personally beyond my comprehension.

To believe in an existence without a cause, at least in the Newtonian's world of cause and effect, is derisive (false), and nothing short of a fairy-tale story that children might buy. But as they mature, they certainly laugh at their own naivety when they are reminded of folktales (myth driven saga) they once saw as truth.

The fact is that if this breathtaking universe and staggering (startling, mind-boggling) cosmos was built from nowhere, as most atheists claim, and out of nothing without a maker, then they should believe in the supernatural, which needs to signify a magical universe manipulated by an infinitely brilliant and enchanting designer.

We ought to bear in mind that every couple of centuries, billions come and go. The truth is that history can only identify with those who make history, great souls such as Moses, Jesus, Mohammad, Buddha, Socrates, Plato, Aristotle, Rumi, Omar Khayyam, Avicenna, Shakespeare, Firdausi, Sadie, Luther, St. Augustine, Descartes, Pascal, Rousseau, John Locke (the father of liberalism), Hobbes, Adam Smith, David Hume, Nietzsche, Bertrand Russell, Pasteur, Michael Angelo, Picasso, Immanuel Kant, AL Rahman al-Sufi (Azophi), Kepler, Galileo Galilei, Nicolas Copernicus, Newton, Edwin Hobble, Einstein, George Berkley, Voltaire, Hegel, Marx (may God bless his soul), and so on, through their miracle work, and in how they reached the essence of their geniuses. So should we identify with the work of God and God's majestic derivatives through "evolutionary creation." The point is that it is a drop of the infinite mind of God, which is sacredly implied within the mind of man in which divine messages are manifested. And since great minds are behind great ideas, it is what drives history and revolutionizes our world from the most primitive to the age of modernity, where civility of mind and manner is accordingly encouraged.

Many of the main principles and fundamental ideas underlining the structure of our contemporary world are barely 200 years old. Modern science depicting democracy and natural rights were all introduced by the enlightenment, a revolution of the intellect that seized Europe between 1600 and 1800, in which they challenged proven ways of dealing with reality.

Some contemporary scientists believe there are as many universes as there are refined sands on planet Earth. This should make one wonder, do physicists and scholarly minded scientists believe The Milky Way and the entire cosmos sprang out of nowhere from a single-celled organism and originated from planet Earth without any purpose, as explained in Darwin's theory of evolution where mutation and natural selection signify Darwin's survival of the fittest theory?

The Hubble telescope is the best instrument available for galaxy counting and estimation. The telescope, launched in 1990, initially estimated about two hundred billion galaxies, and still counting, for billions more as more advanced telescopes are expected to bring thrilling news as science progresses further.

The theory that says all species were created from a single-celled organism; did it also give birth to cosmic existence? Or was it perhaps extraterrestrial, and other planetary inhabitants which made life possible on planet Earth?

Or shall we believe the proponents of the big bang theory, like Professor Hawking and the like, that accept gravity is responsible for creating life as we know it?

Or did life perhaps appear on planet Earth from other universes and galaxies, brought about by extraterrestrials, or caused through any other means under the approval of God?

Meaning, order, discipline, purpose, objectives, beginning, the end, fate, destiny, responsibility, inspiration, dreams, imagination, commitments, sacrifice, good deeds, generosity, awesome precision and flawless management, moral conduct, intelligence, conscious mind, empathy, will power, compassion, relativism, absolutism, sustainability, fate, love, honor, devotion, decisiveness, beauty, good and evil, punishment, reward, and hundreds if not thousands of related sociocultural, ethical, legal, and judiciary concepts should put us on a very slippery road and ought to be redefined, not based on spirituality, justice, integrity, empathy, morality, or any other divine law, but depending on Darwin's survival of the fittest doctrine, where no criminal and atrocious behavior should honestly be condemned.

The strong needs to make the weak perish to survive, rather than cooperate and collectively challenge nature to further conquer the unknown for humanity's sake and comfort, to exercise "live and to let live mentality." Otherwise no genocide, wiping out nations through war of aggression, and via conventional weaponries, cluster bombs, biological and hydrogen bomb, should be damned. And let' not forget this type of toxic and cruel dogma (axiom, principle) has already done so much damage to humanity and is still counting.

And yes, since the key is wisdom, a tiny decimal in gradual brain cells aperture (opening) will result in billions of neurons to spark at trillions of synopses where they juncture to inspire apex creativity in mental and physical makeup to benefit humanity.

The incremental escalation in firing brain neurons eventually takes a positive leap in exalted endeavors, which should mean utter freedom from the clutches of ignorance, where the mind of God is truly signified and curiously discerned. We need to awaken to this undeniable fact that unless we prioritize education and pay more attention to learning and in gaining knowledge, we will be devoid of vital information that can shed light on decisive issues of our time where miracle-like events and beyond imagination breakthroughs become reality, setting the stage for the next paradigm shift in human glory.

Glittering stars become a dancing ground to celebrate the mind of man. In turn, mindfulness emanates wisdom where the power of reasoning should repel stupidity and the human beast is to be far-fetched and to substantiate collective attributes conducive to good deeds and virtuosity with aesthetic behaviors in making progressive task possible. Positive evolutionary perspectives can purport (convey) civil communication and constructive dialogues.

Our subconscious mind, which restores thought pattern and behaviors in a vast reservoir, can be tapped to build modern and revered character where barbaric and inhumane deeds are unanimously renounced.

This should awaken mankind to preserve the sanctity of higher self and strive to access the pinnacle of success in emergency accommodation for the acquisition of denoting education, proper employment, decent housing, and efficient medical programs, constituting genuine safety nets with no-nonsense financial plans for retirees and seniors.

Ethology (a branch of scientific knowledge dealing with human character and with its formation and evolution) can patent time parameter and accord with the era of human consciousness, promenading civility of mind and manner.

Make emergency accommodations not prerogatives or optional, but mandated wisdom to save lives and for people's well-being and prosperity, replacing violence with peace, justice, democracy, and human rights, where stoic actions are not encouraged, and sensitivity and compassion towards others' pain and suffering is positively addressed.

To feel responsible in relentlessly seeking practical resolution to ill criterion and on the actual causes for abysmal hurt (profound) which has forced many to lose hope and integrity in the face of degradation and misfortune, as defective products that are constantly disseminated to create restless atmosphere and anxiety as competent broker of fear and uncertainty structure institutionalized strategy to celebrate people's segregation and disunity with expensive Champaign and caviar.

They choose to manufacture hatred and through improvising vile insure the status quo and the fluidity of enslaving the wretchedly poor and destitute, where cerebral deficiencies and economic benevolence for some has solidified the concept of divide and rule, rendering masses of people incompetent to perceive the truth and not able to expose the prevalence of corporate madness, to unveil culture of falsehood and charlatanism, where God is toyed with to yoke dissidents in his name, as if the poor are reincarnated to live miserably and are condemn to be punished because of their character flaws and misdeeds in previous life.

This, by the way, justifies the Darwinism mentality through the survivor of fittest doctrine, and also pampers the extremist's ideology that says everything is fate-related, and is the God which is sentencing the helpless to tolerate what they deserve; either way, the rich elites are the beneficiary of such cultural nonsense and ill-diagnosed criterions.

The atheist's ideology is tenuous (weak) since its missing links and flaws are existentially too risky to depend on, where they meet with the infidel's extremism that cannot be trusted because of their backward mentality and brute behaviors towards other so-called nonbelievers. This leaves humanity with no choice but to align with cultures that are insightful and scintillating (stimulating, witty) on a metaphysical realm, where heavens are aspiring human souls and the cosmic spirit is permeated into each and every animated being. Exhibiting magic and wonder about the absolute power of the omniscient Creator should inspire humanity to cultivate further into the celestial kingdom and closer to the enchanting (majestic) nature of the universe.

Evidence for Creation › Evidence for God › Design and Purpose › God Caused Meaning

Humans have always wondered about the meaning of life...life has no higher purpose than to perpetuate the survival of DNA...life has no design, no purpose, no evil and no good, nothing but blind pitiless (cruel) indifference.1 – Richard Dawkins

Thermodynamics,

The laws of thermodynamics explain the connection between thermal energy, or heat, and other forms of energy, and how energy influences matter.

The First Law of Thermodynamics states that energy cannot be created or destroyed; the total quantity of energy in the universe stays the same.

The Second Law of Thermodynamics is about the quality of energy. It says that as energy is transformed, some of it is wasted. The Second Law also states that there is a natural tendency of any isolated system to deteriorate into a more disordered position.

Saibal Mitra, a professor of physics at Missouri State University, finds the Second Law to be the most interesting of the four laws of thermodynamics. "There are a number of ways to state the Second Law," he said. "At a very microscopic level, it simply says that if you have a system that is isolated, any natural process in that system progresses in the direction of increasing disorder, or entropy, of the system."

Many scientists believe that all processes result in an increase in entropy. Even when the order is increased in a specific location, for instance by the self-assembly of molecules to make a living organism; when one takes the total system including the environment into consideration, there is always a net increase in entropy. Also bear in mind that no isolated system of any kind, and without any guidance also exhausted of being superbly directed, call it life or anything that you wish, could possibly run its course for 4.54 billion years and not become entirely eradicated.

.

In the meanwhile, now the strongest of our ancestors have managed to get us to where we currently are, as Darwin's survival of the fittest theory states, which signifies the fittest of all creatures, including us people, have successfully managed to transfer their genes, and since we have steadily resin from ape to man.

Some anthropologist and other related fields believe we are here because the most conservative of us all did manage to stay alive to convey their genes, which contradicts Darwin's aggressive behaviors of the fittest. So many also question and say, "from monkey to man, from man to what?"

I am also wondering if evolution has graduated our predecessors from ape to man and progressively turned monkeys to human beings, why then are so many monkeys and apes still around? Perhaps evolution has cursed some of their forefathers, denying them the right of becoming full-fledged humans, and since has excluded them to benefits from what evolution has to offer. If yes, why? I am not being sarcastic, as these questions and millions other should pop into any sensible mind.

WE SURE ARE ALL IN A BUBBLE

Civil life requires civil manner; we cannot have a modern life with primitive behaviors. We must not let industrialization to iron out our mind and mold us into senseless, soulless, and cold machines depleted of humanistic characters, where cruelty can become the norm in absence of compassion and caring.

And as technology progresses and intensifies, it can influence us into acting "robot-like" which in all honesty plenty of alarming socio-cultural and socio-political, and socio-economical signs are activated as they already have infected our thoughts, and in how we see the world.

Because often our collective action is so far off from decency in mind and manner and shifted away from what it manifests as correct paradigms in which if righteous deeds are applicable, they can free us from troublesome, toxic, and superfluous (non-essential, not necessary) environment, they can extricate humanity from acting inhumane. Which one should be reminded of the presence of God in everything that one does. And as Rumi the Persian poet, jurist, theologian, and mystic Sufi said:

If in thirst you drink water from a cup, you see God in it. Those who are not in love with God will see only their own faces in it

All day I think about it, then at night, I say it. Where did I come from, and what am I supposed to be doing? I have no idea. My soul is from elsewhere, I'm sure of that, and I intend to end up there.

Your task is not to seek for love, but merely to seek and find all the barriers within yourself that you have built against it.

Silence is an ocean. Speech is a river. Silence is the language of God, all else is a poor translation.

Out beyond ideas of wrongdoing and right doing, there is a field. I will meet you there.

The breeze at dawn has secrets to tell you; don't go back to sleep. You must ask for what you really want; don't go back to sleep. People are going back and forth across the doorsill where the two worlds touch. The door is round and open. Don't go back to sleep.

"When I am with you, we stay up all night.

When you're not here, I can't go to sleep.

Praise God for those two insomnias!

And the difference between them." Let the beauty of what you love to be what you do.

It should be wisely noted that: contemporary life has weaved us into oneness and as evidenced the repercussion of our conducts do immediately effect even the furthest of the globe culturally, politically and financially as the impact of wrong decisions by the mighty is worst on the poverty-stricken societies. And for those most deprived, this should relentlessly remind us of the improper judicious, and often unjustified human criterions, and to warn us all that yes, we do live in a bubble now which can burst at any time if we keep on misbehaving.

EXISTENCE OF GOD

The being of God is a topic of debate that requires philosophical mastery and scholarly information in religious, popular culture, and faith-oriented subjects, where the power of reasoning and inference needs to play a convincing role, since no one has seen or talked to God. A wide range of controversy in metaphysical arguments for the existence or denial of God, leveraged via empirical, logical, or subjective matters, even with scientific issues, have been raised through the course of human history. Epistemology (the nature and scope of knowledge) in philosophy, science, and vast ontological information (study of the nature of existence), is needed to adequately present the "theory of value," to intelligently manifest the perfection of God.

Plato and Aristotle were the pioneers in Western philosophical culture that set forth the discussion for the existence of God, which now will be regarded as the cosmological argument; Ibn Sina, Ibn Rushd (Averroes), Ajuwayani, Alghazali, Thomas Aquinas, Rene Descartes, John Calvin, were among many classical philosophers whom they intelligently argued for a necessary supreme being.

It was Rene Descartes who stated that the being of a benevolent God is logically necessary for the evidence of senses to be meaningful. Ibn Rushed talked about a fine-tuned universe needing an infinitely intelligent tuner; so did Ibn Sina talk about the unmoved mover in the kalam argument. It was John Calvin who argued for a "sensus divinitatis," which renders human beings with the knowledge for the existence of God, and St. Anselm who put forth the first ontological argument.

Philosophers who argued against the being of God include Immanuel Kant, David Hume, Friedrich Nietzsche, and Bertrand Russell. In modern culture, the question of God's existence has been discussed by scientists such as Francis Collins, Stephen Hawking, Richard Dawkins, Lawrence M. Krauss, Sam Harris, Carl Sagan, Neil deGrasse Tyson, John Lennox, and as well as philosophers including Richard Swinburne, Rebecca Goldstein, Alvin Plantinga, Edward Feser, William Lane Craig, A. C. Grayling, David Bently Hart, Daniel Dennett, Neils Bohr, Sigmund Freud, and Peter Higgs.

Scientists comply with the scientific means, within which theories must hold truth via physical experiment, by material evidence. The overall conception of God posits a being which can absolutely not be examined. Hence, the questions concerning the existence of God, for which no evidence can be tested, may by definition lie outside the horizon of contemporary science.

The commencement of many religions affirms that knowledge of the existence of God is the natural light of human reason. They are faith-oriented beliefs that assert that belief in the existence of God is not compliant to proof or rebuttal, but based on faith alone. Classical theism believes in God as the omnipotent, omnipresent, benevolent, transcendent, and metaphysically ultimate being, a timeless, absolutely sovereign being who is bereft (devoid) of all anthropomorphic qualities. This differs from other ideas like open theism, process theism, theistic personalist, and classical theism, which do not accept that God can be wholly defined. They believe it would discredit the transcendent truth of God for simple humans to define him. Robert Barron says by analogy that "it seems impossible for a two-dimensional object to conceive of three-dimensional humans."

Ibn Rushd, a twelfth-century Islamic scholar, philosopher, and physician, explained with rational philosophical argument that there are only two disputations worthy of coherency, both of which are sought in the "Precious Book" (The Qur'an). Rushd cites "providence" and "invention" in using the Qur'an's parables (genres of symbolic literary representation, Allegorical), to claim the existence of God.

Rushd argues that the Earth's weather structured layout is made to support human life; thus, if the planet is so finely tuned to predicate (assert) life, then it suggests a fine-tuner—God. The Sun and the Moon are not just disorderly (random) objects floating in the Milky Way, rather they serve us day and night, and the way nature works and how life is formed, humankind benefits from. Rushd essentially comes to a conclusion that there has to be a higher being who has made everything perfectly to serve the needs of human beings.

Moses ben Maimon, a Jewish scholar, also talked about the heavenly bodies to prove the existence of God. He stated that because every physical object is finite, it can only contain a finite amount of power. If everything in the universe, which includes all the planets and the stars, is finite, then there has to be an infinite power propelling everything in the universe. He believed the only thing that can describe the motion in all things is an infinite being (meaning God), which is neither a body nor a force in the body. Maimonides believed this argument gives us the premises to know that God, but not an idea of what God is. He believed that God cannot be comprehended or be compared.

Abrahamian's religions of Judaism, Christianity, and Islam encourage preamble faith presupposing belief in God and the immortality of the soul, since any other approach including science, philosophy and other analogies do fall short in proving the existence of God.

St. Paul made this debate when he said that pagans should be without excuse because "since the creation of the world God's invisible nature, namely, his eternal power and deity, has been clearly perceived in the things that have been made." In this Paul implied to the proofs for a Creator, later enunciated by St. Thomas, and others, also originally employed by the Greek philosophers.

Other apologetically school of thoughts inaugurated by Cornelius Van Til, known as Presupposition apologetics, or "transcendental" view of God. The principle difference between this doctoring of thought and the more classical evidentialist is that the presupposition list rejects any common denominator between those who believe in God and the nonbeliever, since the nonbeliever denies the assumption of the truth of the theistic view of the world.

Presupposition lists do not accept that the being of God can be substantiated by beseeching to callous, ceaselessly rough facts, which have similar postulated (theoretical, presumed but not proven) sensing for those masses with a primarily different world-vision, as they discredit such a condition is even possible. They say that proof for the existence of God is the very same belief necessary for condition to the intelligibility of all other human experience and action.

They try to prove the existence of God by referencing transcendental importance, the vitality of this belief indicates that all human intelligence, experiences, knowledge, action, (even the situation of unbelief, itself) is the proof for the existence of God. Because God's existence the necessary requirement for their intelligibility.

What Does Modal Logic Mean?

Modal logic is a kind of logical debate that utilizes words like 'possible' and 'necessary' to reach a conclusion.

Plantinga's Modal Ontological Argument

Here's how it breaks down:

1. If God exists, he must exist necessarily
2. Either God exists necessarily or he doesn't
3. If God doesn't have necessary existence, then he necessarily doesn't

Therefore,

4. Either God has necessary existence, or he necessarily doesn't
5. If God necessarily doesn't have necessary existence, then God necessarily doesn't exist

Therefore:

6. Either God has necessary existence, or he necessarily doesn't exist
7. It is not the case that God necessarily doesn't exist

Therefore,

8. God has necessary existence
9. If God has necessary existence, then God exists

Therefore,

10. God exists

Many spiritual people believe that the deduction and philosophical disputation for and against the existence of God does not grasp the point. The word God, which is interpreted in many cultures and history, does not accord with the beings whose existence is justified by such arguments, assuming they are worthy. The real question is not whether, an "uncaused first cause" or, the omnipotent, omnipresent, and the most benevolent God exists.

The real inquiry should be whether Krishna, Zeus, Chinese Shangdi, Sikhism, Christian Yahweh, Jehovah, Allah, or other Gods exist.

And if so, which one, out of thousands of gods sermonized, is the real God? Millions if not billions of the so-called theists do not seem to have an agreement on the only transcendental God that is beyond space and time, and the only cause for all there is, and all there ever will be.

How God is discussed should be of concern, when often no intelligence and cultural dynamics are available to wisely adhere to reasoning power for knowing God, as time parameter should also raise an issue, as most religion's manifestos have originated in the old times, lacking compatibility with evolution trend of thoughts and robust views on philosophical and modern scientific analogies. They demand inference and competency in theoretical proof to correctly argue the premises of God.

Many theists from monotheistic faiths believe their God is the "Henotheism" (most perfect being) from Greek (henos theos, meaning 'one god') and they worship a single God while not denying the existence or possible existence of other deities. Human salvation can only take place in Heaven above, through what some of them prejudicially preach against the others, and vice versa, and no other God is any good.

This hypocrisy of beliefs has led to so many uncivilized behaviors and violence, beyond anyone's imagination, lacking empathy, in which compassion should play a key role in faith-based entities to help others, regardless of who they are and what they believe in.

Most of these arguments do not resolve the issue of which of these Godheads is more probable to exist, since these debates fail to show the difference between immanent gods and a transcendent God.

For the past couple of centuries, many religions, especially the monotheistic faiths, have been subjected to a relentless bombardment of criticism from scientists who have challenged that many historical religious views are wrong; that the universe, and human beings as well, evolved—they were not created; that many religiously based statements of the universe are primitive and mythological; as views on God and man do not comply, and cannot be reconciled with our modem scientific discoveries.

The atheistic conclusion is that the arguments and evidence both show there is insufficient reason to believe that any gods exist. And that believer's subjective religious experiences talk about the human learning, rather than the nature of reality itself; therefore, one has no reason to accept that a god exists.

Some arguments as cosmological, ontological, and theistic' debate stand out among others for proving the existence of God, as they still fall short to adequately prove the existence of God, where faith plays a major role in many religions, since they emphatically express salvation is by having faith in God. The extreme version of this is known as "fideism," which says, if God's existence were rationally evident, then faith in its entirety would become nonessential.

The Cosmological argument

Thomas Aquinas denied the Platonic tie-in of Augustine's theology and constituted his thought on Aristotle. Hence, Aquinas did not bother with "ontological argument," but rebuilt the "cosmological argument." Referencing the question of learning, the difference between these two debates is fundamentally a difference in epistemology.

Augustine believed one can directly go from the soul to God. He did not see the vitality of starting with sensory experiences; but Aquinas deciphered that "The human intellect is at first like a clean slate on which nothing is written" (Summa Theological I, Q:97, 2). It is sensation that writes on the tabula rasa. The mind has no form of its own. All its contents come from sensation; for Aquinas, perception was the key to unraveling the truth about God.

Aquinas initiated with "motion." He argued, it is perceived, as evident to our senses that in our world, some things are in motion. Now, whatever is moved is moved by another, for nothing can be moved except it is in potentiality to that towards which it is moved; whereas a thing moves in as much as it is in act. Motion is the reduction of something from potentiality to actuality.

But nothing can become lessened from potentiality to actuality except by something in a state of actuality. Thus, that which is actually hot, as fire, makes water hot, as water has the potential to be actually hot, and thereby fire moves and changes it, or fire makes wood hot.

Now it is not probable that the same thing could be in potentiality and reality in the same respect, but only in different respects. For what is actually hot cannot synchronously be potentially hot; but it is simultaneously potentially cold. It is therefore impossible that in the same respect and in the same way a thing should be both mover and moved (i.e., that it should move itself.)

Hence, whatever is moved must be moved by another. If that by which it is moved be itself moved, then this also must need to be moved by another, and that by another again. But this cannot go on to infinity, because then there would be no first mover, and consequently no other mover, seeing that eventually movers move only in as much as they are moved by the first mover; as the arrow moves only because it is moved by the hand of the archer, therefore it is necessary to arrive at the first mover, moved by no other, and this everyone realizes to be God.

Thomas Aquinas' intention is to reference a matter of logic, and not a plausible evidence to believe in God. It claims to conclusively prove that God must of necessity exist.

Bear in mind that human intelligence is designed and only potentiated to recognize the traces of God. It is obviously beyond our capability to see God. Is this to say that we will not perhaps one day be able to conquer the universe, as our malleable brain further evolves?

The biological evolution, including human evolution, is basically propelled by environmental changes. Accidental genetic metamorphism (alteration) and innovative outcomes make the successful adaptation possible. Scientists tell us that human evolution started about 7-8 million years ago in the African savannah, where an upright, vertical position became significantly beneficial.

The main reason for improving manual work and tool-making could be to have more food. Our forefathers obtained more meat due to hunting, resulting in more protein and essential fatty acid in the meal. The human nervous system does not proportionally utilize high levels of energy, therefore, a better quality of food was the preliminary reason for the evolution of huge human brain. The size of the human brain was tripled during 3.5 million years; it increased from the average of 450 cm3 of Australopithecinae to the average of 1350 cm3 of Homo sapiens. A genetic alteration in the system controlling gene expression could have occurred approximately 200,000 years ago, which influenced the development of nervous system, the sensorimotor function, and learning capability for motor processes. This is not to believe that the human brain has stopped growing, and that will not further expand.

www.slideshare.net

(Australopithecines are generally all species in the related Australopithecus and Paranthropus genera, and it typically includes Kenyanthropus, Ardipithecus, and Praeanthropus. All these related species are now sometimes collectively classified as a subtribe of the Hominini tribe called Australopithecina.)

I am certain that we sometime in the hereafter will, which should amaze, and alert humanity to forth notice the traces of God as humanity digs more into the so-called nothingness. We should by now know that what we do not see, produces what we see. Our memories, thought process, intelligence, feelings and emotions, our wisdom, and sanity, and hundreds of other things that are not tangible but play an extremely important role in our lives, without which we will not be able to carry on. When a scientist invents and discovers valuable inventions for advancing humanity into the future and for improving human lives, that is admirable. But they cannot not see the mind of their own and the thinking process which materialized the successful result, they can only see the effect of what they have created. We are inhibited to pass the space and time, and to see the almighty God.

Simply, because is beyond human brain, and the entire nervous system to decipher that.

"Man is the measure of all things" – Protagoras

Having faith plays a very imperative role in our lives. It engages us consciously, especially in crucial times. It is an intangible agenda that will also subliminally affects us, even if we stubbornly refuse to think about it, which I am afraid is taken for granted.

"We are too weak to discover the truth by reason alone" – St. Augustine

Life for millions often is full of obstacles. Many times we are faced with difficulties in our families, our health, our finances, our work, and a host of other issues. We can either overcome our barriers, or barriers can overtake us. Having faith in God will most definitely help us to fight our way through in difficult times.

Almost everything we do is faith-oriented, when in front line defending our homeland, we expect to come home safe, we have faith in having a pregnant lady to deliver safely, we have faith in seeing a healthy child is borne. We have faith to land safely when taking a plane to our destination. We have faith when we expect to get home safe or to work, when driving, we have faith to make it, when undergoing a surgery, we have faith to make it when stricken with some type of cancer, or any other malignant disease. We have faith to win when entering a race.

For heaven's sake, we have faith in not choking on a bite we take to eat. And thousands, if not millions of other faith-related issues that we deal with in our lives. For the faithful, faith in God is not casual. Faith in God is the heart and the soul of everything they do, and live for, it is the nervous system of their entire being. Let's not make mistake by acting religiously fanatical, and for having faith; they are not the same. Faith in God is to have compassion and believe in peace and humanity.

To expect science to locate God is to behave as imbecilic as one can be, since science operates in laboratories, where the results of real experimentations are manifested and can only deal what is apparent. Science does not delve into the metaphysical realms. As we are not made to fly, and should not expect wings to exude from either our rear end or from our sides to one-day fly. This is anatomically not possible, except in fiction-oriented movies or books. So is seeing God, as it is just beyond human ability. But, not detecting the magnificent traces of God is utterly unwise, and frankly, should designate poor orientation.

Ontological argument

An ontological argument is a philosophically based debate for the existence of God dealing with abstract entities, where philosophy, and other contextual words, like dualism, existentialism, dialectical, epistemology, solipsism, sequitur, transcendentalism, and metaphysics, are also discussed. Many arguments fall under the category of the ontological, and they tend to involve arguments about the state of being or existing. More specifically, ontological arguments tend to start with an a priori theory about the organization of the universe. If that organizational structure is true, the argument will provide reasons why God must exist.

Dualism: philosophy, the idea that human mind has a spiritual, non-material dimension that encompasses consciousness, and probably with an eternal attribute, or Good and evil struggling for supremacy. Dualism doctrine in contrary to idealism and materialism, holds that, reality consists of two basic types of substance normally including mind and matter, or two basic sort of entity, mental and physical.

Dialectical thinking indicates the ability to view issues from multiple perspectives and to arrive at the most efficient and reasonable reconciliation of seemingly contradictory information and postures.

Aiming at dialectical reasoning is the process of arriving at truth via a process of comparing and contrasting various solutions. This process, also known as logic, initiated in classical Greece by the philosopher Aristotle and has evolved into the present through the works of other philosophers such as Hegel.

What is Marx's dialectical materialism?

Dialectical materialism is a philosophical view to reality resulting from the ideas of Karl Marx and Friedrich Engels. For Marx and Engels, materialism meant that the material world, perceptible to the senses, has objective reality independent of mind or spirit.

Epistemology is the study of nature and scope of knowledge and justified belief. It analyzes the nature of knowledge and how it connects to analogous (like) ideas such as truth, belief, and what is justified. It also deals with the means of production of knowledge, as well as skepticism about various knowledge claims.

Epistemology is the study of knowledge. Three epistemological factors associated with knowledge procurement (acquisition) are truth, belief, and justification. Truth is an occurrence in which there are no false propositions. Knowledge itself can be defined as "justified true belief." Epistemology basically is a branch of philosophy that investigates the origin, nature, methods, and limits of human knowledge. The terms used to describe epistemological positions differ based on whether it's explaining the origin or the acquisition of knowledge.

Transcendentalism is an idealistic philosophical and social movement that developed in New England around 1836 in response to rationalism. Influenced by Platonism, romanticism, and Kantian philosophy, it arrived at that divinity impregnates (pervades) all nature and humanity, and its members held progressive views on feminism and communal living. Ralph Waldo Emerson and Henry David Thoreau were central figures. A system developed by Immanuel Kant was based on the notion that in order to understand the nature of reality, one needs first examine and analyze the logical process that governs the nature of experience.

Solipsism from Latin souls, meaning 'alone', and ipse, meaning 'self') is the philosophical idea that only one's own mind is certain to exist. As an epistemological position, solipsism holds that knowledge of anything outside one's own mind is unsure; the external world and other minds cannot be known and might not exist outside the mind. As a metaphysical position, solipsism takes an step further to the conclude that the world and other minds do not exist.

A non sequitur is a closure or response which doesn't follow logically from the previous statement. You've probably heard an example of a non sequitur before, therefore bunny rabbits are way cuter than chipmunks.

Non sequiturs are often utilized for comedic effect in movies, novels, and TV shows. When someone says a non sequitur, it usually means the person was off the subject in her own thoughts and not listening to the other person. Image that one girl says, "I'm worried that my mother is mad at me," and her friend responds, "I wonder what you call a male ladybug?" The non sequitur shows the friend clearly wasn't listening.

Idealism

The idealist philosopher George Berkeley believed that physical objects do not exist apart from the mind that perceives them. An item in fact exists merely as long as it is observed; otherwise, it is not only senseless (meaningless), but simply fictitious. The observer and the observed are one. Berkeley does try to show things can and do exist separate from the human mind and our recognition, but only because there is an all-encompassing mind in which all ideas are perceived— in other words, God, who observes all. Solipsism agrees that nothing exists outside of perception, but would say that Berkeley falls prey to the egocentric predicament— he can solely make his own observations, and therefore cannot be truly certain that this God or other people exist to see "reality." The solipsist would say it is better to ignore the unreliable observations of alleged other people and rely upon the immediate certainty of one's own perceptions.

Rationalism

Rationalism is the philosophical position that truth is best discovered by the use of reasoning and logic rather than by the use of the senses.

What is the philosophy of existentialism?

Existentialism is a philosophy that highlights individual existence, freedom, and choice. Its main thesis suggests that human beings identify with their own meaning in life, and try to make rational decisions even though they live in an irrational universe. The essence of existentialism suggests that existence predates essence, which is a central claim of existentialism. It opposes the traditional philosophical understanding that the essence (the nature) of a thing is more fundamental and ironclad (unchangeable) than its existence.

It says that man is essentially selfish, that man is a rational being. Sartre saying that "the essence precedes essence" means a personality is not constructed over a previously model designed with exact purpose, contrary to metaphysics that says, "the essence precedes existence." Because it is the one who choose one's own destiny. Sartre does not reject constraining positions of human's existence. In response to Spinoza, who ratified (affirmed) that "man is determined by what surrounds him," Sartre says: an oppressive situation is not unbearable in itself, but when considered intolerable by those who feel oppressed the situation becomes unendurable, so, by literally projecting my intentions onto my present position, "it is I who freely transform it into action."

To say that existence precedes essence is to confirm that there is no such thing as predetermined essence to be located in humans, and that an individual's essence is defined by the individual through how that individual defines and lives his or her life. As Sartre puts it in his Existentialism is a Humanism: "Man first of all exists, encounters himself, surges up in the world – and defines himself afterwards."

Ibn Sina was actually the first proponent of the Ontological argument (980-1037), it was Ibn Sina who articulated a proof for the existence of God within a priori premise. existence even though It is common to know Anselm of Canterbury (1033-1109) the first advocator of the Ontological Argument. An ontological debate is a philosophical argument for the existence of God that utilizes ontology. Many arguments are constituted under the category of the ontological, and they mean to manifest arguments about the state of being or existing. Particularly ontological discussion tend to start with an a priori theory about the organization of the universe. If that organizational edifice is true, the argument will substantiate the reasons for God's existence.

The first ontological discussion in the Western Christian tradition was suggested by Anselm of Canterbury in his 1078 work Pros logion. Anselm explained God as "that than which nothing greater can be thought," and argued that this being must exist in the mind, even in the mind of the person who denies the existence of God. He believed that, if the greatest possible being exists in the mind, it must also exist in reality. If it only exists in the mind, then an even greater being must be possible—one which exists both in the mind and in reality. Therefore, this greatest possible being must exist in reality. René Descartes the seventeenth century French Philosopher concocted an equivalent argument of a supremely perfect being. the early eighteenth century, Gottfried Leibniz augmented Descartes' ideas in an attempt to prove that a "supremely perfect" being is a coherent concept. In the early eighteenth century, Gottfried Leibniz augmented Descartes' ideas tried to prove that a "supremely perfect" being is a coherent concept. Other arguments have been categorized as ontological, including those made by Islamic philosophers Mulla Sadra and Allama Tabatabai.

Later, Thomas Aquinas rejected the argument on the basis that humans cannot know God's nature. Also, David Hume offered an empirical objection, criticizing its lack of evidential reasoning and rejecting the idea that anything can exist necessarily. Immanuel Kant's critique was based on what he saw as the false premise that existence is a predicate. He argued that "existing" adds nothing (including perfection) to the essence of a being, and thus a "supremely perfect" being can be conceived not to exist. Finally, philosophers including C. D. Broad dismissed the coherence of a maximally great being, proposing that some attributes of greatness are incompatible with others, rendering "maximally great being" incoherent.

The traditional definition of an ontological argument was given by Immanuel Kant.

He contrasted the ontological argument (literally any argument "concerned with being")[3] with the cosmological and physio-theoretical arguments. According to the Kantian view, ontological arguments are those founded on a priori reasoning.

Anselm of Canterbury was the first to attempt an ontological argument for God's existence.

Main article: Pros logion

Theologian and philosopher Anselm of Canterbury (1033–1109) proposed an ontological discussion in the second and third chapters of his Pros logion. Anselm's debate was not shown in order to prove God's existence; rather, Pros logion was a job of meditation in which he presented the idea of God as self-evident to him.

In Chapter 2 of the Pros logion, Anselm defined God as a "being than which no greater can be conceived." He suggested that even "the fool" can understand this concept, and this understanding itself means that the being must exist in the mind. The concept must exist either only in our mind, or in both our mind and in reality. If such a being exists only in our mind, then a greater being—that which exists in the mind and in reality—can be comprehended (this argument is generally considered as a reductio ad absurdum, because the view of the fool is proven to be inconsistent). Hence, if we can conceive of a being than which nothing greater can be conceived, it must exist in reality. Thus, a being than which nothing greater could be procreated, which Anselm sees as God, must exist in reality.

Anselm's argument summarizes that

It is a conceptual truth (or, so to speak, true by definition) that God is a being than which none greater can be envisaged (that is, the greatest possible existence that can be imagined).

God exists as a notion in the mind.

A being that exists as a concept in the mind and in reality is, other things being equal, greater than a being that exists only as an idea in the mind.

Thus, if God exists only as an idea in the mind, then we can imagine something that is greater than God (that is, a greatest possible being that does exist).

But we cannot imagine something that is greater than God (for it is a contradiction to suppose that we can imagine a being greater than the greatest possible being that can be imagined.)

Therefore, God exists.

In Chapter 3, Anselm presented a further argument in the same vein:

By definition, God is a being than which none greater can be imagined.

A being that necessarily exists in reality is greater than a being that does not necessarily exist.

Thus, by definition, if God exists as an idea in the mind but does not necessarily exist in reality, then we can imagine something that is greater than God.

But we cannot imagine something that is greater than God.

Thus, if God exists in the mind as an idea, then God necessarily exists in reality.

God exists in the mind as an idea.

Therefore, God necessarily exists in reality.

This contains the notion of a being that cannot be conceived not to exist. He argued that if something can be conceived not to exist, then something greater can be conceived. Consequently, a thing than which nothing greater can be conceived cannot be conceived not to exist and so it must exist.

René Descartes

French thinker René Descartes proposed several arguments that could be termed ontological.

René Descartes (1596–1650) proposed a number of ontological arguments, which differed from Anselm's formulation. Generally speaking, they are less formal arguments than natural intuition.

Descartes wrote in the Fifth Meditation:

But, if the mere fact that I can produce from my thought the idea of something entails that everything that I clearly and distinctly perceive to belong to that thing really does belong to it, is not this a possible basis for another argument to prove the existence of God? Certainly, the idea of God, or a supremely perfect being, is one that I find within me just as surely as the idea of any shape or number. And my understanding that it belongs to his nature that he always exists is no less clear and distinct than is the case when I prove of any shape or number that some property belongs to its nature.

Descartes argued that God's existence can be deduced from his nature, just as geometric ideas can be deduced from the nature of shapes—he used the deduction of the sizes of angles in a triangle as an example. He suggested that the concept of God is that of a supremely perfect being, holding all perfections. He seems to have assumed that existence is a predicate of a perfection. Thus, if the notion of God did not include existence, it would not be supremely perfect, as it would be lacking a perfection. Consequently, the notion of a supremely perfect God who does not exist, Descartes argues, is unintelligible. Therefore, according to his nature, God must exist.

Gottfried Leibniz

German philosopher Gottfried Leibniz attempted to prove the coherence of a "supremely perfect being."

Gottfried Wilhelm Leibniz saw a problem with Descartes' ontological argument: that Descartes had not asserted the coherence of a "supremely perfect" being. He proposed that, unless the coherence of a supremely perfect being could be demonstrated, the ontological argument fails. Leibniz saw perfection as impossible to analyses; therefore, it would be impossible to demonstrate that all perfections are incompatible. He reasoned that all perfections can exist together in a single entity, and that Descartes' argument is still valid.

Mulla Sadra

Transcendent theosophy

Mulla Sadra (c. 1571/2 – 1640) was an Iranian Shia Islamic philosopher who was influenced by earlier Muslim philosophers such as Avicenna and Suhrawardi, as well as the Sufi metaphysician Ibn 'Arabi. Sadra discussed Avicenna's arguments for the existence of God, claiming that they were not a priori. He rejected the argument on the basis that existence precedes essence, or that the existence of human beings is more fundamental than their essence.[26]

Sadra put forward a new argument, known as Seddiqin Argument or Argument of the Righteous. The argument attempts to prove the existence of God through the reality of existence, and to conclude with God's pre-eternal necessity. In this argument, a thing is demonstrated through itself, and a path is identical with the goal. In other arguments, the truth is attained from an external source, such as from the possible to the necessary, from the originated to the eternal origin, or from motion to the unmoved mover. In the argument of the righteous, there is no middle term other than the truth. His version of the ontological argument can be summarized as follows:

There is existence

Existence is a perfection above which no perfection may be conceived

God is perfection and perfection in existence

Existence is a singular and simple reality; there is no metaphysical pluralism

That singular reality is graded in intensity in a scale of perfection (that is, a denial of a pure monism).

That scale must have a limit point, a point of greatest intensity and of greatest existence.

Hence God exists.

Mulla Sadra describes this argument in his main work al-asfar al-arba'a [four journeys] as follows:

Existence

There are two Gods,

There are two Gods in existence. First, the infinitely ethereal (spiritual projection, occult) God that created man, a universally ubiquitous (ever-present) God which is closer to one than one's aorta. The God of the apocalypse (revelation, divine disclosure), love, peace, compassion, kindness, justice, and generosity. And the Other God that is manufactured by man which maneuvers through hypocrisy (the pot calling the kettle black), violence, force, tyranny, genocides, despicably inhumane wars, atrocities, and extreme inequity, all to exert imposition (assignment) for riveting globally classified nations, to exploit and maim solely to ensure maximizing profit. If one cares to meditate on the traces of both Gods, one will be able to clearly discern which one is which, and if so, then enlightenment can prevent moral and spiritual ebb in one's divinity and confessional state of mind. And once this become oriented in one's conscious. It will identify the real culprit, exposing the epidemically disease stricken agent. That is the first step toward collective healing; to further avoid brainwashing, and for eluding against planting fetal mental illness and denial syndrome. Which I am afraid many societies are plotted against, and infected with; where billions live only nominal to God as they behave callous and practice so many misdeeds beyond comprehension, and up to no good criminal activities as if there is no judgment day.

The Cosmological Argument

Everything that exists must have a cause, only correct in our tangible Newtonian's world. Because according to quantum physics things can pop out of nowhere without any cause. Therefore, no flaws by atheists can be materialized in this rather decisive sub-atomic realm. The atheists question that: if God is the cause of everything, then who caused God? Perhaps a make sense question, but certainly not so in the higher realms, since apparently in higher realms no cause is necessary for something to show out of nowhere. Also, you sure cannot pass the bucket and regress to infinity, the bucket must stop at some rather decisive point. Furthermore, Scientists and the mathematicians cannot really calculate infinity as an integer (whole) number or decimal number in their funding's to meaningfully conclude their formulas. Infinity is just a figure of speech, which reason dictates that at least in our material world no open-ended case or idea should make any sense. God created the universe. Nothing can exist outside the universe, but God. Only God can exist outside of time, space, matter and events. Those two things, time and space are really part of the same thing since reason should dictate that: no time can exist without any apace. We can see that we are moving through space, but we cannot see time in the same way, we can only see its effects. And in answering the atheists that why God is an exception to the rules, and why God cannot be seen. we should simply relate that no maker can be seen in one's makings, only the effects and the awesome traces left by the creator should be noticed. Beside thousands, if not millions of other things cannot be seen starting with one's own mind, emotions, feelings and memories. The effects of the material world on our senses cannot be detected which they impact our nervous system and the brain to manage what we must do daily to get by. Have you ever wondered who are you? And if you are inside of you, and where should you be found or seen? look all you want and search for oneself with the most advanced magnifier and try to find you. I am not talking about the apparent physical you with a bunch of muscles, nerves, blood and bones. I am talking about the real you, the one that thinks, feels, falls in love, fears, plays, laughs, cries, is occasionally sad, and perhaps often happy. There are things that are simply above and beyond our human brain and the nervous system to answer. Further, to conceive of God as not existing is not to propagate (procreate, conceive) God.

The theological argument is that:

The coherency in things is for serving a purpose (for instance, all the complex parts of a watch that allows it to keep time), we need to know that they had a designer who designed them with the function in mind; they are immensely improbable to have arisen by random physical procedures. Saying (A hurricane blowing through a hardware store could not assemble a watch.) Organs of living things, like the eye and the heart, cohere because they have a purpose (for example, the eye has a cornea, lens, retina, iris, eyelids, and so on, which are found in the same organ only because together they make it possible for the animal to see. Further, these things and millions of other products did not have a human designer, hence, they must have had a non-human designer, God. God exists.

The Argument from Irreducible Complexity

Evolution has no ability to predict since each and every piecemeal (gradual, incremental) step must be a progress over the preceding one, letting the organism to subsist and regenerate better than its competitors. In many complicated organs, the removal or metamorphosis (modification) of any part would annihilate the entire functionality of the organ. For instance, the lens and retina of the eye, the molecular components of blood clotting, and the molecular motor powering the cell's flagellum. Call these organs "irreducibly complex." These organs could not have been beneficial to the organisms that possessed them in any simpler forms. The Theory of Natural Selection cannot explain these irreducibly complex systems.

Molecular biology has shown that even the simplest of all living systems on the earth today, bacterial cells, are exceedingly complex objects. Although the tiniest bacterial cells are incredibly small, weighing less than 10-12 gms, each is in effect a veritable micro-miniaturized factory containing thousands of exquisitely designed pieces of intricate molecular machinery, made up altogether of one hundred thousand million atoms, far more complicated than any machine built by man and absolutely without parallel in the nonliving world." — Michael Denton, <u>Evolution: A Theory In Crisis</u>

Michael Behe quote" in Darwin's time all of biology was a black box: not only the cell, or the eye, or digestion, or immunity, but every biological structure and function because, ultimately, no one could explain how biological processes occurred. Michael Behe Time, Black, Eye, Biology, Box, Explain Proteins are the machinery of living tissue that builds the structures and carries out the chemical reactions necessary for life".

The Argument from the Paucity (scarcity, deficiency) of mild Mutations.

Evolution is haphazardly done without conscious decision, or so to speak occurred by random mutations and through natural selection. And since the organism is complicated unlikely systems. Then, by the laws of probability, any change is staggeringly more promising to be for the worse than for the better. The greater numbers of mutation would be detrimental for the organism. Furthermore, the amount of time it would consume for all the benign mutations to assemble an organ to be revealed is ludicrously long time. Therefore, something external, something outside of evolution (the prime Mutator) had to favor the process of mutation, appreciating the number of benign ones, to superintend the evolution to function. The only entity that is both infinitely powerful and purposeful enough to be the essential Mutator is God.

> "New mutations don't create new species; they create offspring that are impaired."
>
> — Lynn Margulis

> "Life did not take over the world by combat, but by networking."
>
> — Lynn Margulis, Micro cosmos: Four Billion Years of Microbial Evolution

> "Natural selection eliminates and maybe maintains, but it doesn't create... Neo-Darwinists say that new species

> emerge when mutations occur and modify an organism. I was taught over and over again that the accumulation of random mutations led to evolutionary change [which] led to new species. I believed it until I looked for evidence."
>
> — Lynn Margulis

The modern argument from The Original Replicator

It says that evolution is the protrusion (progression) by which an organism evolves from simpler progenitors. Evolution by itself cannot answer how the original archetype — the first living thing — came into existence. The theory of natural selection can accord with this problem solely by manifesting that the first living thing evolved out of non-living matter. That non-living matter (call it the Original Replicator) must be capable of first self-replication, second by producing a practical mechanism out of surrounding matter to protect itself against breaking down, and third, surviving moderate mutations to itself which then will result in fairly different duplicators. The Original Replicator is complicated. The Original Replicator is too byzantine (elaborate, complex) to have hatched from purely physical processes. For instance, DNA, which presently holds the replicated design of organisms, cannot be the Original Replicator, because DNA molecules require a complex system of proteins to remain stable and to replicate, and could not have been born from natural processes before intricate life existed. Natural selection cannot explain the complexity of the Original Replicator. The Original Replicator must have been created rather than have been evolved.

Argument from an unjust point of view

The argument against God is that the universe seems to be unbelievably brutal and unfair. But how anyone can get this idea of just and unjust? One does not call a line crooked unless one has some concept of a straight line. What is a man comparing this universe with when he/she refers to it as unjust? If the entire show was evil and in vain why did a man who is supposed to be part of the show, find himself in such a fierce reaction against it? Of course one could have given up one's idea of justice by saying it was nothing but a fad, some sort of fancy and wishful thinking. But if so, then the argument against God collapses too–for the argument leans on saying the world was truly unjust. Thus, in the very act of trying to prove that God did not exist and that the entire reality was senseless – one should find that one had to assume one part of reality – namely one's concept of justice – was making a lot of sense. If the whole universe has no meaning, we should never have figured out that it has no meaning: just as, if there was no intelligence in the universe we wouldn't have known about ignorance, or if no goodness in the universe, we wouldn't have known about evil, if no light in the universe and hence no creatures with eyes, we could never have realized it was dark. Dark would be with no meaning.

The fine tuning of the universe

There are a monumental number of physically potential universes. A universe that would be user friendly to the appearance of life must comply with some very severe situations: Everything from the mass ratios of atomic particles and the number of dimensions of space to the cosmological domain that govern the augmentation of the universe must be just precise for stable galaxies, solar systems, planets, the entire universe and complex life to evolve. The percentage of possible universes that would support life is minuscule. Our universe is one of those diminutively improbable universes. Our universe has been fine-tuned to sustain life. There is a Fine- purposeful Tuner.

Example: neutrons are just a tad heavier than protons. If it were the other way around, atoms couldn't exist, because all the protons in the universe would have decayed into neutrons shortly after the big bang. No protons, then no atomic nucleuses and no atoms. No atoms, no chemistry, no life. Like Baby Bear's porridge in the story of Goldilocks, the universe seems to be just right for life." — Paul Davies

The Argument from the Beauty of Physical Laws

Scientists utilize aesthetic axiom (simplicity, symmetry, elegance) to concoct the laws of nature. They could only use aesthetic principles successfully if the laws of nature were orderly, intrinsically and objectively beautiful. The laws of nature are inherently and equitably beautiful Only a beautiful mind-like being with an appreciation for beauty could have designed the disciplinary physical laws of nature. God is the only being with the power and purpose to design beautiful laws of nature.

The Argument from Cosmic Coincidences

The universe includes so many eerie (unearthly, spooky, uncanny) coincidences, like the diameter of the moon, as observed from the earth, which is the same as the diameter of the sun when is noticed from the earth. That is why we can have exhibition eclipses (when the sun looks like it is completely or partially covered with a dark circle because the moon is between the sun and the earth.) when the corona (a bright circle seen around the sun or the moon) of the sun is shown. Synchronies (coincidences, coexistence) are by definition exceedingly improbable. The overwhelmingly improbable defy all statistical elucidation. These coexistences are such as to ameliorate (enrich, enhance) our petrified appreciation for the beauty of the natural world. Such uncanny coincidences are only possible by an Omnipotent, Omnipresent, Omniscient God. it seems in every situation in which we notice a pattern, someone purposefully set the pattern in our universe to be visualized. Illustrious among the uncanny coincidences that should be injected into this debate are those relating to numbers. Numbers are enigmatic (mystic) to us since they are not physical objects like gravels, chairs, and cars, but simultaneously they seem to be real entities, ones that we can't conjure up with any properties we fancy but that have their own requisite(needful) properties, meaningfulness and relations. Hence, they must, however, exist outside us. We are therefore inclined to attribute magical might to them. And, given the infinity of numbers and the enormous possible ways to make them applicable to our world.

The Argument from Personal Coincidences

Many people experience eerie coincidences in everyday living (for instance, someone you knew long time ago calling you out of the blue just when you're thinking of him or her; or a dream about an episode(event) that proves to have just occurred, or you or a loved one happens to miss a flight which then crashes leaving no one alive. Uncanny Synchronizes (coexistence) cannot be explained by the laws of probability. They are inexplicable but play a significant role in our lives. It sure seems they are as laser likely précised as they are dictated from out of this world. That is why they are known as uncanny behaviors.

The Argument from Answered Prayers

Prayers and curses are energy-oriented thoughts, so is our universe, as people's emotions and feelings are intangible issues as is the prevalent energy in the universe. peoples power of intention has the potential to comply with a prevalently awakened universe which it seems reads people's mind and one's earnest request. which of- course those prayers or curses must justly take place, and not randomly. The reward or the punishment need to be justifying, and not done haphazardly or by coincidence. When a heart-broken mother prays for the life of her only dying child and the child recovers, that is the true power of intention. The well-known phrase that says: what goes around comes around, has infinitely been experienced through the course of human history. It is a definite fact and not just an empty promise. There are many occasions that people have survived death. Patients who flat-line under surgery, or during medical emergencies have indicated an experience of being floated overseeing their bodies and noticed a glimpse of a gloriously shining passage to the other side, all taking place while even being pronounced dead. This out of body experience entails the existence of an immaterial soul.

Argument from Mathematical Reality

Mathematical facts are requisitely true. (There is no probable world in which, can say, 4 plus 4 does not equal 8, or in which the square root of 2 can be expressed as the ratio of two whole numbers. The truths that explain our material world, no matter how elemental (basic, fundamental), are empirical, requiring observational adduce (evidence.) For instance, when waiting for some experimental means to examine string theory, so that we can figure out whether we live in a world of eleven dimensions. Truths that demand empirical evidence are not necessary truths. We request empirical proof because there are probably worlds in which these are not truths, and so we have to test that ours is not such a world. The truths of our physical world are not necessary truths. The facts of our material world cannot explain mathematical truths. Mathematical truths exist on a different realm of existence from physical truths, only something which itself exists on a different plane of existence from the physical can elaborate and describe mathematical truths. Only God can explain mathematical truths. Mathematics is derived through pure reason — what the philosophers call a priori reason — which means that it cannot be debunked by any empirical scrutiny.

The basic question in philosophy of mathematics is: how can mathematics be true but not empirical? Is it because mathematics explains some trans-empirical reality — as mathematical realists accept — or is it because mathematics has no gratification at all and is a purely formal bet agreeing with postulated (posit, stipulate, hypothesis) rules and their consequences? The Argument from Mathematical Reality assumes, in its third premise, the position of mathematical realism, which isn't a sophistry (paradox, fallacy) in itself; many mathematicians believe it, some of them arguing that it follows from Gödel's incompleteness theorems This debate, however, goes further and tries to infer (deduce, conclude) God's being from the trans-empirical existence of mathematical reality.

Trinity Foundation hereby grants permission to all readers to download, print, and distribute on paper or electronically any of its Reviews, provided that each reprint bears our copyright notice, current addresses, and telephone numbers, provided that all such reproductions are distributed to the public without charge. The Reviews may not be sold or issued in book form, CD-ROM form.

It is noteworthy to know that the idea of ethical monotheism, which believes that morality is only possible, coming from God alone, and that its laws are unfaltering, was first instituted in Judaism, but is now a core theology of most modern monotheistic religions, not excluding Zoroastrianism, Christianity, Islam, Sikhism, and the Baha'i faith.

Søren Kierkegaard argued that objective knowledge, such as 1+1=2, is unimportant to existence. If God could rationally be proven, his existence would be unimportant to humans. It is because God cannot rationally be proven that his existence is important to us.

In The Justification of Knowledge, the Calvinist theologian Robert L. Raymond argues that believers should not try to prove the existence of God. He believes all such proofs are basically fallacious and believers should not place their confidence in them, much less resort to them in discussions with nonbelievers; rather, they should accept the content of revelation by faith. Raymond's position is similar to that of his mentor, Gordon Clark, which says that all worldviews are fundamentally based on certain unprovable first parlor (premises, axioms), and consequently are end-all (ultimately) indemonstrable.

Positive atheism (also called "strong atheism" and "hard atheism") is a form of atheism that avow (affirm) that no pantheon (deities, demigod, goddess) exist. The strong atheist vividly professes the non-existence of gods. Some strong atheists further aver (predicate, say) that the existence of gods is logically impractical, stating that the combination of attributes which God may be declared to have (omnipotence, omniscience, omnipresence, transcendence, Omni-benevolence) are logically contradictory, incomprehensible, or farcical (absurd, ludicrous), and therefore the existence of such a god is a priori false. Metaphysical naturalism is a common worldview affiliated (confederate) with strong atheism.

Negative atheism (also called "weak atheism" and "soft atheism") is any type of atheism other than positive, wherein a person does not believe in the existence of any deities, but does not specifically utter there to be none.

Agnosticism is the behold that the truth value of certain claims—especially rights about the existence of any deity, but also other religious and metaphysical claims—is obscure (not known or unknowable.) Agnosticism as a commodious (broad umbrella) term does not survey one's belief or disbelief in gods; agnostics may still see themselves as theists or atheists.

Strong agnosticism is the belief that it is not possible for human-beings to realize if it is, or not, that any deities exist. Weak agnosticism is the belief that the existence or nonexistence of deities is unknown but not necessarily unknowable.

Agnostic theism is the philosophical view that include both theism and agnosticism. An agnostic theist believes in the existence of a god or God, but accept the basis of this proposition as unknown or inherently unknowable. Agnostic theists may also persist on unawareness regarding the characteristics of the gods they believe in.

Agnostic atheism is a philosophical position that contain both atheism and agnosticism. Agnostic atheists are atheistic since they do not hold a belief in the existence of any deity, and agnostic because they claim that the existence of a deity is either unknowable in principle, or presently not known in truth.

The theologian Robert Flint explains:

If a man has failed to find any good reason for believing that there is a God, it is perfectly natural and rational that he should not believe that there is a God; and if so, he is an atheist, although he assumes no superhuman knowledge, but merely the ordinary human power of judging of evidence. If he goes farther, and, after an investigation into the nature and reach of human knowledge, ending in the conclusion that the existence of God is incapable of proof, cease to believe in it on the ground that he cannot know it to be true, he is an agnostic and also an atheist, an agnostic-atheist—an atheist because an agnostic.

An apatheist is someone who is indifferent, and not interested in accepting, or denying any claims that God or gods exist or do not exist. An apatheist lives as if there are no gods and describes natural phenomena without reference to any deities. The existence of gods is not repudiated, but may be indicated superfluous (nonessential), or worthless; gods neither provide intend to life, nor influence everyday life. Apatheism of apathy and theism) is the attitude of apathy towards the existence or non-existence of god(s). It is more of an attitude rather than a belief, claim, or belief system. An apatheist is someone who does not care, and is not interested in rejecting or believing any claim that gods exist or do not. The existence of God, or god(s) is not refused, but may be indicated not relevant.

Ignosticism and theological no cognitivism are similar although whereas the ignostic utters that "every theological situation presumes too much about the concept of God," the theological no cognitivist claims to have no idea anyhow to label as "a concept of God."

The ignostic (or igtheist) usually concludes that the question of God's existence or nonexistence is not worth arguing about since concepts like "God" are normally not clearly enough explained. Ignosticism or igtheism is the theological discussion that every other theological position (including agnosticism and atheism) presupposes too much about the idea of God and many other theological concepts. It can be described as having two related views about the existence of God. The view that a coherent definition of God must be stated before the question of the existence of God can be meaningfully talked about. Furthermore, if that demarcation is unfalsifiable, the ignostic takes the theological no cognitivist position that the question of the existence of God is basically absurd. In this case, the concept of God is not considered meaningless; the term "God" is considered in vain. The second behold is synonymous with theological no cognitivism, and skips the step of first asking "What is meant by 'God'?" before declaring the original question "Does God exist?" meaningless.

Some prominent philosophers have regarded ignosticism as a variation of agnosticism or atheism, while others have considered it to be unlike. An ignostic says that he is not even able to utter whether he is a theist or an atheist until adequate explanation of theism is rendered.

In the Aristotelian philosophy, God is seen as part of the explanatory structure necessary to support scientific finale, and any powers God own are—strictly speaking—of the natural order that emanate from God's place as creator of nature.

In Karl Popper's philosophy of science, belief in a supernatural God is outside the natural parameter of scientific research since all scientific hypotheses must be falsifiable in the natural world. The view suggested by Stephen Jay Gould also believes that the existence (or otherwise) of God is not relevant to and is beyond the territory of science.

Logical positivists such as Rudolf Carnap and A. J. Ayer believe any sought talk of gods as literal humbug. For the logical positivists and followers of similar schools of thought, proposition about religious or other transcendent experiences cannot have a truth value, and are deemed to be without making sense, because such statements do not have any vivid verification standard. As the Christian biologist Scott C. Todd says "Even if all the data pointed to an intelligent designer, such a hypothesis is excluded from science because it is not naturalistic." This argument limits the territory of science to the empirically observable and limits the domain of God to the unprovable.

John Polkinghorne beholds that the closest analogy to the existence of God in physics is the ideas of quantum mechanics which are seemingly paradoxical (offending against logic) but make sense of a great deal of different data.

Alvin Plantinga compares the question of the existence of God to the question of the existence of other minds, believing both are notoriously impossible to "prove" against a resolute doubter.

Other philosophers, like Wittgenstein, suggest what is known as anti-realist and oppose philosophical discussion related to God's existence. For instance, Charles Taylor argues that the real is whatever will not go away, and not quiescent (inactive, dormant) from talks of existence. If we cannot reduce talk about God to anything else, or replace it, or prove it bogus, then may be God is as real as anything else.

George Berkeley contended that a "naked thought" cannot exist, and that a perception is a thought; therefore only minds can be ascertain to exist, since all else is just an idea transmitted by a perception. From this Berkeley argued that the universe is based upon observation and is non-objective, it is not based on facts, rather than feelings or opinions. However, he noted that the universe includes "ideas" no discernible to mankind, and that there must, therefore, exist an omniscient super observer, which perceives such things. Berkeley considered this proof of the existence of the Christian God.

C.S. Lewis, in Mere Christianity and elsewhere, nurtured the argument from desire. He suggested that all natural desires have a natural object. One thirsts, and there exists water to quench this thirst; One hungers, and there exists food to satisfy this hunger. He then argued that the human desire for perfect justice, perfect peace, perfect happiness, and other unseen strongly implies the existence of such things, though they seem unobtainable on earth. He further furnished that the unquenchable desires of this life strongly imply that we are purposed for a different life, essentially governed by a God who can purvey the desired intangibles.

Philosophical arguments for the existence of God

Discussing view from beauty.

One form of the argument from beauty is that the grace of the laws of physics, which have been experimentally contrived, or the elegant laws of mathematics, which are abstract but which have empirically proven to be extremely beneficial, is proof of a creator deity who has set up these things to be beautiful and not ugly.

The argument from consciousness claims that human consciousness cannot be described by the physical mechanisms of the human body and brain, therefore, affirming that there must be non-physical aspects to human consciousness. This is held as not so direct evidence of God, prone to the notions that souls and the afterlife in Judaism, Christianity and Islam would be coherent with such a claim. Critics point out that non-physical aspects of consciousness could exist in a universe without any gods; for example, believe in reincarnation are consonant (agreeable, congenial) with atheism, monotheism, and polytheism.

The idea of the soul was created before contemporary understanding of neural networks and the anatomy of the brain. Decades of experimentation lead cognitive science to consider thought and emotion as physical processes although the experience of consciousness still is not understood. The difficult problem of consciousness stays as to whether different people subjectively experience the environment around them in the same way — for instance, that the color red looks the same inside the minds of different people, though this is a philosophical puzzle with both physical and non-physical descriptions. Aquinas profound ways, arguing for God's existence. First cause, the unmoved mover, argument from contingency, argument from degree, or teleological argument.

In his Summa Theologica, Thomas Aquinas generated his five arguments for God's existence. These disputes are foundered in an Aristotelian ontology and utilizes the infinite regression argument. Aquinas did not mean to fully prove the existence of God as he is orthodoxly conceived (a belief or a way of thinking that is accepted as true, or correct), but proposed his Five Ways as an initial stage, which he concocted upon later in his work. Aquinas' Five Ways argued from the unmoved mover, first cause, necessary being, argument from degree, and the teleological argument.

The unmoved mover argument acknowledges that derived from observation, and experience of motion in the universe (motion being the transition from potentiality to actuality) we can see that there must have been an initial mover. Aquinas debates that, whatever is in motion must be put in motion by another thing, so there must be an unmoved mover.

Aquinas' argument from first cause began with the axiom (assumption) that it is not possible for a being to cause itself (because it would have to exist before it caused itself) and that it is impracticable for there to be an infinite chain of causes, which would result in infinite regress. Therefore, there must be a first cause, itself uncaused.

The argument from necessary being affirms that all subsistence (beings) are contingent, representing that it is possible for them not to exist. Aquinas argued that if everything can possibly not exist, there must have been a time when nothing subsisted; as things are now, there must exist a being with need full existence, regarded as God.

Aquinas argued from degree, indicating the event of estate (degrees of goodness.) He believed that things which are known as good, must be called good in relation to a standard of good—a maximum. There must be a maximum goodness that all other goods can relatively be measured with, an absolute good, which causes all goodness.

The teleological argument affirms the view that things without intelligence are carefully organized, controlled towards a purpose. Aquinas argued that unintelligent objects cannot be ordered unless they are done so by an intelligent being, which conveys that there must be an intelligent being to move objects to their ends: God. The idea of the soul was created before contemporary understanding of neural networks and the physiology of the brain. Decades of experimentation lead cognitive science to consider thought and emotion as physical processes although the experience of consciousness still is not understood. The difficult problem of consciousness remains as to whether different people subjectively experience the environment around them in the same way—for instance, that the color red looks the same inside the minds of different people, though this is a philosophical puzzle with both physical and non-physical descriptions.

Aquinas had profound ways of arguing for God's existence. First cause, the unmoved mover, argument from contingency, argument from degree, or teleological argument.

Subjective argument

The sincere seeker's argument, espoused by Muslim Sufis of the Tasawwuf tradition, posits that every individual who follows a formulaic path towards guidance arrives at the same destination of conviction in the existence of God, and specifically in the monotheistic tenets and laws of Islam. This could only be true if the formula and supplication were being answered by the same divine entity being addressed, as claimed in Islamic revelations. This was formally organized by Imam Abu Hamid Al-Ghazali in such notable works as Deliverance from Error and The Alchemy of Happiness, in Arabic Kimiya-yi sa'adat. The path includes following the golden rule of no harm to others and treating others with compassion, silence or minimal speech, seclusion, daily fasting or minimalist diet of water and basic nourishment, honest wages, and daily supplication towards "the Creator of the Universe" for guidance.

Stephen Hawking and co-author Leonard Mlodinow state in their book The Grand Design that it is reasonable to ask who or what created the universe, but if the answer is God, then the question has merely been deflected to that of who created God. Both authors claim that it is possible to answer these questions purely within the realm of science, and without invoking any divine beings. Christian mathematicians and scientists, most notably Leonhard Euler, Bernard d'Espagnat and Lennox, disagree with that kind of skeptical argument.

A counter-argument against God as the Creator tasks the assumption of the cosmological argument ("chicken or the egg"), that things cannot exist without creators, and applies it to God, setting up an infinite regress. The Grand Design / A Brief History of Time.

In his book The Grand Design, Hawkins's conclusion is precisely contrary to what he stated. Professor Hawkins says the universe is not designed, but appeared out of nothing, and into existence; because of some chancy physical laws that just happen to generate universes at will. Then, in his book A Brief History of Time, he claims that "There is a sound scientific explanation for the making of our world – no Gods required." What Mr. Hawking is actually saying is that science in particular physics, and because of some "laws of physics" we now know everything that is requisite to describe the existence of God, and the existence. Professor Hawking is so extremely focused on the laws of physics, he has become one-track-minded, making him irrelevant to the very laws he is proclaiming. He forgets that no law, or laws can ever create anything, they are discoveries from the womb of mother nature. He, as an award-winning physicist, should be applauded for inventing some of them. It is a universe so finely tuned beyond anyone's imagination which requires a must infinitely intelligent programmer.

Hawking states that the reason the universe requires no creator is because of a "new theory" known as the M-theory, (where "M" stands for "membrane," or "murky"1 it has evolved from "strings" to "membranes," although all forms of the theory leads to extra dimensions (11, in fact). However, M-theory is no single theory, but, rather, a number of theories.

The nature of the universe requires that membranes from M-theory must be on the order of Planck length (10-35 m). Such a dimension is much less than microscopic or even well under subatomic particle proportion. In order to validate such objects, one would need an accelerator of 6,000,000,000,000,000 miles in circumference. It should indicate, therefore, that confirmation of M-theory, based upon observable data, would be impossible. Do such a set of theories that forecast everything but are not verifiable through observational data really fall within the realm of science?

Stephen Hawking says, "Because there is a law such as gravity, the universe can and will create itself from nothing. Spontaneous creation is the reason there is something rather than nothing, why the universe exists, why we exist." However, neither gravity nor any other law of physics delivered a mechanism by which universe can be spontaneously created. professor Hawking, and others alike do not know why laws of physics exist?

Although in the quantum world, it is relevant for things such as particles to pop into existence from nothing, it has never been exhibited that non-quantum-sized objects can show such feats. Even if it were possible, why would it be even possible that such laws of physics should exist in the midst of the universes that are supposedly created from nothing? If nothing, means no things, not a thing, then, it utterly couldn't have included any laws of physics, or gravity. Why wouldn't an actual nothing agrees with no laws of physics and no possibility of anything popping into existence? Bear in mind that the skeptics always question "who created God?" Why is it so difficult to know that nothing created God, since they are overwhelmed with believing that the entire universe was created by the potent force of nothing. And as the atheists also accept that a nebulous set of theories, which they cannot be corroborated via observation data, can create an infinite number of universes, having been created from the laws of physics. During the entire course of human history so many idolatrous so-called theories is being manifested to explain God and existence, to no avail.

Just "as Darwin and Wallace explained how the apparently miraculous design of living forms could appear without intervention by a supreme being, the multiverse concept can explain the fine tuning of physical law without the need for a benevolent creator who made the Universe for our benefit. Because there is a law like gravity, the Universe can and will create itself from nothing. Spontaneous creation is the reason there is something rather than nothing, why the Universe exists, why we exist."

They then explain the basic theory behind the "multiverse," which presupposes that multiple universes exist. "According to M-theory, ours is not the only universe. Instead M-theory predicts that a great many universes were created out of nothing. Their creation does not require the intervention of some supernatural being or god. Rather these multiple universes arise naturally from physical law."

The conclusion of what Hawking and Mlodinow are claiming is:

Claim 1: Spontaneous Creation is the reason that there is something rather than nothing, including the Universe; ("Spontaneous creation is the reason there is something rather than nothing, why the Universe exists"). This applies to all universes, meaning it applies to the entire multiverse.

Claim 2: Spontaneous Creation requires the law of gravity; ("Because there is a law of gravity, the Universe can and will create itself from nothing"; "Rather these multiple universes arise naturally from physical law").

Claim 3: The multitude of universes are responsible for producing fine-tuned physical laws ("the multiverse concept can explain the fine tuning of physical law").

The bottom line of what they are finalizing is that you can't have a universe without it being created, you can't have spontaneous creation without physical laws, like the laws of gravity, and you can't have physical laws without a universe.

As Hawking and Mlodinow admit, with no Creation, there is nothing. To have anything – a universe, a multiverse, the cosmos, the law of gravity, "finely-tuned" physical laws, anything, anything at all – you must first have Creation. And they've pretty much proven that "spontaneous" creation is impossible, since it needs physical laws like the law of gravity. So without Creation, the universe/multiverse couldn't create itself.

Hawking and Mlodinow may be outstanding physicists, but they sure have shown themselves to be as poor philosophers and logicians as one can be.

THE GOD WE DO NOT KNOW

According to Mr. Leonard Mlodinow science explores the world as it is offered to the five senses and the brain, while spirituality considers the universe to be purposeful and imbued with meaning. In Mr. Deepak Chopra's view, the great challenge for spirituality is to offer something that science cannot provide, which is the realm of consciousness. The worldviews try to explore cosmos, the physical universe, life, the human brain, and to cultivate the mystery of God and consciousness. The perspectives are to know where the universe came from, where did we come from, what is our purpose here, to delve into human nature and to know where we are going.

To grasp the mysteries of our universe, and perhaps someday learn where the universe is heading. Many scientists, innumerable philosophers, and scholarly minded individuals argue about evolution, genetics, the origin of life, Metaphysics, and so on. What we should the least agree on is that: in the visible world existence breeds existence, that something indubitably (irrefutably, unquestionably) comes from something; the womb of nature is practically impregnated with the reality of cause and effect.

Contrary to the invisible world, the scientists and many prominent physicists tell us that: in the sub-atomic realm something can come out of nothing, that things appear out of nowhere without any apparent reason, and the same thing can appear in several places at the same time. We identify with that as magic which no finer word than "miracle" can describe it better.

It seems such phenomena are exclusively dealt with by the unseen God, where the invisible concurs (be of one mind, be of the same mind) with undetectable. It is not a fiction but a fact that dynamics are resolutely (purposefully, decisively) different in the unseen world, as the environment cannot be controlled and harnessed as they are in our tangible world. In the meanwhile, let's suppose as some people believe, that we have evolved from nothing to a self-aware being, if so, what better word than a miracle can define it.

Further, we should agree on the only God that loves beauty. Just look around you and meditate on the radiance (blush, bloom) of the four seasons. The breathtaking views of natural scenery, and uplifting images of nature with truly unbelievable and dazzling ocean sites holding millions of superlative creatures of the sea. Encompassing scarce and diversified forestry, majestic mountains with amazing valleys. How about millions of pristine landscapes and woods filled with infinitely colorful birds and the bees, conveying so many exotic plants and animals, with incredibly tall and diversified trees, unparalleled blue lagoons, exquisite rivers, and splendid streams.

The astounding view of descending dawn, gorgeous sunrise, and the incredible view of the sunset. The wonderful Twilight which is time span between dawn and sunrise, or between sunset and dusk, that is when the light is still seen in the sky due to sunlight scattering off the atmosphere. The unsurpassed view of the moon, the pleasant blue sky and strikingly delightful stars, and the incomparably alluring rainbow, and so on. We should agree on the infinitely intelligent God, a generous God with magnanimity (bounty), an unbiased endowment that is beyond anyone's imagination.

We should agree on, an infinitely resourceful God, so compassionate and kind; an absolute provider that has created a world of plenty, conveyed with infinite diversity in food, and with fresh air and crystal clear water. We should also realize that: wherever there is an injustice, a ruse, a transgression or a curse like behavior, we must look for a cruel culprit, an ugly spirited character within the human race, or an ignorant one.

We should know the root causes of man's ill fate is because of his/her unawareness, and lack of information, and not to blame God. And because we are made in the image of God, we as well need to pursue beauty, seek wisdom and intelligence, have compassion, be generous, resourceful, kind and considerate. And definitely for one not to do evil, but to act in good will.

Eckhart Tolle said quote" you do not become good by trying to be good, but by finding the goodness that is already within you and allowing that goodness to emerge. But it can only emerge if something fundamental changes in your state of consciousness." Eckhart Tolle further said quote "do not get trapped into ego. Change your state of consciousness, be still and know that I am God."

We shouldn't forget that in the material world our mind can deceive us into believing something that might utterly be false, where I am afraid anomalies can become the norms. This often occurs due to relentless conditioning and deceitful conducts, as a toxic environment is construed to make sure citizens are as conclusively biased to take side with the elites and those in power.

To ascertain that consumers can comply with oligopoly politics, for the people to accord with the unjust market mechanism, and with what the corporate culture has to offer. Forcing the inhabitants to live in a world which is misleading and filled with bogus information, deliberately orchestrated to cover up terrible inequality that has caused so much suffering and havoc for billions of human-beings beyond comprehension.

Comparably, Metaphysics, God and spirituality are non-profit issues and are not supposed to be capital driven. They are over and above human senses, they lie in an invisible realm of infinite possibilities which they need to be felt and innately sought. Spirituality looks toward a transcendent phase that lies in the domain of consciousness; it seeks awareness, purpose and looks for the meaning of life. it was Carl Jung who said quote "who looks outside, dreams; who looks within, awakens."

It shouldn't be so riddling (enigmatic) for anyone to see the prevalent traces of God, unless denial is due to perhaps having so much orgulous (pride), with carrying a chip on one's shoulder not to admit that: we live in a universe that everything we witness, all which we observe, and the invisible world is all sign of the incredible God. And yes, it is so true that mind and human brain addresses neuroscience, and escalates the entire matter of mind and body; but the issues of God and spirituality refers not solely to a pantheon (God, Goddesses, deity), also to the broader term that conceptualizes a divine presence in our universe, and the surpassed. Which implies to the unseen realm that lies beyond our five sense and is the key to infinite possibilities, hoping that one day we can unfold the limitless potential in human consciousness, perhaps enabling mankind to further concur with the unseen.

It is further fair to concord with the fact that I exist. I exist because I can think, and also agree that I am incomplete. How do I know that I am incomplete? I know because I have desires, that I do not possess the absolute knowledge, I do not possess the absolute intelligence, I do not have the absolute wisdom. I do not have the absolute wealth, the absolute power, the absolute beauty, the absolute generosity, or the utter compassion, and do not have the absolute prestige, the absolute goodness, that I am fragmented, and so on, hence, I am not perfect?

And unless there is an absolute goodness, an absolutely perfect being that I could envision in my mind, and be comparably aware of and locate with, I would have not known that I am not complete.

As human beings we are bound to our intelligence, and cannot go over what is in our mind, to exceed beyond what exists in our memory; unless there is an idea of the ultimate and the most perfect being in our thought, we couldn't have known about perfectionism.

That is exactly why we are aware of our imperfection since we are able to know about what is to be-all. we could viscerally (by instinct rather than tutelage) compare; otherwise, it would have been impossible to realize that we are not complete since the idea of something perfect wouldn't have registered in our mind. We are not extraterrestrial, some sort of Martian to perhaps know otherwise. The very reason we know that we are not whole is that the concept of a perfect being exists in our mind, which comparably delineates and makes us aware of the deficiencies that we behold.

There must exist an absolute being, that is why we have in our mind the image of a perfect character that we can identify with since we are able to compare and realize that we are not as perfect. And because the only way to know of one's shortcoming is to comparably know of something which is complete, to perceive that the apogee (apex), the absolute pinnacle of perfection, the absolute crown holder exists.

It should remind and make one aware of such utter apex impression. Otherwise, one would be truly exhausted by its awareness, of its existence. Which then, the impression of an absolutely perfect being would have been beyond anyone's imagination; since one couldn't have any idea or any trace of it in one's mind. It simply couldn't have registered in anyone's mind. As Eckhart Tolle said quote "no human being can behave beyond the level of their consciousness." And I believe when you only see within the eyes, then you are easy to fool.

Therefore, if one has an idea of something, that something, that entity must exist, otherwise it is not possible to be mindful of something that does not exists; even a utopian issue, a visionary subject must have the potential, the possibility to exist, for one to be able to imagine it. Having the idea of God in one's mind is not optional, it is a realistic matter. The idea of a perfect being, an absolutely infallible God is riveted in our sub-conscious mind, and because all other things are solely relative in comparison. It was Einstein that said, "there is a hidden reality underlining our universe and quite different from the world we perceive with our senses."

Leonard Mlodinow "Science has revealed a universe that is vast, ancient, violent, strange, and beautiful, a universe of almost infinite variety and possibility one in which time can end in a black hole, and conscious beings can evolve from a soup of minerals."

Where the stars are so fast that no time can possibly get a chance when facing the black holes since gravity devours everything. It seems in such universe mankind are not so significant, since our lives on the planet earth are the byproduct of physical laws. Laws which they no longer seem to matter in the world of black holes and beyond. This is not to say that man's curiosity to discern the avalanche of questions is ever halted where the profound and innumerable unthinking atoms can become intelligently potentiated, galvanized, awakened and mobilized to discover our origin, and the nature of our universe, and the entire cosmos.

To authenticate our knowledge of "singularity" since there is no physic of any kind to explain singularity. To learn what are we here for, and where are we heading. To understand consciousness, to discover the nature of the atom and our DNA, and know about our physical traits, and in heaven sake how did the planet earth get here. To know if animals are machines, since they unexceptionally are driven by instinct, as if they have been so accurately programmed with no flaws. The question which remains is the reality of action and reaction, the result of natural laws relentlessly maneuvering via cause and effect, or is it something else?

Either our reality is encompassed by the visible universe, or it is not. was the cosmos created from the meaningless void, from an empty space, or was not. is a programmer, or a network of analysts is in charge of this superb, and extremely complex simulated computer known as life, or not? And millions of other viable questions which should halt any genius, or smart Alek scientist not to jump into conclusion about infinitely complex and intriguing existence.

We often pause in silence to learn how our brain a computer made of fatty tissues chemically, and hormonally decides how we feel, genetically determines how we grow, then live and expire, and all taking place with an invisible programmer, an unseen analyst working to create thousands, if not millions of software at the cost of lump sum of meat and fatty cluster exhausted of intelligence, and without central processing unit (CPU). What is so strange is that the neuroscience does widely believe that: the mind does not exist but is the by-product of our brain. What is even more strange is that: human mind hatched science, which ironically denies consciousness, its sole creator. Where scientists who deny consciousness cannot explain why the very basic unit of nature called atom becomes extremely small where matter breaks down and then disappears.

They deny that we are part of the fabric of creation which should be free, and not to become enslaved by an industrial lifestyle where technology can overpower us, as Einstein warned us, quote" "I fear the day that technology will surpass our human interaction. The world will have a generation of idiots." If we reject our self and the power of reasoning and our rationale. We then behave like primates, and eventually become lowered to machines, where we become vulnerable to senseless programming, vailed by greed and material wealth seeking excessive pleasure of the flesh, rather than peace in our mind, which can result in our further complicit behavior, not responding to priorities of living, but acting callous towards essentially decisive matters, where even no human life matters any more.

And sadly enough religion has become part of the problem, many religions try to protect God by killing other believers in the name of the same God that we are meant to honor. Most religions I am afraid they also follow the insane rat race activities to maximize profit, to fill their own pocket at the expense of devotees and millions of believers that worship God, and try to seek sanctuary in the house of God. The organized religion is not the same as spirituality, the organized religion may have discredited itself, but spirituality suffered no such defeat. Religions should tune it down to what make sense, rather than insisting on issues that breeds hatred and superstition.

That is why Darwin's explanation of man's decent from the primates overcomes Genesis, and why millions look into the big bang as the source of cultivating cosmos, rather than to creation myth populated by one, multiple or many Gods.

In which the story of the six blind men and the elephant should prove handy, as it befits the position of many religions.

Blind Men and the Elephant – A Picture of Relativism and Tolerance

The Blind Men and the Elephant is a famous Indian fable that tells the story of six blind sojourners that come across different parts of an elephant in their life journeys. In turn, each blind man creates his own version of reality from that limited experience and perspective. In philosophy departments throughout the world, the Blind Men and the Elephant has become the poster child for moral relativism and religious tolerance.

The Story of the Six Blind Men

One day, six wise blind men were walking in the zoo and accidentally came across an elephant that somehow got out of the cage. The first blind man walked right into the side of the elephant. He touched to either side, but all he could feel was the big body of the elephant.

"Boy," said the first blind man. "I think I must have walked into a wall. "The second blind man was becoming more and more curious about what was taking place. He accidentally walked over to the front of the elephant and touched and latched on to the animal's trunk.

He hastily let go and shouted, "This isn't a wall. This is a snake! We should step back just in case it's toxic and mortally poisonous." The third man hurried to figure out what was happening and to let his friends know what they had run into.

He walked over to the rear end of the elephant and touched the animal's tail. "This is no wall, and this is no snake. You are both mistaking once again. I know for certain that this is a rope."

The fourth man also became curious and knelt down and felt around the elephant's legs, as the tame elephant stood still, he said "My good friends,". "This is no wall and this is no snake. This is no rope either. What we have here, gentlemen is four tree trunks. And I am sure.

The fifth blind man walked up to the front of the elephant and touched the elephant's two long tusks. "this thing is sure made up of two swords," said the fifth man. "What I am grasping is long and curved with a sharp tip at the end". I am not certain what this is.

The sixth blind man scratched his head and mediated on the problem. He seemed to be the wisest of all of them and asked for the zoo-keeper to solve the conundrum they were facing. The zoo-keeper being worried about the loose elephant reached them, and tightly grabbed the elephant's collar. And when he was asked about the problem. He said "you are all right, the elephant seems like something different to each one of you. And only in sharing what each of you gentleman knows can probably understand, and collectively resolve the puzzling issue.

The only hope for tolerating others, to show compassion and object to what is not justified, is for bettering quality of human consciousness, to further advance in our awareness where make sense ability can replace ignorance and superstition.

The question is if the laws of nature govern, and they decide our actions, our future, and are the answer to millions of unanswered questions. Then, are this laws orderly, are they purposeful, calculated and meaningful, managed, equitable, balanced and objectified, or not? If the answer is no, and these laws that reign us are chaotic, and are not regulated and carry no meaning, and are exhausted of having any purpose. Then, how scientists, the physicists, the astrophysicists and millions of other intelligently minded researchers do formulate their data, compute and solidify the end result of their significant study. And bear in mind that the core of the physicist's undertaking projects relies on mathematics which is the kernel of their findings, making them able to substantiate dependable theories. How on earth, can this ever be possible to achieve in a world that is muddled, that is disorderly? How can any neuroscience, neurophysiologist, bio-researcher? or any other medical technician work with medical tools that couldn't gather precise measurement from an undisciplined world for the very imperative task of saving lives? Then, if the reply is yes; would you not ask yourself that: if it is a meaningful universe that is attentively managed and accurately programmed, then, it must have a programmer. And if so, who is the planner, the designer? who is the coordinator, and the software developer?

VAJABALWOOJOOD

God is vajabalwoojood, which means God existence is a must so that other things can relatively exist, they must depend on God existence. God must exist, because God is the creator of all there is, and all there was, and all there ever will be. God is absolute; every other thing is relative referencing the Omni Potent, Omnipresent, Omni temporal and the Omniscient God. God is the absolute truth, that is true at all times and in all places. God is always true no matter what the circumstances. God is a fact that cannot be altered. like for instance, there are no round rectangular, or the angles of a triangle add up to 180 degrees.

It seems math and geometry are the languages of the divine, they can independently be perceived, as they absolutely are necessary for our lives; but numbers as well must be attached to something, like 100 books, 1000 horses, or 10000 soldiers. They depend on other things; they must be attached to other items to mean something. God is all truths because the existence of God logically makes sense, and is the whole truth. Everything and all that exists depends on God, in which without no relative, or other absolute things can ever exist. Every absolute being depends on the other absolute being, except God. for instance, as long as there is space, time must absolutely exist, there couldn't be time without space. But even time slows down and almost stops for objects going at the speed of light.

There is a phenomenon of relativity known as time dilation, in which time appears to slow down almost to a stop for bodies that approach the speed of light. — Jerry Adler, Newsweek, "Stephen Hawking, Master of the Universe: Our 1988 Cover Story on the Legendary Physicist," 14 Mar. 2018

Is time an absolute? Relating to Newton, absolute time exists autonomous of any beholder and advances at a coherent pace throughout the universe. Thus, every object has an absolute state of motion relative to absolute space, hence, an object must be either in a state of absolute rest or moving at some absolute speed.

There are innumerous absolutes, an infinite number of absolute reasons and issues, but they all one way or another depend on other things, except God. Gravity is an absolute but depends on the Earth mass which is also an absolute, since is the Earth's mass that causes it to have gravity, and so in order to not maintain gravity the Earth must not have mass. But the earth has mass, just like any other solid object does. If the Earth didn't have mass, it wouldn't be there anymore! What we know as an absolute on planet earth, might be relative on other planets, or universes except God that cannot be relative, and is the absolute maker of the entire cosmos. All destructible things are relative, including the entire planet earth' since a couple of colossally atomic bombs can utterly annihilate the entire planet earth, except for God that is the absolute being. All other things either absolute or relative depends on God, the creator of heavens and the earth. The vajabalwoojood argument does not have to be persuasive for piercing the logic of others, it is just a fact since the infinite traces of God are so awesomely impressive that should leave no doubt what so ever for any intelligent mind to decipher.

Notably different experimental truths, all the findings of science, are empirical: they depend on evidence and might be wrong or partial. Also, we can be incorrect about what we think we see or experience. since we rely on science and our senses in practical life. That does not change the fact that absolute truth is only to be found inside a well-defined logical system. That kind of truth may, or may not, correspond to the real world, and if it does in the real world, it must depend on other things, except for God that is absolutely independent.

EXISTENCE PEAKED IN MANKIND

All living creatures are extremely complicated, even the most diminutive(microscopic) single-celled bacteria. However, none exceed the overall complexity of the human being. Each human-being is constructed of trillions of molecules and cells, solely the human brain is filled with billions of cells constituting trillions of trillions of connections. The design of the human brain is rightly remarkable and beyond our comprehension. Every cubic inch of the human brain includes at least a couple of million nerve cells conjoined by ten thousand miles of fibers. It is well known that man's 3-pound brain is the most complicated and orderly arrangement of matter in the entire universe! way more complicated than any sophisticated computer, the human brain is competent for storing and creatively maneuvering infinite amounts of information. Its abilities and potential stagger (offset, displace) the imagination. The more we utilize it, the surpass it becomes. The brain competency of even the smallest insect is astounding. The infinitesimal speck of a brain located in a little ant, butterfly or bee enable them not only to detect, smell, taste and navigate, but even to fly with great accuracy. Butterflies routinely travel tremendous distances. Bees and ants engage in complex social organizations, construction projects, and communications. Comparably these minuscule brains put our computers and aviation to shame.

The prodigy (miracle, marvel) of the bodies of both animals and man are evidently ceaseless. Dr. A.E. Wilder-Smith makes this thought-provoking and humbling statement: When one considers that the entire chemical information to construct a man, elephant, frog or an orchid was compressed into two minuscule reproductive cells (sperm and egg nuclei), one can only be astounded. In addition to this, all the information is available on the genes to repair the body (not only to construct it) when it is injured. If one were to request an engineer to accomplish this feat of information miniaturization, one would be considered fit for the psychiatric clinic.

It is not ambivalent that a machine methodically built by a craftsman cogitate the existence of its maker. It would not be wise to think that time and chance could make a jumbo jet, an automobile a computer, a refrigerator or a typewriter. Where the separate parts could have manufactured by themselves into these elaborate mechanisms based on the physical properties of matter. Yet, life is much more intricate than the most advanced man-made machine. Our planet is filled with infinite forms of life, each conveying massive levels of complexity. Materialists see life in all its wondrous forms concluding merely of atoms and molecules. They acknowledge these atoms and molecules make themselves into millions of complex animals and plants. These kinds of callous behold were materialized of an earlier, unripe period in science when the extreme complexity of living systems was not fathomed. Even if nature could build the necessary proteins and enzymes, it is extremely far away from generating life. Presently so many scientists, the prominent philosopher, and scholarly minded individuals believe that life could have never existed without a highly intelligent planner, a potently wise designer. There is a humongous difference between making a building block and generating a complete operating and serviced 200-story skyscraper made from those building blocks. No building can be erected exhausted of any builder, no program can exist without a programmer, without a studiously smart planner.

When ontology, which is a branch of metaphysics, tests existence and being to prove what it means for something to be a physical object, should one define them by their properties? Is it the size, the color, the shape, or are these properties linked to preceding substance that we need to be aware of? This is referred as the problem of substance, the universal difficulty is posed as how can we know if the problem of color, size or shape are separate from the particular object, and how can a substance or matter change in some ways but still stay the same. Metaphysic examines the essence of mind as contrary to physical object, and if the mind is physical, it is also concern if God exists, and disputes about the nature, space and time. Relating to immaterial issues like beauty, morality, justice, and so on, Plato believed the form was an undeniable fact of nature where principle issues like justice, goodness, beauty are realities perhaps abstract(synopsis) in their own rights.

He pulls distinction between the visible world and the intelligent one, and reckoned it is the absolute fundamental rule and the axiom law that represent a higher form of knowledge which governs and designs the intelligible criterions that are prefect and unchanging. Because our knowledge of the visible world is imperfect and changing, where Plato believed there are those who are stuck in the world of sights and sounds since they relate to human-beings sensory experience; as Plato, a philosopher in classical Greece saw the material world as not real, but rather a shadow of actual world of forms in which nothing alters, and nothing proceeds, and nothing is imperfect, Contrary to the physical world of substance and matter that are constantly altering.

Plato also believed cases of justice in the seen world may be relative, as what seems to one person as just, may seem very unjust to the next individual, but he believed the real world is impregnated with the form of justice itself as absolute and not changeable, in which higher form of intelligent identifies with, so does with beauty, goodness, form of wisdom and host of other vital issues. The world of higher form was the centerpiece to Plato's belief, according to which the object of human experience are just shadows of a higher world of forms that are situated above our sensory world.

Plato's teacher, Socrates, first referred to the idea of the invisible world behind the observable world and the instigator to the world of appearances, that is eternal, immaterial and are inconvertible forms. Hence, the theory of forms is the most vital philosophical and thought provoking idea central to Plato's theme and subject matter referencing the world of unseen, since he believed even though we find so many cases of flaws in justice, goodness and beauty in this world, we still by instinct do sense of true justice, true beauty, true goodness, and what true virtuous conduct is. Plato, like his teacher Socrates, believed soul is what makes us alive and animates us, and it is the spirit or the soul which made life possible. Plato was inspired by the perfect lucidity and durability of mathematics, which was closest to perfect clarity and discipline; he doubted the world of our experience since nothing is perfect or permanent. In his theory he explains that beyond the unfulfilling world of human experience exists a world which holds the form of justice, goodness, beauty and other forms that embodies the perfect expression of these ideas.

In this sense, physics looks into the principles and the reality of nature at its root, which references the idea that there must be invisible principals active in nature relating to which all natural processes can be recognized. And gathered something comes to existence and becomes what it is by obtaining its distinctive form linked to and fed by the essence of nature. For instant a seed which becomes a mature plant, or a baby grown into adulthood, the birds and the bees, the flowers and the trees, and so on. Plato argues that subject matter like justice and beauty exist because they engage in the universal form of beauty and justice as its actual fabric already imprinted in the universe.

In the other hand, Aristotle argues that the universal concept of justice and beauty stems from examples of beauty and justice in this world, since Aristotle places importance on observing the details of this world. Aristotle believes that everything is subject to change and motion, but nothing alters or moves without cause; his theology comprehension is set on his perception that there must be something beyond and above the chain of command for the cause and effect principle to exist, which he sees as the invisible forces and the energy behind the motion and change as a deep mystery.

Aristotle, Plato's student, emphasized on cause and reflected on "change," which ultimately led him to posit the existence of a divine unmoved mover. Aristotle believed what moves the world is consistency in change, he manifested change restlessly takes place in our physical world which is due to motion, and time spent, which in turn requires space. And as much as Plato believed in the invisible intelligent world and its abstract form, Aristotle leaned on the visible world and believed true forms are manifested in substance and the material world we experience.

He believed neither matter nor form can exist without each other; they cannot exist independently. He stated it would not be possible for a form to exist without some matter to depend on. He acknowledged that substance can exist without quality, color, number, or any other category, but it is definitely difficult to imagine any category without substance. He renders an example that illustrates this distinction between form and matter, and to grasp a basic sense of the universe and how laid out it is, via the "bronze statue." The bronze is the matter, while the shape of the statue is the form, which he states even a lump of bronze would have its shape and form.

Aristotle stated that we pay attention to the time that has passed when we notice that something has changed. Put differently, time is a measure of change as space is measure of distance. He denies the possibility of empty time as much as he denies the possibility of empty space, where no time can pass without anything taking place.

Aristotle was the son of a doctor and was interested in biology. He had a keen understanding of anatomy, and in his writing was trying to make sense of the world through biology as a paradigm shift in understanding the world. Aristotle was adamant in finding the purpose to each thing, which he thought was the best way to decipher why things are the way they are, and what goal they are to serve, and pushed on teleology which indicates there must be a reason for everything; where teleological phenomenon (exhibiting design relating to having purpose) is the essence of his doctoring.

I believe every gradual change leads to a new form to serve an exclusive goal, which inevitably sets new agendas and circumstances for the next stage of change to occur, to create new positions and to successively manifest and reach certain objectives, and so on. I believe this is contrary to the idea of accepting infinity, since no change from position or form A to B can ever take place in infinite time, demanding infinite space, where no purpose is ever served or any goal could possibly be reached. Furthermore, the idea of showing out of nowhere and from an infinite time and space sounds ridiculous, because neither time nor space can mean anything without having the inclination to execute a deed.

In today's world, because of advancements of science and technology, the matter in its entirety is in question, since such issues as "antiquark," which means the antiparticle of the quark that deals with the subatomic particle identical in mass but opposite to it in electric and magnetic properties (as sign of charge), that when brought together with its counterpart produces mutual annihilation: otherwise, a subatomic particle not found in ordinary matter, which is big challenge and a game changer for the science to deal with in the world of unseen through the naked eye.

ABOUT THE AUTHOR

Dr. Feridoun Shawn Shahmoradian showed an avid interest in learning about other cultures from a very young age. Shawn's love for people, as well as his need to quench a thirst for learning about others' way of life, inspired him to travel extensively to many parts of the world, including the Middle East, Persia, Turkey, (Istanbul, Ankara), Europe, West Africa, and North America. His travels have rewarded him with an invaluable wealth of knowledge and experience, allowing him to acquire realistic views in the context of diversified culture, philosophical, social, political, economic, and psychological endeavors.

Dr. Shawn attended many spiritual and callisthenic seminars in different parts of the world, including Morocco (Rabat, Marrakesh city, Fes, and Casablanca), Oslo, Paris, Amsterdam, Dublin (Ireland), Toronto (Canada), and Monroe (California), Santiago (California), New jersey, Orlando (Florida), Dallas, Houston, and Galveston (Texas) In the United States of America. He then visited New York, Washington, Las Vegas, San Antonio, Austin, El Paso, Corpus Christi, Texas, New Orleans, Miami Beach, Mexico (Mexico City, Cancun, Cozumel), and Bahamas.

At the age of Seventeen, Shawn attended Crawley College in Crawley England, for three consecutive years, and also attended boarding school at Birchington-On-Sea a village in northeast Kent, England. He visited London several times, resided at Brighton England for a while, and visited Hasting, Canterbury, and Sheffield England. Dr. Shawn then traveled to Fresno and San Francisco, California, and went to Lake Tahoe, Nevada, to teach. Dr. Shawn then left to study at Stockton College in Stockton, California, for two full years, taking philosophy and other social science courses. He then transferred to Galveston Texas College for one more year.

A couple of years later he received his electronic engineering degree from Texas Southern University in Houston Texas. He furthered his studies at Texas A & M and received his master's degree in economics, a minor in finance. His love for social science motivated him to attend the University of Texas at Dallas in Dallas Texas, and there he obtained a master degree in public affairs, with a minor in psychology.

Dr. Shawn obsession with sports and a relentless pursuit for excellence in the art of self-defense that he pursued while facing insurmountable challenges over many years makes him a true embodiment of wisdom and strength. After extensive and thorough research in a variety of arts, Dr. Shawn finally created the Pang- Fang system a very unique and extremely practical system approved by well-known authorities in the field of self-defense. Dr. Shawn's system is highly recommended since it conveys decisive tactics with utterly significant strategy in a life and death situation. Dr. Shawn holds a nine- degree black belt in Hapkido, a Korean martial art, and holds a tenth-degree black belt in the Pang-Fang system of self-defense, second-degree black belt in Judo, first-degree black belt in Tae Kwan do, and third-degree black belt in Wu Shu Kung-Fu. He is acknowledged a prominent figure and as a holder of a nonconventional doctorate in the sport and the art of self-defense. Dr. Shawn is the author of the book Mind fighter, the book of The Anatomy of wake-up calls volume one & volume two, The book of God and the system.

Printed in the United States
by Bookmasters

Printed in the United States
By Bookmasters